The Career Coach

MW01073817

Uniquely combining the latest research into careers with the most up-to-date coaching approaches, Julia Yates shows how to effectively apply coaching techniques to the world of career support. Demonstrating how coaching research explains practice and how practice benefits from research, *The Career Coaching Handbook* is accessibly written with a solid evidence-based foundation.

Presented in three parts, the book covers developments in theory and research and applies this knowledge to the real world. Part I, *Theories of career*, looks at 21st-century career paths, job satisfaction and career changes – both planned and unplanned. Part II, *Career coaching approaches*, examines coaching strategies that are applicable to career coaching in particular. Part III, *Coaching into the world of work*, covers specific real-world situations in which coaching is beneficial, from job-search strategies to CV and interview coaching. Evidence and research is used throughout to demonstrate the most effective strategies for coaching.

The Career Coaching Handbook provides an essential introduction for students or practitioners who are interested in developing their own practice, finding new and improved ways to support clients and understanding the theories that underpin effective career coaching practice.

Julia Yates is a senior lecturer in psychology at the University of East London and runs their MSc in Career Coaching. She has worked as a practitioner, director, trainer and writer in the field of career coaching for 15 years.

The Career Coaching Handbook

Julia Yates

Routledge
Taylor & Francis Group

LONDON AND NEW YORK

First published 2014
by Routledge
2 Park Square, Milton Park, Abingdon, Oxon OX14 4RN

and by Routledge
711 Third Avenue, New York, NY 10017

Routledge is an imprint of the Taylor & Francis Group, an informa business

© 2014 Julia Yates

The right of Julia Yates to be identified as author of this work has been asserted by her in accordance with sections 77 and 78 of the Copyright, Designs and Patents Act 1988.

All rights reserved. No part of this book may be reprinted or reproduced or utilised in any form or by any electronic, mechanical, or other means, now known or hereafter invented, including photocopying and recording, or in any information storage or retrieval system, without permission in writing from the publishers.

Trademark notice: Product or corporate names may be trademarks or registered trademarks, and are used only for identification and explanation without intent to infringe.

British Library Cataloguing in Publication Data
A catalogue record for this book is available from the British Library

Library of Congress Cataloging in Publication Data
Yates, Julia.
 The career coaching handbook / Julia Yates.
  pages cm
 1. Career development.   2. Personal coaching.   3. Executive coaching.
 4. Vocational guidance.   I. Title.
 HF5381.Y3745 2013
 650.14–dc23
                                        2013020123

ISBN: 978-0-415-62786-3 (hbk)
ISBN: 978-0-415-62787-0 (pbk)
ISBN: 978-1-315-86736-6 (ebk)

Typeset in Times New Roman
by RefineCatch Ltd, Bungay, Suffolk

To Hugh, Jack and Ted

Contents

Preface

Career coaching as a professional practice has been around for some time, but as an academic discipline it is fairly new. There is an impressive history of research on career development and career decision making, and a wealth of literature that can tell us about the approaches, tools and techniques that are widely used in coaching. Plenty of self-help books on career coaching are also available, many full of helpful and practical advice if you yourself are looking for a career change. But this book is different. This book is for you if you are a professional, or a trainee career coaching practitioner. It combines the latest evidence from the careers world with up-to-date research from the coaching literature. It's intended to help you to be the best career coach that you can be, but also to understand what goes on behind your interactions. It's a book about theory and practice, and how the two interact.

One great piece of literature that I came across when researching this book was in a paper by Whiston, Sexton and Lasoff (1998) which indicates that career practitioners in training get better results than experienced practitioners who have not continued to study. This suggests that for all of us, keeping abreast of the latest theories and ideas, and reflecting on our practice, should not be optional and that life-long career development is useful not just to keep us fresh, but as a way of providing tangible benefits to our clients. And it's fascinating, too. If you find people's behaviour, choices and jobs interesting, and presumably you do, I think you'll really enjoy finding out what we now know about our relationships with our careers in the current era, and reflecting on ways to incorporate these ideas into your practice.

This book is divided into three parts. The first section concentrates on the evidence and theories about careers. Chapter 1 asks what exactly is career coaching, and identifies the particular features that set career coaching apart from other professional career support. Chapter 2 looks at career paths in the 21st century and highlights how things have changed over the last 50 years. Chapter 3 covers the complex issue of how we make career decisions, focusing on both the factors and processes involved, while Chapter 4 summarizes the wealth of literature that investigates what makes us happy at work. Chapters 5 and 6 both focus on interrupted career paths: in Chapter 5, we look at career changes, what prompts them and how they happen; in Chapter 6, we look at career changes which are in some way forced on an individual.

The second part of the book looks more specifically at career coaching interventions and covers some of the key approaches, tools and techniques that you can use with your clients. The section starts with Chapter 7, which highlights the kinds of issues that clients bring to career coaching, and the next two chapters cover two very widely applicable career coaching models: humanistic coaching (Chapter 8) and the GROW framework (Chapter 9). Chapters 10 to 13 introduce four coaching models: motivational interviewing (Chapter 10), positive approaches (Chapter 11), cognitive behavioural coaching (Chapter 12) and transactional analysis (Chapter 13). The final chapter in this section, Chapter 14, highlights eight favourite career coaching techniques.

The third part of the book looks at the nuts and bolts of actually getting a job, and how coaching can help clients into the world of work. Chapter 15 summarizes some of the major changes and trends in the labour market, Chapter 16 examines the evidence for advice on how to make a job search effective, and Chapters 17 and 18 discuss the evidence that can help a client improve their CV and their interview technique.

The book is intended to be a resource for you rather than a narrative. Each chapter stands alone and you can read the book in whichever order appeals to you most.

Acknowledgements

My heartfelt thanks to all who have helped and supported me along the way. To Nelica, who first introduced me to career coaching and whose expertise, wisdom and support can take the credit for any academic credibility within the book. Thanks too to Aneta and Christian, whose belief in me encouraged me throughout. Thanks to Suzanne and Marlene who allowed me to use their interesting career paths as illustrations, and to each of my clients, students and friends whose career stories help me to understand what it all means. To Louise, Mirella and Sarah, whose friendship brightens each day and to Gwenda and Brian, whose unobtrusive but unswerving support makes everything a little bit easier. And to my parents: to my mother for her endless love, kindness and childcare, and to my dad, who would have been very proud.

Finally, to my family. To Hugh, who inspires me in so many ways, and who has been immensely tolerant and patient throughout, reading and commenting on everything I've thrown at him and making a valiant effort to look interested when I talk about career decision-making theory; and to our boys Jack and Ted, who make everything worthwhile.

Table 5.1, originally published in *The Career Development Quarterly*, 'Voluntary midlife career change: Integrating the transtheoretical model and the life-span, life-space approach' by Susan R. Barclay, Kevin B. Stoltz and Barry Y. Chung (59:5, 386–399, 2011), is reproduced by kind permission of the National Career Development Association.

Table 6.1, originally published in *Journal of Vocational Behavior*, 'Partially testing a process model for understanding victim responses to an anticipated worksite closure' by Gary Blau (71(3): 410–428, 2007), is reproduced by kind permission of Elsevier.

Chapter 1

What is career coaching and how can it help?

WHAT IS CAREER COACHING?

There are many different sources of professional support if you are struggling to make career choices or work out what to do next. Many different job titles exist, however, and it is not easy to find out what the differences are. You might find a careers adviser, a career guidance practitioner, a career counsellor, consultant, an employability adviser, a job coach or a career coach, and when you look more closely you might see that they all claim to be qualified, knowledgeable and experienced. So what are the differences (if any) and where exactly can career coaching fit in?

The most traditional type of career support is that given by a 'careers adviser'. Many of us have had experience of careers advice at school or college. Sometimes the careers advice at school might be by a teacher who has no formal training or expertise but who might know the young people well and understand the processes needed to apply for university, or to find an apprenticeship. Alternatively, the careers adviser might be an independent professional, trained at post-graduate level in career guidance to offer impartial, client-centred career support.

'Career counselling' is a term that we often find in the literature about career practice. This is the standard nomenclature in the United States and since so much of the research is published there, it is the term that is most widely used. We also find it in the UK, indicating a particular style of career support that might help clients to resolve internal conflicts or understand patterns of behaviour. Career 'consultants' by contrast have a slightly more commercial brand, and this title might be chosen by practitioners working as private practitioners.

So where does career coaching fit it, and how does it distinguish itself from the myriad alternatives? These is no widely accepted definition of career coaching. Career coaches come in many shapes and forms and have different approaches, standards and philosophies. Eric de Haan (2008) describes a playing field of coaching approaches, with quadrants defined on the basis of two continuums: suggesting to exploring and confronting to supporting. Career coaches can be found in any of the four quadrants, although in general, coaching practitioners would tend to resist the suggesting/confronting quadrant. You will need to work out where you want your practice to sit. This might depend on your client group, your personal style, the organization you work for and your experience of what actually works in practice. I hope that this book will contribute to your understanding of the evidence for which types of approaches lead to the most positive results for clients.

My professional approach, and the one I will advocate in this book, is firmly in the supporting and exploring quadrant, but with the proviso that challenging – if done from a position of unconditional positive regard – is an important component of effective and ethical career coaching.

In order to crystallize my position, here is the definition that I am working to in this book:

> Career coaching is one or a series of collaborative conversations with a trained professional who operates within an ethical code. The process is grounded in evidence-based coaching approaches, incorporating theories and tools, and career theory and aims to lead to a positive outcome for the client regarding their career decision, work and/or personal fulfilment.
>
> (Yates 2011)

So let me move on now to focus on three elements which, while they are not exclusive to career coaching, are perhaps more likely to be seen in career coaching conversations than in other types of career support interactions.

The first is the evidence in career coaching practice of a wide range of theoretical approaches. Perhaps because coaching is a relatively new discipline, the coaching scholars have taken an eclectic approach to theories, identifying the most relevant approaches from other disciplines. In this book I will cover cognitive behavioural coaching, adopted from cognitive behavioural therapy; motivational interviewing, developed from health therapy; appreciative inquiry, adapted from organizational development; and solution-focused coaching, whose origins are in family therapy. I will also discuss the more traditional humanistic practice that is widely seen in career guidance, careers advice and career counselling. In addition to the approaches represented in this book, there are career coaches who might adopt an existential, a psychodynamic or a transpersonal approach to their coaching practice. Of course not all coaches will use every single one of these methods, but it is not uncommon for career coaches to have two or three favourite approaches that they can deploy when most appropriate. To my mind, it is this versatility which makes our practice much more tailored to our clients' specific needs, and this makes us stand out from other groups of career professionals.

The second element that tends to be more widely seen in career coaching than in some of the other career professions is the use of tools. In Chapter 14, we will explore some of the more common techniques used in career coaching, such as drawing, collage, visualizations and storyboarding, but there are books and websites that can introduce you to many more, and I would also encourage you to develop or adapt your own, based on what seems to work for you and your client groups.

Finally, career coaching has a positive and solution-focused brand. Coaching strives to inspire growth and change by focusing on the positive aspects of human nature. The starting point for coaching is that people want to develop and thrive, and it focuses on finding solutions, and what is called 'optimal functioning' (Grant and Cavanagh 2007). Coaching is seen as a practice that can benefit all, not just those who are struggling, and is a mechanism to help people who are already doing well to do even better.

This positive approach in part determines the clients who choose career coaching over career counselling or other brands, and sets their expectations for their sessions. Even though the practice might not be so different, clients will to some degree self-select based on the brand: clients wanting a positive, action-orientated, future-focused interaction are more likely to choose a career coach than a career counsellor (Yates 2011).

But does it work? The experiences of hundreds of practitioners and thousands of clients gives us a resounding 'yes!', but if it is hard evidence you want, there are plenty of encouraging studies.

DOES CAREER COACHING WORK, AND WHAT MAKES IT EFFECTIVE?

Career coaching is a new discipline. While career guidance has been producing research since 1909 and coaching since the 1960s, career coaching as an academic discipline in its own right is only just emerging: the first academic Masters course in career coaching in the UK was launched at the University of East London in 2011. Good quality studies and large amounts of data specifically about this field are in short supply, but the tools and techniques used in career coaching are shared with other disciplines and if we piece all the evidence together, the picture is reassuring.

There are numerous studies (see Whiston, Sexton and Lasoff 1998 for a summary) that demonstrate that both one-to-one and group career support are effective. They result in increased career decidedness, better vocational identity (i.e. a stronger sense of who you are within the workplace), reduced unemployment and clearer career goals. Clients are also more likely to put plans into action following career support, and also tend to report higher levels of satisfaction with their career choices (Greenwood 2008).

One meta-analysis (Brown *et al.* 2003) explored the particular elements within a career intervention that contributed most to an effective outcome, and what is of particular interest to us is that many of these elements are core to career coaching. The relationship or 'alliance' between the client and practitioner is shown to be important, explaining 12 per cent of the variation in effectiveness (Heppner and Hedricks 1995). Chapter 8 on humanistic coaching explores some of the key qualities that are present in a healthy career coaching relationship. Brown and co-workers (2003) report that the use of exercises within career support is something that makes it significantly more effective, and we know that the use of specific tools and exercises is something that marks career coaching out from other kinds of career support. Finally, the study focuses on how useful clients find it to have some help articulating their goals and identifying specific plans. Goals and action points are of course not exclusive to a coaching approach, but they are fundamental tenets of the GROW (Goal, Reality, Options, Way Forward) model which we look at in more detail in Chapter 9.

Other studies have highlighted the importance of signposting clients to information about the world of work (e.g. Bimrose 2008) and enhancing self-awareness (Kirschner, Hoffman and Hill 1994). Chapter 15 focuses not just on sources of information, but also on the mechanics of how we can help clients to make sense of it and techniques for working on self-awareness can be found in Chapters 11 and 14 (on positive approaches to career coaching and coaching tools respectively).

Finally, there is a body of research that can be applied specifically to coaching. Literature that looks at the perceptions and impact of coaching shows that it does indeed have a significant positive impact on behavioural change (see Grant 2003 for a summary) and there are plenty of studies that put particular techniques or approaches under scrutiny. There is, for example, a good deal of research that focuses on the effectiveness of cognitive behavioural therapy (Department of Health 2001), goal setting (e.g. Lock and Latham 1990) and motivational interviewing (e.g. Hettema, Steele and Miller 2005), all of which are relevant to coaching and career coaching.

More research would be better. For our profession to grow and gain credibility, there needs to be a solid corpus of empirical research that can tell us exactly how we need to practise in order to get the best results within our own professional context. But the seeds are sown. Career coaching practitioners still need to read between the lines and extrapolate from research undertaken in a different setting, but the foundations are in place and we are not having to make quantum leaps to see how the research might relate to us. This book explores a range of evidence-based approaches that have a solid foundation of research underpinning them, and you will be able to judge for yourselves which you feel will be most applicable to your own situation.

REFERENCES

Bimrose, J. (2008) Adult career progression and advancement: A five year study of the effectiveness of guidance. London/Coventry, UK: Warwick Institute for Employment Research/Department for Innovation, Universities and Skills. Retrieved from http://www2.warwick.ac.uk/fac/soc/ier/research/eg/

Brown, S. D., Ryan-Krane, N. E., Brecheisen, J., Castelino, P., Budisin, I., and Miller, M. (2003) Critical ingredients of career choice interventions: More analyses and new hypotheses. *Journal of Vocational Behavior*, 62: 411–428.

De Haan, E. (2008) *Relational Coaching: Journeys Towards Mastering One-to-One Learning.* Chichester: Wiley.

Department of Health (2001) *Treatment Choice in Psychological Therapies and Counselling: Evidence-Based Clinical Practice Guideline.* London: Stationery Office.

Grant, A. M. and Cavanagh, E. M. (2007) Doing good, doing harm, being well and burning out: The interactions of perceived pro-social and antisocial impact in service work. *Journal of Occupational and Organizational Psychology*, 80: 665–691.

Grant, A. M. (2003) Keeping up with the cheese! Research as a foundation for professional coaching of the future. In I. F. Stein and L. A. Belsten (eds), *Proceedings of the First ICF Coaching Research Symposium*, 1–19. Mooresville, NC: Paw Print Press.

Greenwood, J. I. (2008) Validation of a multivariate career and educational counseling intervention model using long-term follow-up. *The Career Development Quarterly*, 56: 353–361.

Heppner, M. J. and Hendricks, F. (1995) A process and outcome study examining career indecision and indecisiveness. *Journal of Counseling and Development*, 73: 426–437.

Hettema, J., Steele, J. and Miller, W. R. (2005) Motivational interviewing. *Annual Review of Clinical Psychology*, 1: 91–111.

Kirschner, T., Hoffman, M. A. and Hill, C. E. (1994) Case study of the process and outcome of career counseling. *Journal of Counseling Psychology*, 41: 216–226.

Locke, E. A. and Latham, G. P. (1990) *A Theory of Goal Setting and Task Performance.* Englewood Cliffs, NJ: Prentice Hall International.

Whiston, S. C., Sexton, T. L. and Lasoff, D. L. (1998) Career-intervention outcome: A replication and extension of Oliver and Spokane (1988). *Journal of Counseling Psychology*, 45: 150–165.

Yates, J. (2011) Can Career Coaching Enhance Our Profession? *Constructing the Future,* VI. Stourbridge: Institute of Career Guidance.

Part I

Theories of career

Chapter 2

21st-century notions of 'career'

The word 'career' will come up hundreds of times in this book. It can mean a variety of things to different people and given the range of interpretation, implications and inferences that can be associated with the word, it is useful to begin by unpicking some of the key concepts.

Perhaps surprisingly, the world of career practitioners has thus far failed to reach an agreed definition of the term. 'Career', 'occupation' and 'vocation' are sometimes used as synonyms and at other times as quite distinct concepts. A career could cover just the time from first job to final job, or could incorporate the pre-occupation and post-occupation eras. It might also refer only to paid work, or may also encompass unpaid or voluntary employment or even work experience. Some feel that a career incorporates a notion of progress and advancement, or perhaps confers a degree of prestige. It has been argued that the term has an innate middle-class bias, as it implies that there has been an active choice, as opposed to an almost predetermined destiny which is more often associated with working-class career trajectories. More recently, there has been an acceptance that a career is a subjective construct, rather than an objective reality – the idea being that if *you* think it is a career, then it is a career. Definitions have also become broader. Arthur, Hall, and Lawrence (1989) suggested a straightforward definition, suggesting that 'career' is the 'evolving sequence of a person's work experiences over time'. I like the all-encompassing and non-judgemental ethos of this definition, and their simple explanation that 'everyone who works has a career' (1989: 9).

Compounding the challenges of agreeing a definition, however, is the rapidly changing nature of the labour market. The opportunities and expectations within our contemporary working lives are in many ways quite different from those of our parents and grandparents. In the first part of this chapter, we will look at the concepts that are central to careers these days by exploring some of the key changes in the labour market over the past 30 years. We will then turn our focus to career theories, and offer an inclusive framework which can help coaches to understand the huge range of academic approaches to career. Finally we will look at ways that we can use these theories to help our clients.

CHANGES IN THE LABOUR MARKET

The labour market has been transformed in recent years and the pace of change shows no sign of letting up. There are four changes that particularly affect the way we work (Kidd 2008).

1. **Globalization.** With the increase in low-cost international flights and the ease of international electronic communication, ever more organizations are trading globally and basing parts of their business in other countries. In many sectors, it has become commonplace to travel extensively, and spending a chunk of your career in another country is not unusual in (for example) the financial or clothing production sectors. Perhaps surprisingly, with globalization has not come an increased requirement for languages: English is now so prevalent as the business lingua franca that the need to be able to communicate in other languages is decreasing as globalization becomes more established.

2. **Technology.** Technology has of course had an impact on many areas of work. It has changed the way that most of us do our jobs – for some, beyond all recognition. The rise of technology has resulted in the dramatic reduction in many routine jobs, roles in which there are cognitive tasks that need to be performed with accuracy and speed. These have tended to be jobs at the semi-skilled level, such as a lay pattern designer or a typist. The result has been a labour market that is tending towards an hourglass shape, with a growing number of roles available in low-level and high-level jobs, but fewer opportunities in the middle, for semi-skilled roles. This is having a knock-on effect on social mobility in the workplace as there is a corresponding dearth of opportunities for workers in low-level jobs to move upwards. The effects of technology haven't always been quite what we had imagined. A decade ago, predictions about a paperless workplace and the demise of the office as people worked exclusively at home were widespread, but these predictions have not become reality: people tend to print off documents that are emailed to them, still prefer face-to-face meetings and enjoy social interactions with their colleagues at their desks.

3. **Industrial society to information society.** The focus has moved away from growing, producing and making things to an economy that values (and relies more on) expertise and intellectual property. The proportion of workers now employed in the manufacturing sector is a fraction of what it once was, whereas professional areas such as business services have grown dramatically over the last few decades.

4. **Part-time and flexible working arrangements.** Legislation, feminism and common sense have led to a dramatic increase in the number of women in the labour market, with an attendant demand for part-time and flexible working arrangements. Although it has been women who have benefited most from these changes, increasing numbers of men are taking career breaks, working

from home or reducing their hours. In his 1994 book *The Empty Raincoat*, Charles Handy proposed the notion of the 'portfolio worker', whose working week would be made up of a variety of types of work – perhaps combining two part-time jobs, or one part-time job, some freelance work and a course. This much-vaunted notion, although more popular than it once was, is not widespread, and tends to be limited to certain pockets of the labour force such as those working in the creative industries.

A job for life?

One change that seems to be widely accepted is that a job for life is a thing of the past. The received wisdom is that there has been a dramatic shift in job security within the last generation, but in fact, neither job turnover within the labour market – nor our attitudes to it – have changed so much in the last 50 years. It is a common misconception that several decades ago, workers were more or less guaranteed a job for as long as they wanted one, joining an organization at the bottom straight from school and then working their way up as far as they could go. This is thought to have been the norm for most, and job changes are thought to have been rare. Today, it is thought that jobs are much more fluid, with frequent changes being both more common and considered more desirable than they were previously – an idea explored in more detail in Arthur and Rousseau's 'boundaryless career' model (1996).

The evidence, however, tells a different story and suggests that, broadly, job security has been pretty stable for the last 50 years, and that although there have been changes over the last generation, the figures 'do not support the view that the dramatic changes in the labour market, technology and competition have spelt the end of "jobs for life"' (Burgess and Rees 1996: 334). There *have* been changes in the number of redundancies annually in the work force, but these have followed economic cycles. There has been a slight decrease in average job tenure (i.e. how long people stay in a particular job) for men but no significant overall change for women. Average job tenure has decreased for lower earning men, but stayed static for the more well-remunerated. Job tenure tends to increase as the economic growth slows down, as people are more likely to hang on to their jobs in a time of economic uncertainty, but as the economy picks up and workers feel more confident about available opportunities, they tend to move jobs more frequently (Burgess and Rees 1996).

The current picture

Since the financial crisis of 2008 and the consequent recession and cuts in public sector funding, we have entered an unprecedented era in the labour market. The long-term impact of the 2008 economic collapse on the world of work is still to be seen, but two trends are worth noting. First, the rhetoric that this recession was going to be a 'white collar' one has so far proved false. Professional jobs have continued to grow over the last three years while the main areas of job loss have been in lower-level roles. Second, unemployment figures aren't nearly as bad as everyone predicted. Given that we fell into the deepest recession since the 1930s, the number of unemployed workers is surprisingly low, with the number of jobs actually rising by 500,000 between 2010 and 2012. Reasons for this are still emerging, but alongside possible explanations that each worker is simply producing less, it is thought that organizations and individuals are using part-time and flexible work as a means of avoiding redundancies or unemployment. Nearly half of the 'new' jobs that emerged during this period (2010–2012) were self-employed roles, suggesting that individuals are using their creative and entrepreneurial skills to maintain an income rather than face unemployment (Office for National Statistics, 2013).

These changes in the labour market have had quite an impact on the way that we conceptualize careers. Modern attitudes to career development have shifted considerably in the last generation (e.g. Savickas 2002). The most noticeable and widespread change is that of agency: who is in charge of an individual's career. These days we are taking more responsibility for our own career development, and rather than relying on the organizations we work for to take charge of our training and career progression, we are more likely to make our own decisions and take matters into our own hands, asking our managers for opportunities to develop or organizing training outside the workplace.

Both the world of work and our attitudes towards career management have changed. Let's now explore the academic community's theoretical response to these changes.

CAREER THEORIES

Career theories are developed by academics to help us make sense of people's experiences and dozens have been developed over the last few decades. The theories come from a wide range of academic disciplines and are sparked off by different stimuli. Some theories focus on the content of careers and career decisions, and others look at processes; some are heavily influenced by psychological theories of the individual while the philosophical origins of others are more sociological. The theories do not try to explain every element of the career process, and aren't intended to be applied to every person in every context. In one way, this piecemeal approach is quite helpful to us as learners in that the theories do not contradict each other: we don't need to choose which one we want to believe. In another, though, it makes our jobs much more difficult in that it is quite a challenge to keep all the different theoretical approaches in our heads at once, and to know how to and when to use them to help us understand our clients better.

One helpful framework is that devised by Inkson (2004) who looked at the range of metaphors that the theories use to illustrate their approaches. The categories below are Inkson's, but I have updated the examples to include more recent career theories and concepts.

1. Legacy metaphor: career as inheritance

These approaches are grounded in sociological thinking and hold that our career paths are (at least to some degree) inevitable, being a product of our family and upbringing, our genes, our geographical location or demographic factors such as our gender or ethnicity. Even some of the more psychological theories which appreciate the role of self-determinism, such as Gottfredson's (2002) theory of circumscription and compromise, acknowledge the career inheritances that we are born with.

2. Craft metaphor: career as construction

This metaphor incorporates many of the key psychological theories that emphasize the agency of individuals and the role that they can play in determining their career paths. This metaphor encompasses the idea of self-creation of career and the idea of career as part of an identity that helps to create a sense of self. The notion of 'craft' marries ideas of both functionality and creativity. Career models that apply this construction metaphor include Super's life-span, life-space model (1996), Savickas's (2002) notion of career construction and the social constructivist theories such as the socio-cognitive career choice theory of Lent, Brown and Hackett (2002).

3. Seasons metaphor: career as cycle

This series of theories assumes that the processes of career planning and development are different at different stages in your life. It includes traditional theories such as Super's (1957) developmental theory and Levinson *et al.*'s (1978) age and stage theories. More recent theories, such as Maniero and Sullivan's (2005) kaleidoscope model, focus on the idea of gender and the varied motivators that drive men and women at specific stages of their careers. Boyatzis and Kolb (2000) conceptualize the cycle as a series of cycles, each building on the last. These theories have been widely criticized for being too inflexible and invoking unhelpful stereotypes (e.g. Paul and Townsend 1993), however.

4. Matching metaphor: career as 'fit'

This has been the dominant paradigm in careers for the last 50 years, since Holland came up with his RIASEC inventory of career interests (see Holland 1997 for a more recent exploration of the theory). The metaphor can be explained by the idea of matching square pegs with square holes, and has also been promoted by Dawis and Loftquist's (1984) theory of work adjustment and Dawis's (2002) concept of person–environment fit. This theory has great intuitive appeal, and in addition is popular with those controlling the budgets for careers services because it appears to lend itself to a quick fix. Matching theories such as Holland's have spawned myriad computer programs that link people's interests, skills and values to appropriate job titles and (in theory) identify suitable occupations. But there are significant problems with this theory (developed in more detail in Chapter 3) in that it is hard to know what individual and job characteristics we should be measuring. In addition, it is a static theory applied to a dynamic and fast-moving workplace, and in any case, our best estimate is that a good person–environment fit accounts for only around 5 per cent of job satisfaction (Spokane, Meir and Catalano 2000).

5. Path metaphor: career as journey

This is perhaps the most common of the career metaphors, and it incorporates the twin notions of movement between place and time. A range of different theories conceptualize the movement in different ways. The traditional notion of a 'career ladder' implies a journey upwards, climbing promotion by promotion to a more senior, better paid role with more responsibility. Driver (1984) describes career journeys as being either 'linear' or 'spiral', and implicit in the boundaryless career (Arthur and Rousseau 1996, examined in more detail below) is the notion of a journey that is no longer limited to a particular route.

This metaphor, perhaps more than any other, has crept into common usage whenever we talk about careers: think about the notion of a career *path*, reaching a *crossroads* in your career, taking a *step* backwards, or finding yourself in a *dead-end* job.

6. Network metaphor: career as encounters and relationships

Careers are not pursued in isolation. The network metaphor explores ideas of career as a social or political institution. The prevalence of networking as a way to get and keep a job, or to generate business highlights the importance of relationships, and a relatively recent wave of relational career decision-making theories (Amundson *et al.* 2010; Blustein 2001) are acknowledging the pivotal and inevitable role that others have in our career choices. There has been an enormous volume of work on work–family conflict, and theories (such as Hakim 2006) demonstrate the importance of family life in career decisions.

7. Theatre metaphor: career as role

The organization can be viewed as your stage with you as the central character of a play, taking on different roles as you move through the story. Notions of role models (e.g. Gibson 2004) help us to better understand how to play the part, and psychological contracts as they are negotiated and re-negotiated (e.g. Rousseau 1995) allow the nature of the role to be clarified and to evolve. Role theory leads us to understand concepts of role conflict and role overload, and Gioia and Poole's (1984) idea of career scripts is based on the notion of a developing and deepening understanding of a role. Other research on possible selves (Markus and Nurius 1986) shows us how we play with the idea of different future roles, and 'try them out' to see how they feel, as a way to make our career decisions.

8. Economic metaphor: career as resource

Originally a metaphor conceptualized from the perspective of the employer, this metaphor is best known in the term 'human resources'. This phrase replaced the term 'personnel management' in the mid 1980s as organizations started to think of the labour force as less of a cost and more of an investment or resource. Within the career development arena, the concept is encapsulated in the notion of 'career capital' (e.g. Inkson and Arthur 2001), which looks at a career in terms of a bank of resources that you build up with every new experience encountered.

9. Narrative metaphor: career as story

The last of Inkson's metaphors is perhaps the one that has most currency in current career development theory and practice. The importance of career stories is grounded in the post-modern concept of multiple truths, which holds that there is no definitive 'truth' about someone's career history. A career history can be told from multiple different perspectives and the same incident can have quite different meanings depending on who sees it and their own take on it. The career story is important because it shows how individuals experience and value their own reality. Our stories about our careers are full of inconsistencies and they change between tellings, but this illustrates the complexities of our careers and our responses to them, and also serves as exploration of how these stories can reveal a great deal about our current situations. Savickas (1989) has developed the 'Career Style Interview', which offers a framework for practitioners to use in order to help clients explore their own stories and make their own meanings from their experiences. Other researchers have also made use of this metaphor. Osland (1995), for example, makes links between career 'archetypes', such as individual journeying and heroism, and ancient mythology. Nicholson and West (1988) even go so far as to suggest that careers are myths, 'fictions about the past to help us feel good about the future' (1988: 94).

CAREER DEVELOPMENT THEORIES

I will explore some of the theories above in more depth later on in the book, particularly in Chapter 3, which focuses on career decision making, but I now want to highlight four of the theories that specifically focus on the life span, evolution and trajectory of entire careers. These are the boundaryless career (Arthur and Rousseau 1996), the protean career (Hall 1996), the kaleidoscope model (Maniero and Sullivan 2005) and the life-span, life-space model (Super 1996).

The boundaryless career

The boundaryless career (Arthur and Rousseau 1996) has caught our collective imagination, finding currency with the public, media and academic communities. Proposed over 15 years ago, it told of the end of traditional, organizational careers in favour of more fluid, more flexible career paths. The psychological contract had changed: organizations were no longer in a position to offer a secure job and steady promotion prospects in exchange for lifelong devotion. The 'boundaries' are most often interpreted as those of the organization: in the traditional view of a career, an individual moved up the career ladder, but within one organization. Now an individual can move sideways, upwards, diagonally or indeed into a totally different field. Other boundaries that Arthur and Rousseau suggest are mutable these days are geographical (as people commute far further to get to work and might follow their careers from one region or from one country to another) and occupational (as people make major career changes throughout their working lives).

Critics (e.g. Rodrigues and Guest 2010) respond to the model at both a conceptual and an empirical level. First, they suggest that although the metaphor of a boundaryless career is easy to understand, it is an oversimplification and poorly represents the complexities of career development and career moves. The evidence suggests that there hasn't actually been a great change in work behaviour in the last 30 years. Careers were thought to have changed from organizational to boundaryless in the mid 1980s, but as we discussed above, looking at employment data in the US, UK and the rest of Europe from the 1970s onwards, there is only a marginal shift towards shorter tenure and more frequent turnover, much of which can be accounted for by economic cycles.

The second main criticism is around the idea of agency (i.e. who calls the shots). The theory holds that traditional careers were controlled by the organization while new-style boundaryless careers are controlled by the individual. In truth, the evidence seems to suggest that although modern careers may include more changes from one organization to another, the impetus for the move more often than not stems from the organization and not the individual – so the move from one firm to another is the result of changes in the business that result in redundancies or a lack of opportunities for development, rather than an individual's proactive decision to take control (Swinnerton and Wial 1995). A recent survey (Wittekind *et al.* 2010) showed that 66 per cent of employees are hoping for a stable, secure career with a single employer, where only 15 per cent are actively aspiring to a boundaryless career.

Case study

Suzanne's passion in life was art history and she was delighted to get a job at the Victoria and Albert Museum (V&A) for decorative arts in London when she left university. She got involved with a range of activities at the museum, including co-curating a major exhibition, and developed a strong portfolio of skills and a good network. But with the arrival of children and a move to York with her husband's work, things had to change. She gave up her permanent contract at the V&A, but stayed on to work for them on an occasional project basis, commuting down to London when she needed to. Alongside this she started building up her freelance profile, writing articles for art magazines and becoming involved in lecturing in different contexts. She did some media work, including appearances on *Women's Hour* and various BBC4 documentaries, but the work began to dry up and she needed to find a new angle. She approached her husband's publishers with a book idea and they agreed to give her an advance on a new biography of Effie Gray, a key figure in the Pre-Raphaelite movement. She heard that a film was being made about the same topic and did some digging around to find out whether she could make some links with the film producers. Although there were no opportunities to get involved in any way with that particular film, her contacts did open up another door for her and she was invited to work as the historical consultant on a film about the life of Charles Dickens.

The thread of Victorian art history has run throughout Suzanne's career history, but she has combined full and part-time employment with project and freelance work, and has moved between curating, writing, teaching, lecturing and consultancy. Her interesting and diverse career has been the result of circumstances, contacts, determination and a proactive approach, as well as great expertise and a genuine love for her field.

The protean career

Building on the emphasis on agency within the boundaryless career, Hall (1996) developed the protean career model, which is a proactive and values-driven approach to a career. Named after Proteus, an Ancient Greek sea god who was able to change his shape, the model proposes that in today's rapidly changing work environment, workers need to be able to respond to the needs of the workplace and adapt to meet their employers' demands. The author argues that a career that does not follow this model is likely to be dependent, based on the values and choices of others, and thus less likely to be fulfilling. Self-directed workers engage in active networking, building up formal and informal contacts to support them professionally, and manage their own professional development, seeking out opportunities to learn new skills.

Critics argue that while this approach may suit those who have the luxury of being able to make their own career decisions, it may seem aspirational, perhaps to the point of being fanciful, for the less privileged. As Kidd (2008: 5) puts it, 'one might ask, however, how far will those who are less advantaged socially and educationally be able to achieve the personal skills and level of autonomy to manage their own careers?'.

Case study

Jacob had joined Amnesty International as a teenager and was an active campaigner on their behalf throughout his time at college and university, so it felt like a natural step to apply for a permanent job when he graduated. He got a job as a researcher on their Africa desk but soon found the organization too corporate and too hierarchical, and left to do an MA in African Studies. He then worked for some time for Jubilee 2000, campaigning against third world debt, before moving on to the World Development Movement, a small collective non-governmental organization (NGO) with a socialist and collaborative structure that focused on African development from a political standpoint. After a while, Jacob decided to reduce his hours at the NGO and networked his way to some freelance work teaching, running campaigns and working as a consultant to a variety of charities and government agencies, including Gordon Brown's office when he was Chancellor of the Exchequer, to supplement his income. During this time, he developed an interest in organic farming and started volunteering for a local cooperative. When a part-time paid opportunity came up with the organization, Jacob decided to leave the charity sector and take the job. He is now working in their café, doing their accounts, filling veggie boxes and teaching permaculture to local community groups.

It is clear to see how influential Jacob's values have been in every one of his career decisions, both in terms of the content of the roles he has taken and the culture and structure of the organizations he has worked for. Control, the other key element of the protean career, can also be clearly seen in Jacob's story: he has remained firmly in control of his decisions, moving from one organization to another when it felt right for him.

The kaleidoscope career

The body of career research has often been accused of being very male-centric: theories developed by men using male participants to devise approaches that explain male career paths. Our third model for modern careers, by contrast, stemmed from research into women's career trajectories. The role of women in the labour force has changed quite substantially over the last generation or so, with more women working, more women occupying senior roles, and a widespread acceptance of the part-time and flexible arrangements that working mothers have demanded.

Maniero and Sullivan (2005) developed the kaleidoscope model of careers to explain some of the different decisions that men and women are likely to make in their career paths.

> Like a kaleidoscope that produces changing patterns when the tube is rotated and its glass chips fall in to new arrangements, women shift the pattern of their careers by rotating different aspects of their lives to arrange their roles and relationships in new ways.
>
> (2005: 106)

They describe women's careers as fundamentally relational, and their studies suggest that women are much more likely to evaluate every career decision in the light of its impact on their family. Career and context are inextricably linked. The kaleidoscope model proposes three key motivators in career decisions:

1. Authenticity. Can I still be myself in the midst of all this?
2. Balance. If I make this career decision, can I balance the other parts of my life to make a coherent whole?
3. Challenge. Will I be sufficiently challenged if I accept this career option?

Most career decisions will involved some interaction of all these elements, but the balance will change over time, and Maniero and Sullivan found that the dominant influence tends to differ between men and women. Their research suggests that early career choices for both genders are dominated by the desire for challenge. This can manifest itself in different ways, but often includes a desire for prestige, high salaries and status, and perhaps an opportunity to develop expertise or gain a qualification. In the mid-career years, the relative importance of these factors decreases, particularly for women. Women tend to be more drawn to roles and opportunities that will allow them to fulfil other areas of their lives such as caring for their young children or ageing parents, or devoting some time to their interests or voluntary work. Critics point out that women who have children are under more pressure and tend to have greater motivation to focus on their work–life balance during their mid-career years but the authors hold that their model applies to women regardless of their personal and family circumstances. Men at this stage are still often motivated by the extrinsic rewards of status and salary, but tend to focus more on developing and determining their professional identity – discovering who they are and what that means to them within the workplace. In the later career years, perhaps when the external demands of caring for family members have typically diminished, women then are more likely to start to explore their professional identities, and make choices that align their professional and personal selves more closely. For men, this period is characterized by a focus on their work–life balance, perhaps in preparation for retirement and a new life chapter.

Table 2.1

	Women	Men
Early career	Challenge	Challenge
Mid-career	Balance	Authenticity
Late career	Authenticity	Balance

The model could be criticized as being simplistic and overly generalized, but it has a great deal of resonance with many women in today's work force.

Case study

Fiona left university with a degree in maths and in common with many of her contemporaries, she applied for a graduate training scheme with a firm of accountants. The training was tough but it was well paid and she enjoyed being part of a large team. After her children were born, she continued to work for a few years but when they started at school it became clear that it was not a career that fitted in very well with her family life. It was hard to find any part-time opportunities at an interesting level, and unless the job was on her doorstep, she would never be able to get back to pick up her children from after-school club. She decided to re-train as a maths teacher. She found a part-time job in a local school and for the next ten years managed, with a little help from her partner and various childcare options, to pick up her kids from school and look after them in the holidays. During this period she gradually built back up to a full-time role but when her children were in their sixth form, she felt that she was ready for another change. Teaching had worked out extremely well while her kids had been at home and she had genuinely enjoyed some elements of the role, but the bureaucracy, admin and endless marking had taken their toll on her enthusiasm. The best part of the job for her had been working with the parents and helping them plan ways to support their own children. Fiona had taken a course in coaching while working as a teacher and now decided to set herself up as a parent coach, using her networks within the school and council to obtain some referrals. The work is steady, but she's developing a good reputation in the field and has a few regular contracts with the council as well as some private clients.

Fiona feels positive about all three different phases of her career, but each was clearly motivated by different values. In the early days, she enjoyed the prestige, salary and intellectual challenge of accountancy, loved the social life associated with it, and was happy to live and breathe her firm. When her children came along, she needed something that would allow her to fulfil her role as 'mother', and in her final phase, free of the demands of parenthood and the need to establish her status and identity, she felt that she had free rein to choose something that genuinely meant a lot to her.

Life-span, life-space

One of the most influential thinkers within the history of career research is Donald Super. His developmental model, which explored the different stages of vocational development throughout our working lives, was popular with practitioners in the late 20th century, and later on in his career, responding to criticisms that his early model was too rigid, he developed the 'life-span, life-space' model (1996). The model is a broad one that acknowledges the influences of individual factors, circumstances and the experiences and opportunities that present themselves to us. One of Super's key ideas is that of the self-concept. Your self-concept is how you see yourself and is linked to the notion of 'identity' that we will explore in more detail in Chapter 3. It is a product of your self and your environment and how the two interact. Super's model holds that working lives are most fulfilling when your work allows you to implement your self-concept, i.e. to be the person that you think you are. Your self-concept develops throughout your life, and Super identifies a series of stages of vocational development that we go through, from growth and exploration in childhood and young adulthood, establishment and maintenance in our mid-career period and decline around retirement. The sequence of stages is proposed as fairly stable, but the model allows for considerable flexibility around the specific timing and duration of each stage, and proposes that we go through a mini-cycle of each of the stages every time we face a transition or a period of de-stabilization in our careers.

Using these theories in coaching practice

Clients often present with career histories that on the surface just don't seem to make sense, sometimes even to the clients themselves. The absence of a coherent narrative can be quite troubling for clients as they struggle to understand the decisions that they have made. If you as a practitioner can share a theory or a metaphor with your clients, you can give them a framework that might allow them to understand their own stories better, and it can be a powerful way to validate their choices. In one of the case studies above, we saw Jacob make a career change from studying African politics to organic farming. An appreciation of the protean career model can help us to see this as a choice that fits perfectly into a value-driven career, rather than an unconnected move. A client such as Fiona might be feeling that she is letting herself down in some sense by opting for a lower level, part-time job when her children came along. Understanding that this is a well-trodden 'kaleidoscope' path for many women may allow her to enjoy the choices that she is making. The theories can encourage clients to see their choices as progression and development rather than as illogical decisions.

The theories, metaphors and frameworks can support your interactions with clients, even if you don't share them directly. It can give you some clue as to the kind of language and ideas your clients are likely to respond well to, and perhaps most valuably, it can help to enhance your empathy for your clients.

New career theories are being created and published all the time. Every new angle, every change in the labour market, and every new academic paradigm will spawn a range of new theories, building on the old and shifting to accommodate new ways of thinking. Keeping up with them all and making sense of how they all fit together feels like a daunting task, but having an awareness of this framework of metaphors can help communication with your clients as you listen to the language that they choose and respond appropriately. Eventually you will develop your own bank of the ideas and concepts that you feel best explain your clients' stories and help them make sense of their choices.

REFERENCES

Amundson, N. E., Borgen, W. A., Iaquinta, M., Butterfield, L. D. and Koert, E. (2010) Career decisions from the decider's perspective. *Career Development Quarterly*, 58(4): 335–351.

Arthur, M. B. and Rousseau, D. M. (eds) (1996) *The Boundaryless Career: A New Employment Principle for a New Organizational Era*. Oxford: Oxford University Press.

Arthur, M. B., Hall, D. T. and Lawrence, B. S. (1989) Generating new directions in career theory: The case for a transdisciplinary approach. In M. B. Arthur, D. T. Hall and B. S. Lawrence (eds), *Handbook of Career Theory*, Cambridge: Cambridge University Press.

Blustein, D. L. (2001) The interface of work and relationships: Critical knowledge for 21st century psychology. *The Counseling Psychologist*, 32(4): 603–611.

Boyatzis, R. E. and Kolb, D. A. (2000) Performance, learning, and development as modes of growth and adaptation throughout our lives and careers. In M. Peiperl, M. Arthur, R. Goffee and T. Morris (eds), *Career Frontiers: New Conceptions of Working Lives.* Oxford: Oxford University Press.

Burgess, S. and Rees, H. (1996) Job Tenure in Britain 1975–1992. *The Economic Journal*, 106: 334–344.

Campbell, E. (1968) *Hero with a Thousand Faces*. Princeton, NJ: Princeton University Press.

Cochran, L. (1998) *Career Counseling: A Narrative Approach*. Newbury Park, CA: Sage Publications.

Dawis, R. V. (2002) Person–environment correspondence theory. In S. D. Brown and R. W. Lent (eds), *Career Development and Counseling: Putting Theory and Research to Work*. Hoboken, NJ: Wiley, pp. 3–23.

Dawis, R. V. and Loftquist, L. H. (1984) *A Psychological Theory of Work Adjustment*. Minneapolis: University of Minnesota Press.

Driver, M. J. (1984) Career concepts – a new approach to career research. In R. Katz (ed.), *Career Issues in Human Resource Management*. Englewood Cliffs, NJ: Prentice Hall.

Gibson, D. E. (2004) Role models in career development: new directions for theory and research. *Journal of Vocational Behavior* 65: 134–156.

Gioia, D. A. and Poole, P. P. (1984) Scripts in organizational behavior. *Academy of Management Review*, 6(3): 449–459.

Gottfredson, L. S. (2002) Gottfriedson's theory of circumscription, compromise and self-creation. In D. Brown *et al.* (eds), *Career Choice and Development*, 4th ed. San Francisco: Jossey-Bass, pp. 85–148.

Hakim, C. (2006) Women, careers and work-life preferences. *British Journal of Guidance and Counselling*, 34(3): 279–294.

Hall, D. T. (1996) Protean careers of the 21st century. *Academy of Management Executive*, 10(4): 8–16.

Handy, C. (1994) *The Empty Raincoat: Making Sense of the Future*. London: Hutchinson.

Holland, J. L. (1997) *Making Vocational Choices: A Theory of Vocational Personalities and Work Environments*, 3rd ed. Englewood Cliffs, NJ: Prentice-Hall.

Inkson, K. (2004) Images of career: nine key metaphors. *Journal of Vocational Behavior*, 65: 96–111.

Inkson, K. and Arthur, M. B. (2001) How to be a successful career capitalist. *Organizational Dynamics*, 30(1): 48–61.

Kidd, J. (2008) Mental capital and wellbeing: Making the most of ourselves in the 21st century. *State-of-Science Review: SR-C10 Careers at Work*. London: The Government Office for Science.

Lent, R. W., Brown, S. D. and Hackett, G. (2002) Social cognitive career theory. In D. Brown & Associates (eds), *Career Choice and Development*, 4th ed. San Francisco: Jossey-Bass, pp. 255–311.

Levinson, D. J., Darrow, C. N., Klein, E. B., Levinson, M. H. and McKee, B. (1978) *The Seasons of a Man's Life*. New York: Knopf.

Manieiro, L. A. and Sullivan, S. E. (2005) Kaleidoscope careers: An alternative explanation for the 'opt-out revolution'. *Academy of Management Executive*, 19(1): 106–123.

Markus, H. R. and Nurius, P. (1986) Possible selves. *American Psychologist*, 41: 954–969.

Nicholson, N. and West, M. (1988) *Managerial Job Change: Men and Women in Transition*. Cambridge: Cambridge University Press.

Office for National Statistics (2013) *Labour Market Statistics*. London: Office for National Statistics.

Osland, J. S. (1995) *The Adventure of Working Abroad: Hero Tales from the Global Frontier*. San Francisco: Jossey-Bass.

Paul, R. J., & Townsend, J. B. (1993) Managing the older worker – don't just rinse away the gray. *Academy of Management Executive*, 7(3): 67–74.

Rodrigues, R. A. and Guest, D. (2010) Have careers become boundaryless? *Human Relations*, 63(8): 1157–1175.

Rousseau, D. M. (1995) *Psychological Contracts in Organizations: Understanding Written and Unwritten Agreements*. Thousand Oaks, CA: SAGE Publications.

Savickas, M. L. (1989) Career style assessment and counseling. In T. Sweeney (ed.) *Adlerian Counseling: A Practical Approach for a New Decade*, 3rd ed. Muncie, IN: Accelerated Development Press, pp. 289–320.

Savickas, M. (2002) Career construction: A developmental theory of vocational behavior. In D. Brown & Associates (eds), *Career Choice and Development*, 4th ed. San Francisco: Jossey-Bass, pp. 149–205.

Spokane, A. R., Meir, E. I. and Catalano, M. (2000) Person–environment congruence and Holland's theory of careers: A review and reconsideration. *Journal of Vocational Behavior*, 57: 137–187.

Super, D. E. (1957) *The Psychology of Careers*. New York: Harper & Row.

Super, D. E. (1996) A life-span, life-space approach to career development. In D. Brown, L. Brooks & Associates (eds), *Career Choice and Development*, 2nd ed. San Francisco: Jossey-Bass, pp. 197–261.

Swinnerton, K. A. and Wial, H. (1995) Is job stability declining in the US economy? *Industrial and Labor Relations Review*, 48(2): 293–304.

Wittekind, A., Raeder, S. and Grote, G. (2010) A longitudinal study of determinants of perceived employability. *Journal of Organizational Behavior*, 31: 566–586.

Chapter 3

How people make career decisions

Before we launch into the theory underpinning career decision making, it is worth spending a moment questioning a key assumption, which is whether we do all actually make decisions about our careers. Clearly some groups of people have more options than others. The number of career options you have to choose from is determined by a vast range of factors including personality, abilities, qualifications, location, class, ethnicity, gender, age, health, economic climate, role models, luck, attitudes and family background. Some may feel that their career paths are a product of their circumstances and to a degree, pre-destined by factors such as geography and social class. Bimrose and Barnes (2011: 2) wonder: 'Are individuals actually able to navigate their way effectively and "choose" their career biographies, or do the social structures within which they make decisions constrain freedom to determine their own destiny?' The options open to each of us vary tremendously, but pretty much all of us will be involved in career decisions at some level, and certainly those who engage with a career coach tend to be in the throes of career choice. So what do we know about how people make career decisions and how can the theory help us?

Career decision making is one of the areas where there is least synergy between theory and practice, and is generally the aspect of career learning that is least understood and most poorly communicated. But it is important. Too often inter-actions with a career professional focus on generating options rather than making decisions, and clients leave the session expecting that the right answer will magic-ally emerge. Sometimes, of course, it does, but as practitioners we need to under-stand the processes so that we can support those clients who need extra help.

There is a whole psychological discipline devoted to human decision making, looking at how and why we make the choices that we do, and whether there are good and bad ways to make a decision. Some of these theories have been applied to, and tested on, career decisions and in this chapter we will look at some of the key ideas, the big names and the significant studies within this arena.

There are two elements to the decision-making process and we will look at them in turn. The first part of the chapter will explore the factors that influence us when we make decisions, and in part two we will turn to the actual thinking processes involved when we make our choices. In the third part of the chapter we will look at a few models of decision-making styles, some of which link both factors and processes. In some ways these distinctions are artificial ones – in practice, the different elements happen simultaneously and are interlinked – but this distinction will serve as a useful framework for exploring the ideas.

THE FACTORS: WHAT DO WE BASE OUR CAREER DECISIONS ON?

We'll look now at the three most significant groups of decision-making theories within vocational research that examine the kinds of factors that we base our decisions on: trait and factor, relational and post-rational.

Trait and factor or 'matching' approach

The trait and factor or 'matching' approach has been the dominant approach to career support within career guidance and occupational psychology in the UK and the US for years. The empirical evidence around these ideas raises serious questions about its usefulness and its limitations as a process, yet its intuitive appeal means that policy-makers, clients and practitioners remain firmly wedded to it. It provides a clear, easily understood framework and, important for policy-makers at least, a decision made this way can be done relatively quickly, and with only one professional intervention.

The premise of the theory is that people are more satisfied and more effective in jobs whose principal characteristics reflect their interests, values and skills. So, for example, if you like animals, you should seriously consider working as a veterinary nurse; if you are good at listening to people, you might want to think about counselling.

The biggest name within this arena is John Holland's (1959), whose prolific research has dominated the field for the last 50 years. Holland interviewed a large number of people doing all sorts of different jobs and categorized their vocational interests in one of six interest areas: Realistic, Investigative, Artistic, Social, Enterprising and Conventional (RIASEC). He then devised a questionnaire for clients that identifies an individual interest profile (based on their top three interest areas) and generates a list of jobs that might be suitable. Holland's work forms the basis of many interest inventories that are available online such as 'Prospects Planner' at the Graduate Prospects website (www.prospects.ac.uk).

The intuitive appeal of this approach is clear, and as a basis for a conversation around options and ideas, there is some value in these methods. As noted earlier, however, the empirical evidence is mixed and certainly suggests that this approach isn't the only one we need.

There has been plenty written about matching theories but the research has never really explored (or at least, not conclusively) the extent to which they are applicable in the real world or useful to practitioners. Instead it has focused on the internal structure of the theories – whether the traits are distinguishable from each other, and how accurately we can measure them. There are, therefore, several questions over this approach to career decision making that remain unanswered.

First there is an issue about whether this approach, initially developed more than half a century ago, is helpful in the current labour market: a theory whose premise is that relatively stable characteristics such as personality and values should predict career choice doesn't seem to be terribly appropriate in a labour market characterized by rapid change. The theory has been shown to be too culturally specific for our multicultural workforce and its relevance to women's careers has been queried. The theory doesn't appreciate the idea of personality development or the dramatic way that interests can change, and finally it has been estimated (see Spokane, Meir and Catalano 2000 for a review of the literature) that even if everything else goes to plan, congruence (by which we mean the degree to which you 'match' your job) accounts for only around five per cent of job satisfaction.

Holland's research continues to dominate but other variants of the trait and factor approach have emerged, including Dawis and Loftquist's (1984) theory of work adjustment which acknowledges a bilateral influence that an individual and their workplace have on each other.

These models of career decision making are prescriptive – they show us how we *ought* to make decisions. We'll move on now to more recent approaches that, although not yet quite as widely embraced by practitioners, have much closer links to making occupational choices in the real world.

Relational approaches

A growing body of work has looked at the impact of relationships and 'relational processes', by which we mean individuals' connections to others within their communities and the impact of society on their decisions. This approach to career decision making has traditionally been considered a poor way to make choices, with the prevailing view being that decisions ought to be made autonomously and that the role of the career practitioner should be to help clients to identify and dismiss any hint of influence from others. As Shultheiss *et al.* (2002: 302) put it, 'Traditionally, theory and practice have been based on the merit of independent thought and judgement'; as Blustein (2004: 605) points out, however, we 'do not make career decisions in a relational vacuum' and the evidence showing not only how widespread, but also how positive these influences are, is becoming hard to ignore.

In their 2010 study, Amundson *et al.* (2010) showed that an impressive 94 per cent of the participants based career decisions at least in part on a feeling of 'connectedness', and the research is beginning to paint a picture of the different ways in which all those close to us influence our decisions. Much of the research has been conducted with young people as participants, so the impact of parents has been particularly under the spotlight, but data is emerging on the role of siblings, friends and partners (Schultheiss *et al.* 2002; O'Brien 1996). One interesting study (Brousseau *et al.* 2010) looked at the different impact of male and female partners (in this instance in heterosexual relationships) and found differences in the kind of support they are likely to give when their partners are facing a career choice. Female partners were shown to be more likely to help increase their partner's self-awareness and suggest jobs that might suit them. Male partners were more likely to encourage risks and help to dispel dysfunctional myths with a bracing 'go for it!' attitude.

In fact, a wide range of people and roles have been shown to sway our career decisions, with friends, colleagues and families (including even deceased relatives) all being shown to have an impact on our job-related decision-making processes. In general, the message is that the involvement of our nearest and dearest has a positive impact on our ability to make career decisions and on our levels of satisfaction with the decisions we make.

The empirical evidence for the relational aspect of career decision making has been related in particular to two psychological theories: attachment theory and relational theory. Attachment theory was first proposed by Bowlby (1969) and concerns long-lasting relationships, focusing largely on the impact that early childhood relationships can have. Relational theory (which has grown out of the work of Jean Baker Miller 1976) holds that much of our motivation in life is driven by a desire to connect with others, and it is only through these connections that we identify ourselves. We can only touch on these theories in this book, but Blustein (e.g. 2001) and Schultheiss (e.g. 2003) have both written widely on their role within career decision-making processes.

It can be a valuable exercise within the coaching session to stimulate a discussion by using conversations that your clients have had with others. Sometimes clients' friends and family can give the advice or voice the concerns that you, as a coach, can't and asking clients not so much about what they have been advised, but what their reaction has been to that advice, can be very insightful. Conversations along these lines can also validate clients' choices to involve their loved ones in their decision, acknowledging, valuing and evaluating what others' views can bring. A discussion with a coach can allow clients to consider whether a negative comment from a friend is a valid warning or was said through a lack of understanding. It can also encourage them to explore why they are so quick to believe one particular opinion.

Post-rational career decision making

The third group of theories are collectively known as 'post-rational'. They are drawn from different theoretical backgrounds, but all accept that the kind of trait and factor matching approaches explained above are neither always realistic nor universally desirable. Quite a range of ideas fit into this broad category, including

Gelatt's (1989) theory of positive uncertainty and Bloch's (2005) application of chaos theory to a career model, but in this section we will focus on two theories that seem to have strong resonance with career decision makers these days.

Planned happenstance

Arguably the most popular of these theories, gaining currency both with academics and practitioners over recent years is Mitchell, Levin and Krumboltz's (1999) notion of 'planned happenstance'. This is a prescriptive approach that acknowledges the role of luck in career paths and career decisions. It encourages people to engage in behaviours that increase their chances of finding opportunities, and to be open to opportunities that come their way. This approach might lead a client to engage with a wide variety of work experience placements, even those which ostensibly may not sound all that appealing, on the off-chance that one leads to something. It might also encourage a client to be open to any opportunities that result from, for example, a fortuitous meeting at a party.

Alongside the obvious intuitive appeal of this theory (how many times have you heard someone explain their career decision by saying 'I just fell into it. . .'?), there is some empirical evidence to support this theory. Murtagh, Lopes and Lyons for example (2011) showed that career decisions are often based on some past activity or event that was undertaken with no thought of a career: the student whose gap year holiday job involved working children may go on to pursue a career in social work, for example, or the employee who once embarked on an Italian evening class may some years later apply for a secondment overseas.

One other useful element acknowledged in this approach is the time that it takes to reach a career decision. There can be an expectation, perpetuated both by clients and practitioners, that a client who arrives at a coaching session with a career dilemma should leave an hour later with all decisions made and a ten-year career path clearly mapped out. Planned happenstance highlights that decisions can take time – the participants in Murtagh's study took on average two years to make their choices.

It's not what you do, it's who you are: career identities and possible selves

The second of the post-rational theories is that of career identities and possible selves. This is a useful approach for coaches to get to grips with as it has a great deal of resonance with mid-career changers.

Identity is all about the meanings given to an individual by others and by themselves. These meanings are built up through a complex web of experiences and behaviours, including social roles, group memberships (social identities) and personal character traits that they display (personal identities). Identities are built up through individuals portraying themselves in a certain way and others responding to them. Your identity is who you are within a social context, and your professional identity is just one aspect of your whole identity. A professional identity that is closely aligned with a personal identity is more likely to lead to a sense of authenticity in one's work life and to job satisfaction.

The concept of professional identity was first proposed by Schein (1978) who described it as a 'relatively stable and enduring constellation of attributes, beliefs, values, motives and experiences in terms of which people define themselves in a professional role'. Your professional identity is your image of yourself at work. It is what you conjure up in your mind's eye when you talk about your work self, and it is how you think others judge you when you tell them what you do. It is based on what you know about your profession and your work life and how people respond to you when you talk about it.

From a career decision making point of view, what is important within this context is your own opinion of your professional identity. Does it convey what you want it to about you? When you tell people what you do, do you like the assumptions and judgements that you imagine they are making? In general, if you are comfortable with your professional identity, you are more likely to be comfortable with your job, and identifying what specifically makes someone feel uncomfortable with their professional identity can be very revealing. Your 'possible' self (or a possible identity) is your own image of yourself in a different role in the future. Pizzolato (2006: 58) defined possible selves as 'what we would like to become, what we could become and can be what we are afraid of becoming'.

> A very straightforward question to get your clients thinking about their own feelings regarding professional identity is to ask them how they respond (and how they feel about their response) when asked 'and what do you do?' in a social situation. One interesting linguistic tic to watch for here is whether they say 'I am a . . .' or 'I work as a . . .'. Those who say 'I am a . . .' are often reflecting a positive professional identity in their language – defining themselves by their roles; those who say 'I work as . . .' are putting some distance between themselves and their professions, perhaps reflecting a desire not to be defined by their job.

Career, work and professional identities and the idea of possible selves (or possible identities) are important concepts in career choice and career change. They can help people to dream, plan and reject. Possible selves can be used within career development both to aid career choice, and to make a career change more likely to be successful.

Schemas and niches

The idea of a schema has been around within the discipline of psychology for decades. A schema is a tiny package in your brain that stores all the information that you have about a particular thing. These schemas evolve and change, and are based on your experiences and your social learning within the world. Brower and Nurius (1993) have applied the idea of schemas to the world of occupational choice and suggest that each of us has a schema for every different occupation we are aware of. Some of these schemas will be fully formed and some based on reliable evidence or experience. Others might be scant or vague, or in large part based on culturally constructed stereotypes, but they still exist.

Elements of the schema for a particular occupation may be widely shared, but individuals will also have their own personal take on it. For example, take the schema of a plumber. For some, the idea of a plumber will conjure up a strong sense of autonomy – the concept of being your own boss and making your own decisions about what jobs to take. It might make you think of an image of driving around in your own van, in charge of your working week. An alternative schema of a plumber, held by others, could centre around the ideas of manual work and problem solving, focusing on the logical processes needed to identify a fault, the expert knowledge of plumbing systems required, and the manual strength and dexterity needed to fix it. For a third group, the schema might highlight the social nature of the role and the notion of going round to people's homes, having a chat and a nice cup of tea, and restoring their freezing cold rooms to warm and cosy homes.

So the 'schema' is our image of the job. The 'niche' as described by Brower and Nurius (1993) is our idea of what goes on in that person's life when they leave work, and it can encompass pretty much everything about their lives and lifestyles. It is about the house that they live in, the car they drive, their family, the holidays they go on and the way they spend time at the weekends.

When playing around with possible selves, we imagine our possible self not just in the working schema that we have, but also in the lifestyle niche that we conjure up. We then make a judgement about whether this is a possible self we would aspire to and could imagine inhabiting.

If you are the kind of person who would like to be going skiing during their holidays, who reads *The Independent* but also subscribes to *Grazia* and who saves every penny up for the latest Jimmy Choos, you may well feel much more comfortable with the niche and the identity of a PR executive than that of a plumber, even if your particular skills are more suited to plumbing than PR.

One effective way to use possible selves in career coaching is through visualization. Ask your clients to close their eyes and then get them to explore a day in the life in a possible professional identity. Ask how they're feeling about going in to work and encourage them to tell you about their colleagues, their environment and their tasks. You could then get them to explore the niche that they associate with the job – asking them to visualize their home, weekend and holidays. When they have finished the visualization, you can use it as the basis for discussion, encouraging them to analyse how they felt in the role.

THE PROCESS: HOW WE MAKE THE DECISION

We've looked so far in this chapter at some of the types of factors on which people base their career choices; whether it's how well a job matches their skills, interests and values, what their friends and family think, what opportunities happen to come their way and how they feel about living the life they associate with a particular role. We are now going to examine the processes that take them from these ideas to an actual decision.

There is a huge body of work conducted by psychologists over the last 40 years into how people make decisions. The received wisdom is that there are two complementary thinking systems that our brains use to make decisions. Sometimes they operate concurrently, at other times consecutively. One is the conscious, rational, logical approach and the other is our unconscious instantaneous, gut instinct.

Conscious reason

The first (and still the most influential) decision-making theory proposes that decisions are, and should be, grounded in conscious reason. The basic premise is that you need to identify the factors that are important to you, and then use a deliberate, rational process to work out which one is going to give you the best return.

One of the most influential theories in decision making in the 20th century was 'expected utility' decision-making theory, which has been applied to the process of making career choices by, for example, Pitz and Harren (1980) and it is an example of this thinking. If using expected utility to make a career choice, one would decide which factors matter and assess all the jobs imaginable against these criteria in order to find which option would give the best overall outcome.

Here is an example of how this might work. An individual might be considering the following five jobs: nurse, advertising executive, police officer, plumber and novelist. She might have identified four criteria which are particularly important to her within a work context: autonomy, the opportunity to help people, a job they find interesting and a fun environment to work in. The individual would then put all these factors into a spreadsheet, and give each job a rating for each factor. A simple calculation would then lead her to see that being a police officer would be most suitable for her.

Table 3.1

	Nurse	Ad exec	Police officer	Plumber	Novelist
Autonomy	5	6	7	9	9
Helping people	9	2	7	7	3
Interesting	6	7	5	3	9
Fun environment	4	8	6	2	1
Total	**24**	**23**	**25**	**21**	**22**

You might add some weighting to these categories, acknowledging that perhaps autonomy is more important to you than working in a fun environment, and you might factor in the probability of success: the novelist might lead you to the optimal outcome but your chances of making a living pursuing that option might be slim.

This may all sound well and good (and indeed is the basis of many careers education workshops, one-to-one sessions and books today) but in reality, that is just not how we make decisions. To begin with, we couldn't possibly work with a spreadsheet big enough to incorporate all possible job options. The weighting system and an estimate of probability also make the calculation complicated. And finally, in turns out that in practice, we are non-compensatory in our career decision making: that is, the presence of one good thing cannot make up for the absence of something else. If, for example, a job is badly paid, (and for us, this is a key factor), we won't take it, even if it ticks every other box for us, in that it is interesting, near home and has nice colleagues.

Gati (1986) proposed the 'sequential elimination' model, which expands the expected utility model and incorporates some new ideas. Rather than deciding between all the options at once, Gati's model proposes a gradual narrowing down of options, factor by factor, as a person choosing a degree course might gradually eliminate subjects in this way:

No scientific subjects

⇓

subjects compatible with A levels in French, English and History

⇓

subjects requiring 3Bs or less at A level

⇓

subjects involving some kind of literature

⇓

subjects also involving history

⇓

subjects including a gap year

⇓

subjects including a gap year in an English-speaking country

⇓

American Studies

The sequential elimination model has been shown to be much more aligned to the way that we usually make decisions, and is a more realistic framework that clients can use to help structure their decision making.

Conscious, rational reasoning is a decision-making style that is much admired by proponents of the trait and factor approach outlined above: traditional careers education programmes would always advocate a very deliberate and structured plan for identifying skills, values and interests and then matching them up with job ideas. But they are not one and the same thing. This type of conscious reason can be applied to any of the factor approaches we covered above; for example, you could use a conscious process of reason to decide to go with the job that your dad suggests (following a relational model) or you could apply an expected utility model of decision making to decide to work out the job in which your professional image is the most caring (professional identity).

Challenges presented by conscious reason

It seems that, however hard we try, it's nigh on impossible to keep our gut instinct from interfering with our conscious, rational minds. Another challenge we face is the amount of data that we need to absorb. A conscious, rational decision should assess all the information available and only then compare one thing with another. When it comes to the arena of careers, there is simply too much information even for our remarkable brains to cope with. So our brains take a few short cuts: rather than researching and absorbing every piece of information available to us, we are more likely to choose a subset (Gati and Tikotzki 1988) such as limiting the number of options we consider or selecting one criterion, such as promotion opportunities, for a broad review. Another technique our brains use in an attempt to cope with the volume of information available is something that Brownstein (2003) calls 'motivated reasoning'. Our gut instinct sneaks in and makes an early decision, and as our conscious mind is processing the information, it selects only the data that supports the instinct's choice.

Finally, it seems that our assumption that it is good for clients to have a wide range of options is being called into question. It has been well documented over the years that having a choice is helpful in decision making, allowing us to feel in control and making us happier with our final choices. However, research has recently suggested that more options are not always better and the optimal number of options tends to be around seven (Iyengar and Lepper 2000). When the number of options reaches 25 to 30, people really start to struggle to reach a decision, are more likely to put off making a choice altogether and tend to be less satisfied with the outcome. If we start to struggle at 25 options, what impact, I wonder, would the 665 occupational clusters that exist in the UK have on us?

Gut instinct

For most people, gut instinct plays an important role in our career decision making. Some of us put great faith in our instincts while others are more enthusiastic about trying to analyse and evaluate the reasons behind our initial preferences, but in one way, shape or form, the gut instinct is there and has a great impact on our choices. Greenbank and Hepworth (2008) conducted a study into the career decision-making processes of university students and found 'no evidence of any rational decision making at all' in the student population.

The phenomenon of gut instinct (or as the scholars lovingly call it, 'System 1') has received considerable attention within the journals focusing on decision making, but has not been tried and tested very widely within the careers arena. Gut instinct is an unconscious, automatic process. It is based on reason, but the reasoning process happens extremely quickly through a range of short cuts and the processing all happens in our unconscious minds, so we don't have access to these reasons. We may not quite understand how they work, but we do know that our gut instincts have evolved over the years into extremely smart systems, and are able to make perceptive judgements in an instant.

Instincts work in different ways, using a range of heuristics (or rules of thumb) that are often consistently reliable. In Gerd Gigerenzer's book *Gut Feelings* (2007), the author describes experiment after experiment that demonstrates how gut feeling can outperform conscious reason in a wide range of situations including trading on the stock market, choosing good schools, diagnosing heart conditions and predicting which political candidate will win an election.

It tends to be your instinct that allows you to be creative, seeing patterns and making links that your conscious thought processes might not, and from this perspective it is an extremely valuable element of a career decision, enabling individuals to generate ideas and solutions to their career dilemmas.

Gut instinct is shown to be particularly helpful in making decisions where it is not possible to process all the information thoroughly and for decisions that will inevitably be about shades of grey, rather than those with a definitive right answer, both of which suggest it might lend itself well to choices around occupations and jobs.

Challenges presented by gut instinct

The main challenge presented by gut instinct lies in the unconscious nature of the information processing. This means that conclusions and decisions made on this basis are susceptible to a whole range of flaws, biases and prejudices that we are both unaware of and unable to control, and the literature is full of evidence of the biases commonly found in instinctive thinking. In his book *Thinking Fast and Slow* (2011), Daniel Kahneman, one of the leading scholars within the field of rational decision making, describes a range of experiments that have shown us some of the most common biases that our instinct is susceptible to. As a whole story, it would make one question instinctive decision making as a reliable way to make major life choices, but there are some biases that seem particularly significant within the field of career decision making.

We are susceptible to bias when selecting information to trust. Our conscious, rational mind would take a piece of career information and consider a range of factors such as how many people agree with this view or how reliable is the source. The instinctive mind has a different set of criteria. Our instincts are likely to believe small sample sizes, and trust messages that are delivered with confidence over those which are communicated in a more measured style. Our instinct is very susceptible to priming. Many intriguing experiments have been conducted that show the impact that reading a particular word, or seeing a particular image can have on our decisions. As with much of the evidence within this section, it has not all been applied directly to the field of career decisions, but we can see how this kind of phenomenon might have an impact. A brief glance at a screensaver with a dollar sign on it, for example, has been shown to increase our individualistic behaviour – making us less likely to help a stranger, and more likely to turn the chair that we're sitting on to face away from someone. We could imagine that this might well have an influence on our career decisions. An injudiciously placed pound sign could reduce your chances of performing well in the 'teamwork' exercises at a selection centre, but could make you more likely to find banking an attractive career path.

If our instinct finds a question too challenging, it will often answer a different question, but make us think it is responding to the original one. When asked 'how happy are you with your life these days?', people usually answer the question 'what mood are you in right now?'. I wonder what impact this might have on some of the challenging questions that career coaches ask? Could our gut instincts respond to the question 'what sort of job do you think you'd enjoy?' by answering 'what sorts of jobs do other people enjoy?' or 'what sorts of leisure interests do you enjoy?'.

Instincts can be learned, and those very experienced in a particular situation tend to have better instincts. Gigerenzer (2007) cites the example of chess grandmasters, whose many thousands hours' practice have led them to being able to look at a chess board and make an instantaneous judgement about where to move next. Whether this is useful in a career context is a moot point. Even the most insatiable of us is only likely to make half a dozen career changes during a working lifetime, and this doesn't come close to the time that it takes to hone a chess player's instinct. It is also useful to note that in general, we tend to overestimate our own ability to make instinctive judgements, over-rating our chances of getting it right.

So where do we go from here? If we can't rely on either our conscious logic or our gut instinct, then how do we ever move forward? Much of the benefit of this kind of evidence is simply to raise our clients' awareness of what is going on inside their own heads, so that they can understand their own thinking and make more informed decisions. This information can also be used to help us think about how we present information to our clients, as we learn that adding an anecdote to some statistics might have more impact than the statistic alone, and encouraging clients to reduce their number of options to six or seven will help to prevent them from becoming overwhelmed with choices.

Decision-making styles

One further area of related scholarly activity over the last few decades has been that of individual decision-making styles. Proponents of these models believe that each of us will have a 'typical' style of decision making that we are more likely to apply to any decision. These styles are thought to be learned responses rather than personality traits, and there is some evidence that we can adopt different styles when faced with different decisions.

Decision-making styles have been classified in what seem to be hundreds of different ways. Here we will look at three models of decision-making styles that can be applied to the career arena, and how practitioners can make use of them.

Maximizers and satisficers

The first model of decision-making styles we will focus on has been around for nearly 60 years and it splits decision makers into maximizers and satisficers. This model has been widely tried and tested, and has been applied specifically to the careers arena. The distinction was identified by Simon (1955) and suggests that people typically fall into one of two categories in their decision making. Maximizers are those who prefer to identify all the options, compare them based on different criteria and work out which one is the best. Satisficers have a minimum acceptable threshold and will trawl the options until they find one that surpasses the threshold, upon which they will stop their search.

Maximizers, for example, as they are choosing a university course might decide they want a course that will give them a chance of getting a well-paid job after graduation, a good tutor to student ratio and a town-based location that would give them access to plenty of lively nightlife. They would be looking to find the single course that would score most highly on all three of these criteria, so would explore all possible courses in the UK and find out how they each perform on each of these measures before identifying the one that best fits. This approach puts us in mind of the expected utility model explained earlier, although one of the key things about the maximizers is that they are keen to explore *every* available option. This is of course a great way to identify a perfect course, but takes considerable time, relies on all the relevant information being available and comparable and entails rejecting a lot of pretty good options.

Satisficers might have the same three criteria, but rather than simply looking for the best overall combination, they would set a minimum level: they might want a course whose destination statistics show less than six per cent unemployment after graduation, which gives access to weekly seminars with fewer than 20 students in a class and whose Student Union offers at least three gigs on campus each year. Satisficers might then start looking through an alphabetical list of courses to see whether they meet the criteria, and stop at, say, Cartography at Cumbria University, when they find the first course that meets the minimum requirements. This approach is clearly much quicker, but of course means that the individual may never find out about Youth Studies at York, which might score considerably higher on all three measures.

Career decision-making styles

Let us look now at the work of Bimrose and Barnes (2007), whose longitudinal qualitative study of career decision making led them to identify four career decision-making styles:

1. **Evaluative careerists**. These focus on self-awareness and identifying their own needs, values and abilities before looking around for options that might suit them. This style tends to involve some change and uncertainty over the long term as needs, values and abilities alter over time. Bimrose and Barnes also noted that this group of decision makers showed the least confidence about the paths that they had chosen. This style of decision making has some resonance with the trait and factor matching approaches.
2. **Strategic careerists**. This group of decision makers is rational in its decision-making processes, assessing options, weighing them up against certain criteria and then working out which one is going to be meet their needs. This group might be most comfortable making career decisions in a rational way.
3. **Aspirational careerists**. These people focus on long-term goals and tend to view their futures holistically, seeing career goals as inextricably linked to life plans. This group might find the notion of career identities, schemas and niches and possible selves particularly appealing.
4. **Opportunistic careerists**. Individuals with this kind of career decision-making style tend to see and take advantage of opportunities that are presented to them. Rather than making proactive decisions or plans, they wait and see what life throws at them and respond to chances. These careerists may respond well to the idea of planned happenstance.

Career decision-making profiles

The final model we will look at here is by Gati *et al.* (2010) and as with the Bimrose and Barnes (2007) classification, this was developed specifically to apply to career decisions. Gati moves away from the notion of a stable career decision-making style towards the more flexible and adaptable idea of career profiles, proposing a model of 11 dimensions according to which an individual can be characterized:

1. Information gathering (comprehensive – minimal)
2. Information processing (analytical – holistic)
3. Locus of control (internal – external)
4. Effort invested (much – little)
5. Procrastination (high – low)

6. Speed of making final decision (fast – slow)
7. Consulting with others (frequent – rare)
8. Dependence on others (high – low)
9. Desire to please others (high – low)
10. Aspiration for ideal occupation (high – low)
11. Willingness to compromise (high – low)

This profile is pretty comprehensive, covering aspects of personality, motivation and the factors individuals consider as well as elements of the process themselves. Its all-embracing nature can be both a plus and a minus in terms of its practical use within a coaching session, but if decision making broadly seems to be blocking a client's progress, it can provide a useful framework within which to explore the different dimensions. This career styles profile is available free of charge on the web (at Gati's own website: www.cddq.org), so coaches could also suggest that clients might find it helpful to complete the questionnaire and start thinking about their own styles between sessions.

WHICH TYPES OF DECISIONS BRING THE BEST OUTCOMES?

So after all this theorizing, what is actually the *best* way to make a decision? Strangely, given the wealth of research in this area (and believe me, there is plenty more out there), we don't really know.

One of the big gap areas within the career decision-making literature is that there has been little research linking career decision-making processes with outcomes. We are beginning to build up a sketchy picture of how we make these decisions, but there is little reliable evidence of how well the processes work. One notable exception is with the career decision-making styles of maximizers and satisficers.

In their 2006 paper 'Doing better but feeling worse', Iyengar, Wells and Schwartz looked at these decision-making styles when applied to occupational choices and compared the outcomes of decisions made in these two different ways, trying to find out which process led to 'better' outcomes. Of course, one of the difficult things in this kind of research is that it is extremely difficult to identify what 'better' means. In this experiment, they used the objective measure of salary and the subjective measure of self-reported job satisfaction. They also asked participants to rate how happy they were with their own decision-making process. Their results were interesting. Maximizers in general ended up with jobs that paid more, so you could argue that from an objective perspective, they had 'better' jobs and therefore had made 'better' decisions. But satisficers reported higher levels of job satisfaction, and were more content with the process of decision making and with the outcome of their decisions. As the title of the paper suggests, the maximizers may have been doing better, but they were feeling worse.

Iyengar *et al.*'s (2006) theory to explain this counter-intuitive result is two-fold. First they suggest that because maximizers have put such a lot of thought into their career choice, they end up with high expectations of how good the result should be: after all that effort they ought to end up with the perfect job, and it is hard for any outcome to meet such high expectations. The second explanation is that in choosing between a range of potentially suitable jobs, the maximizers end up having to reject a number of relatively good options. This is likely to lead to a sense of regret, and to thoughts of 'I wonder what would have happened if . . .?'. The satisficers stopped looking when they met the first option that crossed their threshold of the minimum acceptable level, so were not faced with rejecting any suitable options.

The final study we will look at in this chapter is by Singh and Greenhaus (2004). This research compared the decision-making processes of career changers with the person–environment fit found in their eventual job. They found that the best fits were obtained by those who had used a combination of career decision-making processes. Although the person–environment fit is only one measure of job satisfaction, this is still a very interesting finding and one that gives us a clue as to how to use all this information in our coaching practice.

Using these theories with clients

In general, these theories are useful for coaches in one of two ways. First, coaches can use these theories to inform their own practice, style of questions and structure of the intervention with clients. For example, if a coach thinks that clients seem to be showing characteristics of an opportunistic career decision-making style, helping them to see that actively looking for – and preparing for – opportunities may maximize their chances of success.

The second and arguably more useful way for a coach to use these theories is to share them with their clients in order to start a discussion about their style of career decision making, the impact their style has had on their career path, and alternative strategies that they could use.

Case study

Janice is in her mid 30s and visited a career coach because she was struggling to work out what to do next. She felt that in her career thus far, she had never really made an active career decision, but had just 'fallen into' job after job, with no thought of why she was doing it or where it might lead. Janice felt that she wasn't in control and was anxious that her lack of direction had wasted years of career development.

Her career coach asked her to talk through some of the career transitions she'd had and shared with her the theory of planned happenstance. Janice immediately recognized this in her own experiences and as she talked with her coach, they identified a number of specific decisions that Janice had actually made in order to enable her to take advantage of the opportunities that came her way. Janice felt much more positive about her proactive involvement in her career history to date.

The coach then asked Janice to tell her how she described her current role to people, and how she felt when she did so. This led to a discussion about Janice's career identity, and enabled Janice to identify where the mismatch was between her work identity and personal identity. Armed with a greater self-efficacy around her career decision-making ability, and a clearer sense of what was wrong with the current situation, Janice was in a strong position to start thinking about new options.

Career decision making is extraordinarily complex, and our understanding of the process is by no means complete, but decades of research and hundreds of studies have given us considerable insights into the conscious and unconscious factors involved. There are many concepts to get to grips with and still plenty of things remain unclear, but overall it is a rewarding body of literature to engage with. An understanding of the literature will enable us to support our clients appropriately and offer a range of useful alternative frameworks and approaches that will make career decisions swifter and more effective.

REFERENCES

Amundson, N. E., Borgen, W. A., Iaquinta, M., Butterfield, L. D. and Koert, E. (2010) Career decisions from the decider's perspective. *Career Development Quarterly*, 58(4): 336–351.

Bimrose, J. and Barnes, S. A. (2007) Styles of career decision making. *Australian Journal of Career Development*, 16(2): 20–28.

Bimrose, J. and Barnes, S. A. (2011) *Adult Career Progression and Advancement: A five year study of the effectiveness of career guidance.* Warwick: IER Bulletin 99.

Bloch, D. P. (2005) Complexity, chaos, and nonlinear dynamics: A new perspective on career development theory. *Career Development Quarterly*, 53: 194–207.

Blustein, D. L. (2001) The interface of work and relationships: Critical knowledge for 21st century psychology. *The Counseling Psychologist*, 29: 179–192.

Blustein, D. L. (2004) Moving from the inside out: Further explorations of the family of origin/career development linkage. *Counseling Psychologist*, 32(4): 603–611.

Bowlby, J. (1969) *Attachment and Loss.* London: Hogarth.

Brosseau, D. C., Domene, J. F. and Dutka, T. W. (2010) The importance of partner involvement in determining career decision-making difficulties. *Canadian Journal of Career Development*, 9(2): 35–41.

Brower, A. M. and Nurius, P. S. (1993) *Social Cognition and Individual Change: Current Theory and Counseling Guidelines.* Newbury Park, CA: SAGE Publications.

Brownstein, A. L. (2003) Biased predecision processing. *Psychological Bulletin*, 129(4): 545–568.

Dawis, R. V. and Loftquist, L. H. (1984) *A Psychological Theory of Work Adjustment.* Minneapolis: University of Minnesota Press.

Gati, I. (1986) Making career decisions: A sequential elimination approach, *Journal of Counseling Psychology*, 33(4): 408–417.

Gati, I. and Tikotzki, Y. (1989) Strategies for collection and processing of occupational information in making career decisions. *Journal of Counseling Psychology*, 36: 430–439.

Gati, I., Landman, S., Davidovitch, S., Asulin-Peretz, L. and Gadassi, R. (2010) From career decision making styles to career decision making profiles: a multi-dimentional approach. *Journal of Vocational Behavior*, 76(2): 277–291.

Gelatt, H. B. (1989) Positive uncertainty: A new decision-making framework for counselling. *Journal of Counseling Psychology*, 36: 252–256.

Gigerenzer, G. (2007) *Gut Feelings.* London: Penguin Books.

Greenbank, P. and Hepworth, S. (2008) *Working class students and the career decision-making process: A qualitative study.* Report for the Higher Education Careers Service Unit (HECSU), Manchester.

Holland, J. (1959) A theory of vocational choice. *Journal of Counseling Psychology*, 6: 35–45.

Iyengar, S. S. and Lepper, M. (2000) When choice is demotivating: Can one desire too much of a good thing? *Journal of Personality and Social Psychology*, 76: 995–1006.

Iyengar, S. S., Wells, R. E. and Schwartz, B. (2006) Doing better but feeling worse. *Psychological Science*, 17(2): 143–150.

Kahneman, D. (2011) *Thinking, Fast and Slow*, London: Allen Lane.

Miller, J. B. (1976) *Toward a New Psychology of Women.* Boston, MA: Beacon Press.

Mitchell, K., Levin, A. and Krumboltz, J. (1999) Planned happenstance: Constructing unexpected career opportunities, *Journal of Counseling & Development*, 77(2): 115–124.

Murtagh, N., Lopes, P. N. and Lyons, E. (2011) Decision making in voluntary career change: an other than rational perspective. *The Career Development Quarterly*, 59: 249–262.

O'Brien, K. (1996) The influence of psychological separation and parental attachment on the career development of adolescent women. *Journal of Vocational Behavior*, 48: 257–274.

Pitz, G. F. and Harren, V. A. (1980) An analysis of career decision making from the point of view of information processing and decision theory. *Journal of Vocational Behavior*, 16: 96–105.

Pizzolato, J. E. (2006) Achieving college student possible selves: navigating the space between commitment and achievement of long-term identity goals. *Cultural Diversity and Ethnic Minority Psychology*, 12(1): 57–69.

Schein, E. H. (1978) *Career Dynamics, Matching Individual and Organizational Needs.* Reading, MA: Addison-Wesley.

Schultheiss, D. E. P. (2003) A relational approach to career counseling: Theoretical integration and practical application. *Journal of Counseling & Development*, 81: 301–310.

Schultheiss, D. E. P., Palma, T. V., Predragovich, K. S. and Glassock, J. M. J. (2002) Relational influences on career paths: Siblings in context. *Journal of Counseling Psychology*, 49(3): 302–310.

Simon, H. A. (1955) A behavioural model of rational choice. *Quarterly Journal of Economics*, 59: 99–118.

Singh, R. and Greenhaus, J. H. (2004) The relation between career decision making strategies and person–job fit: A study of job changers. *Journal of Vocational Behavior*, 64: 198–221.

Spokane, A. R., Meir, E. I. and Catalano, M. (2000) Person–environment congruence and Holland's theory of careers: A review and reconsideration. *Journal of Vocational Behavior*, 57: 137–187.

Chapter 4

Job satisfaction
What makes us happy at work?

We saw in the last chapter that many factors come into play when one makes a career decision. Many of them, such as location, working hours and salary are usually relatively predictable, but how much you are going to enjoy your job is much less tangible and far harder to anticipate. As career coaches, we spend a good deal of our working lives trying to help our clients become more fulfilled at work, so a clear sense of the factors that are generally likely to make for a satisfying professional life will enable us to help clients make more informed predictions about their own future.

Fortunately for our purposes, there have been hundreds of studies that have contributed to our understanding of the influential factors. Results are not always conclusive – indeed some are downright contradictory – but several substantial meta-analyses help us to make sense of the data. In this chapter we will summarize and discuss some of the key findings.

> Think about your own career history and rate each different job on a scale of 1–10. Then take the highest and lowest scores and analyse which factors made your experience there so positive or negative.

How happy you are in your job is determined by a combination of work factors as well as your personality and life events, and we will look at each in turn. Work factors are likely to be the most relevant to our practice as career coaches as it is these that are most easily controlled and changed. They also constitute the most influential group, accounting between them for 55 per cent of our work satisfaction, so that is where we will start.

WORK FACTORS

Many studies have explored the work factors that contribute to job satisfaction, but six factors consistently emerge as the most influential (e.g. Roelen *et al.* 2008).

1. **Task variety.** The work factor most likely to influence our job satisfaction is how much variety there is within our work. Jobs with a high level of variety are much more likely to lead to a happier workforce.

2. **Colleagues.** Good colleagues make an enormous difference to how much we enjoy our working days, and the key thing is having a sense of community. Although having one great friend in the workplace does have an impact on how much your enjoy your job (Rath and Harter 2010), it is not as important as feeling that you are part of a team who get along well, share common goals and values, and who care about each other personally as well as professionally. The research linking colleagues and job satisfaction has found strong links between peers and day-to-day happiness in the workplace, but limited evidence of links between a good relationship with your supervisor and your job satisfaction. This may seem a little counter-intuitive, but the absence of a link is thought to be down to the relatively small amount of time each day that most workers spend in close contact with their boss.

3. **Working conditions.** The conditions within which we work are often given considerable weight when we are considering a job. The office environment, locale and facilities all play their part in how attractive a job seems from the outside, and indeed how much satisfaction we might derive from the job when we're in post. This category also includes organizational culture, which has been shown (e.g. Bellou 2010) to have a small but significant impact, with concepts such as a culture of creativity, fairness, enthusiasm for the job and a good reputation enhancing satisfaction. Conversely, satisfaction is constrained by issues such as cultural aggressiveness, an over-emphasis on meeting goals and a focus on beating the competition.

4. **Workload.** This is divided into overall workload and specific work demands. Workload includes perception of time pressure, and the concept of work demands covers factors such as being forced to take on extra work, and the job insecurity or the emotional commitment required by a role. It is usually measured subjectively, so is a measure of an individual's experience of the load and demands rather than an objective assessment of work volume. Although too small a workload can lead to boredom within the working day, it is work overload which is most clearly associated with lower levels of job satisfaction.

5. **Autonomy.** Having a reasonable degree of autonomy over one's working day has been shown to have quite an impact on job satisfaction, and is one of the most widely documented contributory factors. In this context, the concept consists of two distinct but closely linked ideas. The first is that of individual responsibility for work – having elements of your job that are clearly down to you, and getting credit when things go well, and accepting blame when things don't. The second element of the concept is the more traditional interpretation of the word, referring to having control over one's own decisions – being able to make choices about what to do and how to do it, being able to implement ideas and work out solutions to problems.

6. **Educational opportunities.** The last of the key work factors is the degree to which your job allows you to develop. This refers not just to the opportunities to work towards formal qualifications (although they can be a very attractive element to a role), but the chance to grow, learn and develop through work. The inclusion of this concept links to the self-actualizing tendency which holds that people are naturally inclined to want to develop and learn.

These factors can be some of the most useful morsels of information that you can share with your clients but it is of course important to bear in mind both that these factors won't apply in the same way to all clients, and that many of them are very subjective. For example, what constitutes a 'good' colleague will vary from one person to another. A concept such as 'task variety' can be interpreted in different ways: one person's 'It's so boring – I spend all day, every day on the phone' could be another person's 'It's fantastic, I talk to 20 different people every day and no two calls are alike'. Sharing information about the evidence can lead to productive discussions about your clients' perceptions of these factors and their own priorities.

CAREER SUCCESS

One area that has received some attention in the academic journals is the extent to which objective and subjective measures of success interrelate. In other words, to what extent does career success bring, or correlate with, job satisfaction?

Overall, some meta-analytic studies conclude that objective career success (measured by status and promotion) does have a small but significant correlation with job satisfaction at around 0.3 (e.g. Dette *et al.* 2004). This finding has some links with the list above, in that seniority tends to bring autonomy and therefore a greater opportunity to incorporate more task variety in your day. More negatively, however, more senior roles often have heavier workloads, and tend to be more isolated.

The quest for a higher salary is a great motivator in many careers, and is often a key factor in a career decision. Many studies have looked at the impact of salary on job satisfaction, and the conclusion is clear that better pay has only a small correlation with job satisfaction and life satisfaction: a good pay packet does make you happier at work and may mean you enjoy your weekends more, but only marginally. This is perhaps what you might have expected. What *is* surprising – and certainly less well documented – is that a higher salary doesn't actually make you much happier with your salary overall. Pay has only a small correlation with pay satisfaction, which means that the big cheeses in your firm earning more than £100k a year are only a little more content with their salaries than the lowly junior clerks on less than £20k (Judge *et al.* 2010).

As objective career success has a small positive influence on job satisfaction, so job satisfaction increases your chances of promotion and a pay rise. Subjective success, as measured both by job satisfaction and by how well you think you are doing compared to your peers, has an impact on objective success: those who are happier at work are more likely to get promoted and to earn more (Abele and Spurk 2009). Researchers aren't entirely sure of the reasons for this but it could be that a perception of success makes an individual more confident, which tends to bring more motivation and action.

We've looked so far at the factors associated with the workplace that can have an impact on job satisfaction. As far as our professional practice is concerned, these are the most useful factors to consider as they are the ones our clients are most able to control within their working lives: if a role is unrewarding because it lacks task variety and autonomy, a client could look for another role that allows for greater responsibility and control. We're now going to look at the individual factors that have an impact on job satisfaction and with these, the changes required are more tricky; finding a job that affords you more autonomy is easier for most than developing more of an extravert personality. I would be cautious about discussing these with clients, but I am including them here as it can be useful for you as a practitioner to understand the individual as well as work factors, giving you a fuller picture.

Individual factors

Around 45 per cent of the variance in job satisfaction is attributable to individual factors, including age, gender and personality (Judge *et al.* 2002).

Personality traits

Personality is one area that has been shown to have a substantial influence on job satisfaction. Early research on the links between personality and job satisfaction suggested that there was a single distinct job satisfaction trait that predisposed you to being content at work. Subsequent research indicates that the personality most likely to enjoy higher job satisfaction is in fact composed of a range of different elements. Judge *et al.* (2002) conducted a meta-analysis and found some clear links with four out of the 'Big Five' personality factors, with openness to experience the only factor that does not relate to job satisfaction.

The personality type most likely to enjoy their work lives, regardless of job, is that which scores low on neuroticism and high on extraversion, conscientiousness and agreeableness.

Neuroticism is negatively correlated with job satisfaction (by which I mean that people who score high on neuroticism are more likely to score low on job satisfaction). High scores on neuroticism indicate people who are quick to experience negative emotions and who are drawn to situations that make them feel negative; they are likely to find themselves discontent, whatever their circumstances. Extraversion, in contrast, is strongly linked with positive job satisfaction. Extraverts are predisposed to experience positive emotions and as they tend to get more out of social situations (and nearly all jobs involve contact with others), the nature of the work environment is likely to bring social satisfaction to them. Conscientiousness is linked with high levels of work involvement so people with high scores on conscientiousness are more likely to work harder, work longer hours, and be more actively engaged with their work and work life. As a result, they are more likely to gain both formal rewards, such as pay and promotion, and informal rewards, such as recognition and feelings of achievement, within the workplace. Finally, those of us with high scores on agreeableness tend to be highly motivated to develop intimacy with colleagues, which is likely to lead to a satisfying work environment.

Age and gender

The research around age and gender is a little contradictory, but the general consensus currently is that women and men gain job satisfaction from different factors. Issues such as work environment and colleagues are more significant for women, whereas for men, factors such as pay and promotions have more of an impact (Okpara *et al.* 2005). Clark *et al.* (1996) examined how gender and age interrelate to impact on job satisfaction and found that for men, the correlation between age and job satisfaction forms a U-shaped curve, indicating that they tend to get greater satisfaction at the beginning and end of their careers. For women, the pattern is a little different, with women's career satisfaction tending to be more linear, indicating that women in general become more satisfied with their careers as they get older.

Congruence

Congruence is the term used to describe the degree to which the individual and the job match, so marries up the two sections above, examining the interaction between work factors and individual factors.

It could be argued that this area has received disproportionate attention both in the research literature and in career practice, in part because of the huge influence of one academic. Holland's (1959 and 1985) original theory of vocational types, which we examined in more detail in Chapter 3, has underpinned most careers education in the US and the UK and continues to dominate today, even though the empirical evidence has prompted Holland himself to revise his theories (Holland 1997).

As noted above, Holland devised an interest inventory which measures subjective interests and categorizes people with a three-letter code, based on an individual's top three interest areas from the options of Realistic, Investigative, Artistic, Social, Enterprising and Conventional (RIASEC). This code is then matched against a database of jobs and a list of suitable jobs generated.

This approach was the dominant theory of decision making in the 1970s and 1980s, and it is a very attractive way for clients – especially young people who have had very little experience of the world of work – to narrow down the vast array of options into something more manageable. The approach also appeals to commonsense; it feels intuitively obvious that having a job that matches your interests, skills and values is going to make you more fulfilled at work. But countless empirical studies show that while it does make a difference, that difference is small, with a correlation of around 0.25 (Spokane *et al.* 2000) and explaining perhaps 5 per cent of the variance in job satisfaction. There is one interest type that does show a clear link with job satisfaction; it is consistently found that people presenting with a strong sociable profile are significantly happier in a sociable environment.

One interesting piece of research has been into the idea of 'incongruence'. Dik *et al.* (2010) have suggested that avoiding incongruence is more important than finding congruence. The evidence seems to be that moving away from an area that you're reasonably interested in to one that you're very interested in only marginally improves your job satisfaction. In contrast, a shift from a sphere that you have no interest in whatsoever to one that you find reasonably engaging makes a far more dramatic difference. This is a particularly useful piece of information to bear in mind when working with career changers, or those who are unhappy in their current roles.

Life satisfaction

Work is, of course, only one part of our lives. There is inevitably an interdependence between how we feel about work and our home lives. With the rise of dual-career couples and single-parent families, research on the interaction between work and families has attracted some attention. The conflict is conceptualized in two directions: work–family conflict, where work has an impact on family life, and family–work conflict, where family life has an impact on work. It will come as no great shock to find that a role conflict has an impact on job satisfaction, but what is perhaps less obvious is the direction of this impact. Family–work conflict is associated with low levels of job satisfaction: as issues such as childcare and family health affect work life, one's satisfaction with work decreases. Work–family interference, by contrast, has no impact on job satisfaction. You might imagine that a work role that forces you to work late, miss the kids' Christmas play and cancel a weekend away would be a less satisfying experience that one that allows you a satisfying home life on top of your office job. But it does not appear to be the case; perhaps because work–life balance is something that we can control to some degree, those who are likely to feel negative about work interfering with family can usually ensure that it doesn't have a significant impact.

Specific events in one's life can also have an impact on one's satisfaction at work (Georgellis *et al.* 2012). Events usually considered happy ones, such as a wedding or the birth of a child, have a positive impact on job satisfaction for the year or so preceding the event. The positive mood that accompanies the anticipation of the event spills over and influences all sorts of aspects of your life, including your work. Job satisfaction gradually returns to its previous levels around a year after the joyful event unless you are a woman who has just had a baby, in which case it continues to descend until your child is around five when it gradually and gently starts to work its way back up.

A challenge for many clients lies in the link between job satisfaction and self-esteem. A high level of job satisfaction has a positive impact on other elements of life, including your mental and physical health, and your self-esteem (Faragher *et al.* 2005). In a virtuous circle, these factors influence how likely you are to make a career change, and how successful you will be at interview (Kanfer *et al.* 2001). You are more likely to manage a successful career transition, then, if you're fulfilled in your current role.

Clients who choose to seek out a career coach, however, are often in the throes of the vicious countercycle. Low job satisfaction leads them to you, but this low job satisfaction can have a detrimental effect on their self-esteem and therefore their chances of making a successful career move. It can often be important to first work with clients on improving how they feel about their current position before you move on to think about a career move. Chapter 11 on positive approaches offers several straightforward exercises which can boost positive mood, and some of the goal-setting tools in Chapter 14 may also help.

Case study

Sarah didn't really know what she wanted to do when she graduated, but with good people skills, an interest in commerce and a love of shopping, a career in retail seemed ideal. She was thrilled to get a place on a prestigious retail graduate training scheme, but that was where things started to go wrong. She was busy in her new job, the days went quickly and she loved her interactions with the customers, but she just didn't feel inspired and her managers were beginning to ask why. Sarah knew that she was in the wrong job, but couldn't quite put her finger on what was wrong, and this made her very anxious about choosing another direction: if she didn't know what was wrong, how could she be confident that she would get it right next time?

Sarah went to see a career coach and together they tried to figure out why the role was unrewarding. Sarah explained that she loved working with the customers, but somehow felt isolated. The coach explained that a strong component of job satisfaction is a like-minded group of colleagues all pulling together, and Sarah saw that this was something that was really lacking in her role. They also talked through the idea of task variety, and Sarah was able to identify that although her day was varied in one sense – she had a range of responsibilities and a large number of different stock lines to look after – she actually found it very repetitive. Even though she was involved in many different tasks each day, one day was very much like another.

Armed with a clearer understanding of some of the things that were contributing to a lack of fulfilment in her work, Sarah felt much more confident about her ability to choose another role that she would find more satisfying.

Job satisfaction is one of the most widely researched areas within careers literature. There are research experiments and published data sets that examine different aspects of job satisfaction, and that look at the specific factors associated with job satisfaction in different industries or professional groups. But it is proving a hard one to nail, and we have not yet found a formula to predict which people and which jobs are going to score highest. Encouragingly, research into job satisfaction is moving on apace at the moment and academics are leaving no stone unturned. Positive psychologists have identified job satisfaction as a fundamental pillar of life satisfaction (Rath and Harter 2010) and are beginning to add evidence to the existing pool of occupational psychology and career research. Song and Arvey (2011) have even linked molecular genetics to job satisfaction and for those interested in this level of biological detail, I can reveal that there are 'two genetic markers, dopamine receptor gene DRD4 VNTR and serotonin transporter gene 5-HTTLPR, weakly but significantly associated with job satisfaction'!

One thing that I found interesting when reading the research into job satisfaction is that although it is widely accepted that being happy at work is important, the factors that actually give you satisfaction are not very widely known about, tend not to be the sorts of things that people base their career decisions on and are usually quite hard to research. When considering a new role, factors such as pay, location, seniority and area of interest are common key considerations, but looking at the list of factors reported in the research, they are not nearly as influential as, for example, autonomy or task variety in determining overall job satisfaction. The first list is much easier to find out about – it is usually clear from the job ad – but the level of autonomy and variety is trickier to identify. Sharing your knowledge of these factors can be enormously helpful to clients, as they can research these factors and take them into consideration as they are making their choices.

REFERENCES

Abele, A. E. and Spurk, D. (2009) How do objective and subjective career success interrelate over time? *Journal of Occupational & Organizational Psychology*, 82(40): 803–824.

Bellou, V. (2010) Organizational culture as a predictor of job satisfaction: The role of gender and age. *Career Development International*, 15(1): 4–19.

Clark, E. A., Oswald, A. J. and Warr, P. (1996) Is job satisfaction U-shaped? *Journal of Occupational and Organizational Psychology*, 69: 57–82.

Dette, E. D., Abele, A. E. and Renner, O. (2004). Zur Definition und Messung von Berufserfolg – Theoretische Überlegungen und metaanalytische Befunde zum Zusammenhang von externen und internen Laufbahnerfolgsmaßen (Defining and measuring occupational success – theoretical considerations and meta-analytical findings on the relationship between external and internal measures). *Zeitschrift für Personalpsychologie*, 3: 170–183.

Dik, B. J., Strife, S. R. and Hansen, J. C. (2010) The flip-side of Holland types congruence: Incongruence and job satisfaction. *The Career Development Quarterly*, 58: 352–358.

Faragher, E. B., Cass, M. and Cooper, C. L. (2005) The relationship between health and job satisfaction: A meta-analysis. *Occupational and Environmental Medicine*, 62(2): 105–112.

Georgellis, Y., Lange, T. and Tabvuma, V. (2012) The impact of life events on job satisfaction. *Journal of Vocational Behavior*, 80(2): 464–473.

Holland, J. (1959) A theory of vocational choice. *Journal of Counseling Psychology* 6: 35–45.

Holland, J. L. (1985) *Making Vocational Choices: A Theory of Personalities and Work Environments*, 2nd ed. Englewood Cliffs, NJ: Prentice Hall.

Holland, J. L. (1997) *Making Vocational Choices: A Theory of Personalities and Work Environments*, 3rd ed. Englewood Cliffs, NJ: Prentice Hall.

Judge, T. A., Heller, D. and Mount, M. K. (2002) Five-factor model of personality and job satisfaction: A meta-analysis. *Journal of Applied Psychology*, 87(3): 530–541.

Judge, T. A., Piccolo, R. F., Podsakoff, N. P., Shaw, J. C. and Rich, B. L. (2010) The relationship between pay and job satisfaction: A meta-analysis of the literature. *Journal of Vocational Behavior*, 77: 157–167.

Kanfer, R., Wanberg, C. R. and Kantrowitz, T. M. (2001) Job search and employment: A personality–motivational analysis and meta-analytic review. *Journal of Applied Psychology*, 86(5): 837–855.

Okpara, J. O., Squillance, M. and Erondu, E. A. (2005) Gender differences and job satisfaction: A study of university teachers in the United States. *Women in Management Review*, 20(3): 177–190.

Rath, T. and Harter, J. (2010) *Well Being: The Five Essential Elements*. New York: Gallup Press.

Roelen, C. A. M., Koopmans, P. C. and Groothoff, J. W. (2008) Which work factors determine job satisfaction? *Work*, 30: 433–439.

Song, Z., Li, W. and Arvey, R. D. (2011) Associations between dopamine and serotonin genes and job satisfaction: Preliminary evidence from the Add Health Study. *Journal of Applied Psychology*, 96(6): 1223–1233.

Spokane, A. R., Meir, E. I. and Catalano, M. (2000) Person–environment congruence and Holland's theory of careers: A review and reconsideration. *Journal of Vocational Behavior*, 57: 137–187.

Chapter 5

Planned career changes

Trying to define exactly what constitutes a career change is tricky. How different does a job have to be to constitute a change in career? An investment banker changing to a primary teacher would definitely qualify as such, but what about a journalist who starts to lecture in journalism? Or a teacher who becomes a head teacher? Or a librarian who leaves the local authority library for a librarian job at a law firm? Each of these examples could be argued either way. Perhaps the terminology doesn't matter all that much, but an awareness that 'I want to change career' can mean a range of things may help us to keep a check on our own assumptions. Career changes feature prominently in the work of many career coaches, so it is important that we have a good understanding of what causes them, how they work and what effect they have.

There are, of course, all sorts of precursors to a change of career or even of job. In this chapter we'll focus on career changes that are more or less the choice of the individual, and then in the next chapter we will go on to explore career changes that, for a range of reasons, are likely to be beyond the control of the individual. This distinction might seem somewhat artificial: many of those who are apparently choosing to change career are in fact responding to a hint from management that they are not cut out for this line of work, and many who are forced into redundancy are secretly delighted to have the opportunity to make a change. This does, however, seem to be a sensible way of categorizing the information so here we'll start the topic with a look at the antecedents of career change, and then move on to explore the career change process. We will then examine in a little more detail the midlife transition that precipitates many career changes, and the advice we can find for career coaches working with this client group. Chapter 6 will then move on to examine the impact of job loss and the specific contexts of redundancy, dismissal and parenthood.

WHAT MAKES PEOPLE DECIDE TO CHANGE CAREERS?

There has been a considerable amount of research into why people change career, and it seems that whether or not we do so is determined by a complicated web of factors incorporating issues to do with the job itself, the individual and their community. An understanding of some of these factors and how they can combine to determine an individual's behaviour can be useful as we try to understand our clients' choices.

Carless and Arnup (2010) conducted a meta-analysis that scrutinized approximately 40 smaller studies and identified a pretty statistically robust set of factors predicting career change, each of which we will now look at in turn.

Individual factors

Individual factors can be split into those based on personality, demographics, attitudes and circumstances.

Personality

In terms of personality, those scoring highly on the 'Big Five' personality factors of extraversion and openness to change are more likely to change career, as they often enjoy change for its own sake and tend to get bored easily. Those with a high risk-taking style will usually also take the plunge.

Demographics

Demographic influences suggest that younger people (linked to fewer dependents, shorter occupational tenure and less time spent in a particular community as outlined below) and men are more likely to make career changes. Those with higher education levels tend to have more transferable skills, so will usually find opportunities to change.

Attitudes

Our attitudes are quite significant in predicting whether or not we change career. People's attitudes towards career change differ on a number of counts, and those who have a positive view of it, who feel a social pressure to change and who feel that they are in control of their behaviour in this regard are more likely to change their career. An anxiety around job insecurity and a high motivation for skill development will also make an individual more likely to move.

Circumstances

Circumstantial factors that will make a change more likely include low geographical barriers (i.e. not being tied to a local area for schools, spouse's work or caring responsibilities) and a familiarity with a new work arena.

Cultural and community factors

The communities within which you live, work and socialize will have quite an influence on whether you decide to change your career. In terms of individual's local communities, there are two factors that make a difference. People are more likely to make a career change if they haven't been in their local community for long, and if they haven't been in their job for long. Those who have not made either a work or a home move for some time will find it harder to change. The other community that is quite influential is that at work, and individuals who find that they don't particularly fit the professional culture they find at the workplace are more likely to make a move. Finally, individuals can find that their community either overtly or covertly puts them under pressure to change career and this can have quite an impact. If, for example, you come from a 'high achieving' family or group of friends and your job is not one that is afforded great status within this group, you are more likely to try a new career avenue.

Work factors

The last, and perhaps most obvious, category are the work-related factors. It is no surprise to learn that dissatisfaction with the workplace in various forms will lead to an increased chance of changing career. Specific factors include job insecurity, bullying, low job satisfaction and low work involvement.

The balance of individual, community and work factors involved will vary from one career change to another but it is particularly helpful for coaches to remember that the impetus to stay or go is based on more than the job itself.

HOW DO CAREER CHANGES HAPPEN?

Every person's experience of a job or career change is different but there is some evidence from the literature that can help us to support our clients. Here I will present first Prochaska *et al.*'s (1992) transtheoretical model of change as a framework to help understand the process of career change as a sequence of stages. We'll then look at some evidence that acknowledges the role of chance (Mitchell *et al.* 1999 – see Chapter 3 for a more in-depth treatment) that we can see in many career changes.

The transtheoretical model

The transtheoretical model of changes (Prochaska *et al.* 1992) is a widely used psychological model that explains in some detail five stages of change. 'Transtheoretical' refers to the fact that its origins are drawn from a range of different theoretical approaches, and although it was originally developed for use in health settings – with weight management and smoking cessation, for example – it has been applied in and developed for a range of other contexts. Criticisms (e.g. West 2005) have been raised, suggesting that in practice the stages are in fact not quite as discrete as the model might suggest, but it remains a useful framework to bear in mind when working with clients who are in the process of making a change.

The model involves five stages of change (Prochaska *et al.* 1992):

1. **Precontemplation.** The individual is not happy but is not ready to accept that a change is needed.
2. **Contemplation.** The individual becomes aware of some of the reasons underlying their unhappiness and starts to consider the possibility of a change.
3. **Preparation.** The client is experimenting with new possible selves and exploring ideas.
4. **Action.** The individual translates their ideas into plans and their plans into actions.
5. **Maintenance.** A period of consolidation and stabilization.

One of the specific arenas in which the model has been developed is that of career change. Barclay *et al.* (2011) have applied the model to this context and offer a range of emotional and practical responses that are typical of each stage, to help us, as practitioners, understand where our clients are. They also offer some suggestions for appropriate career coaching behaviour at each stage which you might find useful (see Table 5.1).

The role of planned happenstance in career changes

Murtagh *et al.* (2011) conducted a study that looks at the role of chance in career changes, and in their findings you may recognize some ideas and themes from the theory of planned happenstance that we covered in Chapter 3. In this study, the researchers highlight the importance of positive emotions, unplanned action and building certainty over time. They found numerous examples of individuals who engaged in a particular course of action or activity for interest, and subsequently found that as a result of a change in circumstances, that 'hobby' provided them with the means to pursue a particular career path. An evening class in art taken purely for pleasure, for example, could lead a few years down the line to a job working for the local adult education college, or some voluntary work at a local charity could inspire a change in direction.

As noted earlier, it has been shown (Murtagh *et al.* 2011) that it takes roughly two years from deciding to change to actually making the transition. Clients can sometimes put themselves under great pressure to make a change quickly and may become frustrated if the process takes longer than they wish. Sharing this information about the average length of career decision and job search can help them to manage their expectations.

Table 5.1 The stages of a career change

Career changer: Typical behaviour exhibited when career changer is in each stage	Career coach: Suggested behaviour to help career changer develop self-awareness and move on to the next stage
Pre-contemplation • Experiencing discouragement (although not fully aware of the reason) • Loss of interest in work tasks/ industry • Letting go of work and old work identity	• Listening empathically • Relationship-building • Motivational interviewing • Helping client to explore ambivalence and emotions concerning work and self-concept
Contemplation • Growing awareness of job dissatisfaction • Concern for the future • Initial thoughts of a possible career change • Expressions of doubt regarding a career change • Weighing pros/cons of a career change • Emotional expressions – increasing personal control/self-efficacy	• Helping career changer to identify, clarify and explore the problem • Narrative approaches/soliciting and helping career changer to rebuild the career narrative • Exploring life themes • Aiding client in learning about self
Preparation • Increased motivation to change careers • Willingness to explore interests/ skills through assessments • Willingness to explore educational opportunities • Crystallizing, specifying and implementing	• Administration/interpretation of career assessments • Providing career listing resources • Supporting career exploration
Action • Managing stress • Redefining self • New life roles (e.g. student, new employee/trainee) • Determined/committed • Stabilizing, consolidating and advancing	• Educator and consultant roles • Supporting changes in social connections • Designing and supporting stimulus control plans • Encourager and emotional supporter
Maintenance • Building coworker relationships • End of formal educational pursuits • Career change complete • Holding on, keeping up and innovating	• Supporting the expansion of changes to broader environments • Consultancy role

Barclay *et al.* (2011). Used by permission.

Midlife career transition

Career changes can happen at any point in a career and be sparked off by a range of factors, but one common time to reconsider your career is during your midlife transition. Career decisions that are made during this phase of life can involve some psychological processes and emotional responses that are quite different from those that tend to be important in initial career decisions or in the 'first bounce' career changes (those that tend to happen just a few years into a career). And it is for this reason that it's useful to understand something of the midlife transition and the impact that it can have on our career.

Career theories from the 20th century that looked at a career as a series of stages (such as Super's influential 1990 'life-span, life-space' theory of career development), tended not to include a midlife transition. Bejian and Salomone (1995) suggest that this may be simply because career changes were so much less common for many decades, and that mid-career transition did not become widespread until the turn of the millennium. The concept of a midlife transition (referred to and experienced by some as a 'crisis') is one that can be explained through the lens of psychodynamic theory. The theory of the midlife transition is grounded in the work of Carl Jung who likened the transition to the moment at midday when the sun stops rising from the east and starts setting towards the west. Jung identified two key processes that occur in midlife that can engender an emotional reaction. First is the process of 'individualization', when we work out who we are and develop a deeper self-awareness and an insight into our own identities. We also gain a better understanding of what our life means to us and how we fit into the 'bigger picture'. Second is the external changes that happen and that we must respond to. These could include redundancy, children leaving home, the realization that we are never going to have children, or the death of a parent, any or all of which result in an increased awareness of our own mortality.

There are then, according to Levinson (1978), three key tasks in mid life. The first is that we need to reappraise the past. This can include thinking about past goals, some that perhaps haven't been achieved, and thinking about time wasted. Time becomes a more pressing concern in midlife as we start to be sometimes painfully aware that our lives are limited and we can see towards the end of our working and physical lives with greater clarity than before. Secondly we need to modify our life structures, often in the light of this reappraisal, which can lead to major changes such as getting divorced or changing career. The third key task is to reconcile some of the inner dilemmas raised by the process of individuation (as we reconcile the different elements of our personality, our experiences and elements of our psyche to see ourselves as a coherent 'whole'), the most pressing of which is usually a reappraisal of our position in the young/old dichotomy. As midlife approaches, we have to work out where we stand. We're not young any more, and in some ways this has significant benefits; we become more confident and more experienced, for example. As we develop this maturity, however, we become more aware of our own mortality and this leads to a heightened need to find meaning in life.

Much of the research used men as its subjects, but there have been some studies that have looked more specifically at the experiences of women. Broadly speaking, working women tend to experience the same midlife career transitions as men, although one of the key differences (Lieblich 1986) is that women are more likely to make meaning of our midlife questions by drawing on our personal relationships.

Case study

Ben had shown great potential throughout his life. The brightest child in his class at school, he got straight As at A levels and a first class degree in English Literature at university. He got a job in an NGO whose mission he really believed in and worked his way up the ladder, eventually overseeing the organization's communications, publications and their website and becoming the youngest member of the senior management team. But it soon became clear that professionally, Ben had gone too far too fast and he found that he wasn't quite coping. He decided it was time to go it alone, resigned from his job and started to freelance. He had a young family and was excited about the idea of being able to spend more time with his little boy. Things started off reasonably well, and by agreeing to do anything and everything that he was asked to, he gradually built up a client base which gave him enough work to pay the mortgage. While he was enjoying the flexibility that freelance employment gave him, he soon realized that he was gaining a reputation and repeat business as a quiz writer for women's interest websites – a far cry from the values-driven roles that he'd had in his early career. For Ben, things came to a head one day when he was writing a quiz about handbags on the high street and he remembered the aspirations he'd had in his early 20s. The gulf between his young adult goals and his mid-adult achievements was painful and he decided to find a career coach to help him find his way.

In the first few sessions, the coach adopted a very humanistic approach and worked with Ben to get him to understand his feelings of loss and grief over his unfulfilled ambitions and to allow him to come to terms with the differences between his early aspirations and his current reality. Ben started to realize that he could judge his status by more than his seniority in work and began to gain a more balanced perspective. The next sessions with the coach were more forward-looking, as Ben started to play around with ideas for the future and a more flexible interpretation of 'success'. He was able to identify what he wanted to keep and what he wanted to change in the future, and accepted that although not as young as he once was, he still had a considerable time ahead of him before retirement and that there was plenty of time to achieve his new goals.

Midlife transitions and the career coach

An understanding of the emotional and psychological impact that the midlife transition can have on an individual is an important starting point for a career coach. This will ensure that you spend enough time allowing your clients to make sense of their feelings and to grieve for what they may view as their lost youth and unmet goals, or acknowledging how they wish to build on the past. Simply understanding some of these common processes and reactions can allow you to support your clients and to give them the space they require to explore their feelings and come to terms with their situation. But there are some other approaches and techniques that you might find particularly helpful.

Values

It is often fruitful to focus on values with mid-career transition clients. We mentioned above that a midlife transition can cause individuals to start to reconsider their values as they search for meaning in their work lives. Brown (1995) provides a good summary of a range of techniques that can be used to help clients to explore this area. Her suggestion is that an examination of values needs to encompass two stages:

1. crystallization – where you become so clear about your values that you can put a name to them;
2. prioritization – where you identify which values mean the most to you.

There are a number of techniques that you can use to help clients to crystallize their values. Quantitative measures such as the Life Values Inventory (Crace and Brown 1992) or the Strengths Finder (explored in more detail in Chapter 11) provide a list of ready-made values and pose questions to which your responses will suggest the values that may be most important to you. These tools will also provide some information on the way that you have prioritized the values through the assessments. Constructivist methods (where individuals need to generate the words themselves rather than selecting from a pre-existing list) may be more time-intensive but will allow clients to define and describe their own values. You could ask your clients to identify people that they admire and help them to unpick what makes those people so estimable. Corlozzi (2003) proposes an extremely effective method called the 'Depth Orientated Values Extraction', which focuses on people's preferred leisure activities. Asking clients to think about the times when they feel happiest can help them identify their values. You might then go on to ask them to identify life's peak and worst experiences as another way of helping them explore. Finally, using visualizations can help clients identify possible selves, which can reveal the things that matter most to them.

Sometimes the identification process can uncover a sense of prioritization, as crystallization can clearly expose priorities. If clients need a little further help, you can draw on some other techniques that can help. The most revealing way tends to be to present clients with choices and see how they react and which they choose. Visualization can provide interesting insights. You could, for example, ask clients to imagine two different possible selves and to compare the different emotions that the images produce. Alternatively, ask them to imagine a fork in a road, with two value-driven goals at the end of either path. Which one will they take?

> [A]t the end of one path is great career success, a large salary and lots of international travel; at the end of the other is a fulfilled family life, where you get to pick the kids up from school each week and weekends are spent together in family activities.

Asking for instant answers to questions that juxtapose competing values can lead to productive discussions.

Holistic focus

Bejian and Salomone (1995) suggest that career coaching which focuses on issues beyond work, such a voluntary activities, hobbies and relationships, can be of great benefit when working with clients who are in the throes of a midlife transition. Living through this transition may highlight that an individual has been relying too much on their professional identity as a source of status, and they may find that they need to rebalance their lives in order to gain more meaning from elements of their life beyond the workplace.

Future orientation

Clients facing a midlife transition can find themselves so focused on the past that they are unable to move forward. One exercise that you could try with clients in this situation is a technique called 'career time perspective'. This was developed by Savickas (1991) and has been shown to increase clients' 'future orientation', or the degree to which they can free themselves from focusing on the past and start thinking about their futures. Having a future orientation has been shown to be critical in career development, and it is a quality that can be developed. The career time perspective is a series of three exercises: orientation, differentiation and integration. In the orientation exercise, clients are asked to draw three circles, representing their past, present and future, and to arrange them to show how they feel about the inter-relation of their past, present and future. They are then encouraged to reflect on the reasons for the relative size and position of the circles. In the differentiation phase, clients are asked to draw a life line from birth to death, plotting ten future life events and specifically thinking about the answers to the questions 'what will I do?' and 'who will I be?' for those events. During the final, integration, phase, clients are invited to link present behaviour with future outcomes, and devise their own step-by-step plans for the future.

Finally, let us look briefly at the outcomes of career change, and ask is a career change worthwhile? Happily for our clients, the research clearly tells us that it is. Those who have taken the plunge are usually more satisfied with their careers ultimately (Thomas 1980), specifically reporting higher levels of job satisfaction, increased feelings of job security and shorter working hours than those who stayed put (Khapova 2006). The group who overall tend to be most pleased with their changes are those who were interested in the new role itself; those who changed for a better salary, status or benefits reported to be generally less delighted with their choice (Green *et al.* 2007). Clearly this evidence is generalized but these are useful nuggets of information to share with clients who are contemplating a move.

REFERENCES

Barclay, S. R., Stoltz, K. B. and Chung, Y. B. (2011) Voluntary midlife career change: Integrating the transtheoretical model and the life-span, life-space approach. *The Career Development Quarterly*, 59: 386–399.

Bejian, D. V. and Salomone, P. R. (1995) Understanding midlife career renewal: Implications for counseling. *Career Development Quarterly*, 44(1): 52.

Brown, D. (1995) A values-based approach to facilitating career transitions. *Career Development Quarterly*, 42: 137–142.

Carless, S. A. and Arnup, J. L. (2010) A longitudinal study of the determinants and outcomes of career change. *Journal of Vocational Behaviour*, 78: 80–91.

Corlozzi, E. A. (2003) Depth-orientated values extraction. *Career Development Quarterly*, 52: 180–189.

Crace, R. K. and Brown, D. (1992) *The Life Values Inventory*. Minneapolis, MN: National Computer Systems.

Green, L., Hemmings, B. and Green, A. (2007) Career change and motivation: A matter of balance. *Australian Journal of Career Development*, 16(1): 20–27.

Khapova, S. N., Arthur, M. B., Wilderon, C. P. M. and Svensson, J. S. (2006) Professional identity as the key to career change intention. *Career Development International*, 12(7): 584–595.

Lieblich, A. (1986) Successful career women at midlife: Crises and transitions. *International Journal of Aging and Human Development*, 23(4): 301–312.

Levinson, D. J. (1978) *The Seasons of a Man's Life.* New York: Alfred Knopf.

Mitchell, K., Levin, A. and Krumboltz, J. (1999) Planned happenstance: Constructing unexpected career opportunities. *Journal of Counseling and Development*, 77(2): 115–124.

Murtagh, N., Lopes, P. N. and Lyons, E. (2011) Decision making in voluntary career change: An other than rational perspective. *The Career Development Quarterly*, 59: 249–262.

Prochaska, J. O., DiClemente, C. C. and Norcross, J. C. (1992) In search of how people change: Applications to addictive behaviors. *American Psychologist*, 47: 1102–1114.

Savickas, M. L. (1991) Career time perspective. In D. Brown and L. Brooks (eds), *Career Counseling Techniques.* Boston: Allyn & Bacon, pp. 236–249.

Super, D. E. (1990). A life-span, life-space approach to career development. In D. Brown and L. Brooks (eds), *Career Choice and Development*, 2nd ed. San Francisco: Jossey-Bass.

Thomas, L. E. (1980) A typology of midlife career changers. *Journal of Vocational Behavior*, 16: 173–182.

West, R. (2005) Time for a change: Putting the transtheoretical (stages of change) model to rest. *Addiction*, 100(8): 1036–1039.

Chapter 6

Unplanned career changes

We looked in the last chapter at the nature, provenance and outcomes of career changes that are within our control. But many of the changes that we make in our working lives, whether they are changes of career, sector, job or working arrangements, are not always our decision or at time of our choosing. In this chapter we will look at the impact of some of the circumstances that can lead to an unplanned career change. We will begin by examining the impact that job loss can have, and then look more specifically at what the research can tell us about issues such as redundancy, dismissal and parenthood and how they can affect both our emotions and our careers. It may seem surprising to include parenthood in a chapter on unplanned career change – after all, most of us have some degree of control about whether we have children, when we have them and to what extent their existence interferes with our careers. But in practice, things are often not that simple. Although having children *can* happen to order and may have pre-cisely the impact on the parents' careers that they were anticipating, for many people the arrival of children can throw life and careers into great confusion, and even if the decision to begin a family is planned, the associated changes often are not.

JOB LOSS

Work fulfils two crucial functions for subjective well-being (Jahoda 1982). The first is that it provides a social institution which fulfils basic psychological needs such as time structure, social contacts, a collective purpose, status and regular activity. The second is that it provides a source of personal identity and meaning. Work fills our days and gives us a reason to get up in the morning.

It is no great surprise to learn, therefore, that an involuntary job loss does little for our self-worth. It is well documented (e.g. Guindon and Smith 2002) that a forced job loss is likely to lead to higher stress levels, depression and anxiety, and lowered self-esteem. Identity can be lost, self-worth can plummet, and assumptions about life and the world are often shattered. The psychological impact of job loss and subsequent unemployment can last for years, well into an individual's new career (Clark *et al.* 2001). Coupled with this are the economic challenges usually associated with a job loss and the removal of a social network that would often mitigate the effects of a crisis. Individuals need to re-create themselves in a new role, and find a way to integrate themselves in society in a different way.

The emotional impact of a redundancy or dismissal can mirror the stages of grief that people experience with a major loss such as a bereavement. Kubler-Ross (1969) came up with a model which identified five stages of grieving that individuals need to work through to come to terms with a loss: denial, anger, bargaining, depression and acceptance. Kubler-Ross suggests that an individual's emotions become progressively worse through the stages and hit rock bottom in the depression stage; thereafter, an individual can start to feel more positive about his or her situation and the future.

Blau and Devaro (2007) applied the Kubler-Ross model to job loss and have identified some thoughts (Table 6.1) that might be associated with each of the stages which you could use to help you understand your clients' current position

Table 6.1

Denial

1. I can't believe I am losing my job at Company X.
2. I am in total disbelief that I must leave Company X.
3. I can't believe this is happening to me.

Anger

1. I am angry about being laid off.
2. I feel a lot of hostility towards Company X.
3. I feel furious that this could happen to me.

Bargaining

1. I think I should be able to make a bargain with Company X about being laid off.
2. I should be allowed to make a deal to avoid being laid off.
3. Some sort of compromise position should be offered to me.

Depression

1. I am very sad about leaving Company X.
2. I feel depressed about leaving this company.
3. Sometimes I feel like crying about being laid off.

Exploration

1. Maybe a positive opportunity will come out of my leaving Company X.
2. I am willing to explore the possibilities this job loss will create.
3. I am going to try and keep an open mind about leaving.

Acceptance

1. I am accepting that I will eventually leave Company X.
2. I think I can handle leaving Company X.
3. I will prepare for the coming change I need to make.

Blau (2007). Used by permission.

in their grieving process. This model includes an additional stage, that of exploration, which links the depression stage with acceptance.

If you have clients who are facing redundancy, this can be a very useful model to share with them. It can validate their current feelings and make them feel that they are reacting in a very 'normal' way; it can lead them to the realization that they are trapped in a particular stage, or it may encourage progression to the next stage. It can help them understand where they are now, and allow them to feel hope for the future.

Boundaries

The emotional impact of job loss can be profound and long-lasting. As a career coach, this is something that you should be aware of, so that you can feel confident that the support you offer is suitable for your clients at this time. As noted above, the emotional response to an unwelcome job loss can be as all-encompassing as that following a bereavement. Individuals who have worked in a particular role for a long time, who have dependents and who did not receive adequate notice that their job was ending, commonly experience the emotions of grief, including 'feelings of despair, anger, hostility, social isolation, loss of control, depersonalization and death anxiety' (Brewington *et al.* 2004: 81).

As a career coach, it is helpful if you are sensitive to these feelings, as clients will need to come to terms with them before they are likely to be able to move on productively to a new position. You will need to be very clear about your own professional boundaries when working with clients who are suffering after a job loss. If you feel that their emotional response to the job loss is preventing them from making any progress towards their career goals, you may judge that it is time to have a discussion with them about the potential value of seeing a counsellor.

Of course, each person is different and no two sets of circumstances are the same. A considerable amount of research has been conducted into the factors that make people more likely to adjust well and cope with job loss. We will look now at several of the factors that can have an impact, including class, gender and community.

There is some evidence that class may have a significant influence on the impact of job loss. Andersen (2009) found that a period of unemployment has a much more negative effect on subjective well-being for those with medium-status roles than for those with lower and higher status jobs. His argument is that while for the high-status professions, a period of unemployment provides a release from a highly stressful job, and for the lower status roles, it offers an escape from an unsatisfying job, for the those in the middle, a job loss removes a role that is relatively satisfying and not too stressful.

Gender seems to make a difference in reactions to job loss and unemployment. Forret *et al.* (2010) studied parents who had been made redundant and found that the men were highly likely to see the redundancy as a traumatic loss, whereas the women were much more likely to see it as an opportunity.

The community that you find yourself in also makes a difference. At a cross-national level, there is some evidence that different cultures respond in different ways. Carroll (2007) showed that Australian men are less likely to suffer psychological distress during a period of unemployment than German or UK men.

High levels of unemployment within your local community are linked to an increased ability to cope with job loss, as the job loss carries less stigma (Clark *et al.* 2001).

Finally, being surrounded by a strong support network makes a big difference, both to how you feel about losing your job and to how quickly you find another position (Kanfer *et al.* 2001).

Post job-loss career growth

But it's not all doom and gloom. There has been a lot of research in the last few years into the idea of post-traumatic growth which refers to people who have lived through extremely challenging times and as a result of their difficulties, have ended up with increased life satisfaction. This approach has been applied more recently to the arena of careers, and a number of scholars have explored the idea of 'post job-loss career growth', where a redundancy or other forced break can eventually result in the individual finding greater job satisfaction and subjective career success than they would have experienced had they remained in their previous role.

So what can we do to make our clients more likely to experience post job-loss career growth? Eby and Buch (1998) identified three categories of factors that make post job-loss career growth more likely, and while most of these factors will be beyond our clients' control, there may be some that they might usefully learn from. Within the category of 'individual characteristics', Eby and Buch found that individuals who were at a mid-career stage, who had not been particularly happy in their previous roles and who stayed active during their job search, were more likely to secure a new job that they found fulfilling. In terms of an individual's environment, it helps to have some financial resources at hand to reduce the pressure of having to find work as quickly as possible. The support of friends also aids resilience, as does having flexible family arrangements that allow you to pick and choose from a wider pool of opportunities, such as jobs further afield or roles that entail shift work. Finally, Eby and Buch identified the impact of what they call 'transition process characteristics' which incorporate how the job loss was handled, how long the between jobs period lasts and how successfully the individual resolves their feelings of grief and anger.

So that concludes a brief exploration of some of the more generic aspects of job loss. We will now move on to look at some of the research from three specific types of job loss: redundancy, dismissal, and traumatic life events. We will end the chapter with a summary of the considerable research that has gone into the experiences of parents, and in particular mothers.

Redundancy

By far the biggest group of forced job losses contains those whose positions have been made redundant. As career coaches, we are also more likely to see a high proportion of clients from this category, as redundancy or outplacement counseling or coaching is now often offered as part of the redundancy agreement.

The details of how the redundancy was handled by the employer can give an indication of the emotional impact that the job loss may be having. Eby and Buch (1998) explored the impact of an 'ethical' approach to making employees redundant and found the employees who had advance warning of their job loss felt that the organization cared more about their future, which led to better emotional acceptance of their situation. They also reported that the white-collar workers in their survey were given significantly longer notice periods than the blue-collar workers, which may link back to the evidence cited earlier on the impact of job status on post job-loss experiences (Andersen 2009). Employees were also shown to have greater emotional acceptance if they had been told about their job loss by the HR department or the senior managers in the organization rather than by their line manager. Although perhaps rather counter-intuitive, employees felt that it made them think that the organization as a whole cared about them if the notice came from someone central. The third factor uncovered in this study was that having a good reason for the redundancy made a positive difference to the employee's subsequent health and emotional acceptance.

Forced exits

The career changes we will look at in this chapter are by no means all negative, but what defines them is that the timing of them (and for some the change itself) is not entirely in the hands of the individual.

One area which is almost always a negative experience is the forced exit or dismissal. There is relatively little written about people who have been sacked. It is a tricky area to research, partly because those who have been sacked are often not terribly enthusiastic about talking about their experiences, and partly because relatively few people actually end up getting dismissed – more often than not, they are re-structured out of a job, they go before they are pushed or their employer makes them an offer it is in their best interests to accept.

The reasons for dismissal are more complex than simply poor performance or inappropriate behaviour on the part of the individual; Klaas *et al.* (1998) identify a series of organizational factors which predispose a manager to making a decision to fire an employee. The HR policies within the organization have a part to play, with managers who have had interview and performance management training in organizations with dismissal policies and well-represented unions being far less likely to make dismissals. The economic situation also makes a difference: employees recruited in a time of economic prosperity stand more of a chance of dismissal than those recruited when times are hard, as in general employers have a wider choice of better applicants during a recession so are more likely to be able to pick the candidate who is just right. An employee is also more likely to face dismissal if the organization is not performing at capacity – it is only when there is some slack in the system that managers can afford to let even a poor performer leave. Finally, there is some evidence that race plays a part, with dismissals less likely when there is racial congruence between the manager and the member of staff.

One area that has proved easier to track than others is that of CEO dismissals, and these findings may be of use if this is a client group that you encounter. Ward *et al.* (1995) followed the future career paths of a group of CEOs who had been forced to leave their posts and came up with some interesting results. They analysed the different reasons for the CEOs' departures, categorizing them as negative (for example, poor performance and illegal or improper behaviour) or neutral (such as a merger, an ethical stance or a strategic disagreement), and found that the reason for the CEOs' dismissal had no impact on their future career path. What did have an impact, however, was the age at which the CEOs had been fired. If they were let go before the age of 50, they were likely to find another active role in a similar organization. If fired after 60, they tended to find one or a range of advisory roles. If their dismissal came during their 50s, their chances of future career success were greatly reduced. This information could be of use to clients facing this kind of situation as they try to position themselves strategically in the job market.

Career transitions necessitated by traumatic life events

Most of the career changes that we discuss in this chapter stem from the workplace. But for a significant number of people each year, career transitions are the product of a traumatic life event, usually a physical injury. Haynie and Shepherd (2011) conducted a quite moving piece of research into career changes of soldiers who had sustained serious injuries through their military careers, which gives some clues to the emotional responses of others in parallel situations.

Their research focused on the qualities that were likely to be associated with a more positive attitude to their new career and identified two key stages of development that were needed. The traumas the participants had undergone were such that they shattered participants' fundamental assumptions 'that the world is benevolent, meaningful and that [they] had self worth' (2011: 509). The study found that the individuals needed to find a way to make sense of their trauma in the context of the world, society and their lives in order to reinstate some of their core beliefs about the world. Those who managed this successfully were able to come up with a sense-making narrative that told a coherent personal story and linked their previous life and career with their future plans. The study also found that those looking for roles about which they were passionate made the transition better than those looking for financial rewards.

Parenthood

Fathers

The evidence is clear that it is overwhelmingly women whose careers are interrupted when children come along, but fathers' careers are not completely untouched. We do know that fathers are likely to work longer hours than men without children, as a response to their 'father as breadwinner' role (Biggart and O'Brien 2010). Men's working patterns have changed over the last 40 years; the proportion of men working part-time, for example, has increased to around 10 per cent. One might suppose that this is a response to changing attitudes towards childcare, but in fact, a higher proportion of non-fathers are working part-time compared to fathers, suggesting that while opportunities and attitudes have changed in many ways, the gendered role of male as the main provider is proving more difficult to shift. Biggart and O'Brien provide some evidence that men's careers are more likely to be more successful *after* they have children – their earnings are likely to increase and they are more likely to be promoted. This may be a consequence of the increased hours of work, but there are also suggestions that objective career success is linked to the perception of masculinity, with the appearance of masculine qualities helping male workers win promotion. Biggart and O'Brien (2010) suggest that having children makes men appear more masculine but makes women seem more feminine, which contributes to the different pace of promotion in parents.

Mothers

Women's relationship with the workplace has changed dramatically over the last generation. Female participation in the workplace has increase from 43 per cent in 1970 to 73 per cent in 2013 (ONS 2013), with the increase especially noticeable in professional and managerial fields. But although the proportion of women in higher status jobs and at more senior levels has increased significantly, it is nowhere near proportionate (women form 45 per cent of the workforce but only 16 per cent of the senior management – Burke and Vinnicombe 2006). There are plenty of theories and reasons to explain this. One that has captured the attention of the world's media is the idea that women are somehow 'opting out' and are making the choice not to aim for the highest level, but there is plenty of evidence that the reasons are more complex than that.

Women's career paths are likely to be different from men's and are far more likely to be non-linear and disjointed (Maniero and Sullivan 2005). One major reason for this (although not the sole one) is motherhood, although women's own choices and employer organizations' responses to mothers and their needs also play important roles. Patton and McMahon (2006: 119) describe the situation starkly, identifying a negative relationship for women between marriage and number of children and 'every known criteria of career involvement and achievement'.

Pregnancy

The impact of motherhood on women's careers starts in pregnancy. Millward (2006) conducted a qualitative study into the impact of pregnancy on women's careers and found two major themes. The first was the change of identity that her participants reported, talking about gradual invisibility as a valued employee linked to a growing insecurity about their future status.

The second change found was in the psychological contract between these women and their employers. The women interviewed reported significant feelings of guilt about the impact that their pregnancy was having on their work performance as a result of, for example, time taken for ante-natal appointments, fatigue or other pregnancy-related symptoms. They also found that their professional aspirations, commitment and productivity were questioned by colleagues and supervisors.

Career breaks and returning to work

The percentage of women returning to work after having children has doubled since 1983, with two-thirds of new mothers back in work within nine months. This does not, however, necessarily indicate quite the leap towards equality that you might think, as around 40 per cent of those return either part-time or in more junior roles than before. Hakim (2006) proposes a model to explain women's choices. She categorizes women into the home types (20 per cent), work types (20 per cent) and adaptive (60 per cent). The adaptive women are those who are most interested in working in a way that fits around their family needs, such as part-time, across flexible hours or taking a less stressful job. Those in the work type category will return to their previous roles if this is viable for them; women in this category tend to have higher pre-natal salaries, so resuming their role post-birth is more likely to be feasible financially. Those with a home orientation will not return to work if at all possible, and are shown to be more likely to choose partners whose earning capacity will probably allow them to stay at home after maternity leave.

Women's work choices are, of course, not the only factors that determine what they end up doing. Women's post-birth behaviour is, for the most part, pretty consistent with their pre-birth intentions (Houston and Marks 2003), but 24 per cent of those who planned to return to work find that they can't, mostly because they find that work commitments don't sit comfortably alongside family commitments, or because they encounter issues around the cost of childcare and lack of organizational support.

Cabrera (2006) examined women's reasons for taking a career break and found a whole web of factors involved. Childcare was the biggest single factor that led to taking a career break, but this was by no means the whole picture. Lack of suitable childcare constitutes the sole reason for 30 per cent of women, but is only a contributory reason for a further 50 per cent. Other influential factors include the lack of opportunity within the workplace, sex discrimination, sexual harassment, and a sense that the prevailing male culture in many organizations is at odds with women's more relational approach to decision making. Half the women interviewed for Cabrera's study reported a change in career focus after having children, citing a reduced interest in corporate careers, a new area of career interest, or the desire to make a difference.

Career opportunities for mothers

One of the factors keeping women out of the workplace is a sense that they aren't getting the promotions or opportunities that their male colleagues are. There is some clear evidence that women need to outperform their male counterparts in order to achieve the same status (Blau and Devaro 2007; Lyness and Heilman 2006).

The situation for women at work has clearly moved on by leaps and bounds in the last generation, but there is still a way to go. The glass ceiling does still exist, but is situated considerably higher up the corporate ladder than it once was. Formalized anti-discriminatory HR policies in recruitment have made a great impact on the fairness of job selection for entry level jobs, but recruitment for senior jobs is far more likely to rely on informal networks.

Women still struggle to get full and fair access to these networks. For a number of reasons, networking is likely to be more difficult for women than for men. Women report that they often feel excluded from the kinds of networking events that men are likely to engage with (such as a round of golf), and there is some evidence that mentors, although widely used by women, do not provide the same access to networks for both genders. Time out for children makes this problem worse for women, as they will often lose touch with their colleagues altogether during their maternity leave or career break, and even if they do return to work full-time, they are more likely to be the parent who has to rush back to relieve the child minder, or who arranges to work from home one day a week, thus missing out on the 'water-cooler' moments or drinks after work during which these networks are consolidated.

Mothers also need to overcome barriers of perception. There is some evidence (Hoobler et al. 2011) that managers are more likely to think that mothers will probably suffer from work/family conflict more than fathers, and that this has an impact on their perceived promotability. Nearly half of women who return to work do so part-time, and this brings its own set of pre-conceptions for mothers to deal with. Broschak et al. (2008) found that while part-timers are shown to put in extra effort at work in gratitude for the flexible working arrangements and are shown to be more productive per hour (as a result of lower work fatigue), they are thought by managers to be less committed, harder to motivate, harder to manage and less caring about their jobs, their departments and their customers. They tend to receive lower pay, fewer fringe benefits, fewer opportunities for promotion and less training and because they are less likely to be members of a union, they have lower job security.

Putting these factors all together, Poduval and Poduval (2008) have coined the phrase the 'maternal wall' to sit alongside the glass ceiling, suggesting that even maintaining a professional level can be quite a challenge for mothers.

Clients typically choose to come to see us when things are not going so well in their careers, so the scenarios we have described in this chapter may well be familiar to you as practitioners. It is of course vital to remember that the research quoted here is based on generalizations; every client will have his or her own story, with individual circumstances and an individual response. Having an understanding of some of the common experiences and the range of reactions that are frequently experienced can help you to feel empathy with your clients, and sharing some of the stories embedded within the research can help clients to validate their own responses, which can help them to see a way towards a brighter future.

REFERENCES

Andersen, S. H. (2009) Unemployment and subjective well-being: A question of class? *Work and Occupations*, 36(3): 3–25.

Biggart, L. and O'Brien, M. (2010) UK fathers' longer worked hours: Career stage or fatherhood? *Fathering: A Journal of Theory, Research, & Practice about Men as Fathers*, 8(3): 341–361.

Blau, G. (2007) Partially testing a process model for understanding victim responses to an anticipated worksite closure. *Journal of Vocational Behavior*, 71: 421–428.

Blau, F. D. and Devaro, J. (2007) New evidence on gender differences in promotion rates: An empirical analysis of a sample of new hires. *Industrial Relations*, 46(3): 511–550.

Brewington, J. O., Nassar-McMillan, S. C., Flowers, C. P. and Furr, S. R. (2004) A preliminary investigation of factors associated with job loss grief. *The Career Development Quarterly*, 53: 78–83.

Broschak, J. P., Davis-Blake, A. and Block, E. S. (2008) Nonstandard, not substandard: The relationship between work arrangements, work attitudes, and job performance. *Work and Occupations*, 35(1): 3–43.

Burke, R. J. and Vinnicombe, S. (2006) Supporting women's career advancement. *Women in Management Review*, 21(1): 10–16.

Cabrera, E. F. (2007) Opting out and opting in: Understanding the complexities of women's career transitions. *Career Development International*, 12(3): 218–237.

Carroll, N. (2007) Unemployment and psychological well being. *The Economic Record*, 83(262): 287–302.

Clark, A. E., Georgellis, Y. and Sanfey, P. (2001) Scarring: The psychological impact of past unemployment. *Economica*, 68: 221–241.

Eby, L. T. and Buch, K. (1998) The impact of adopting an ethical approach to employee dismissal during corporate restructuring. *Journal of Business Ethics*, 17: 1253–1264.

Forret, M. L., Sillivan, S. E. and Maniero, L. A. (2010) Gender role differences in reactions to unemployment: Exploring psychological mobility and boundaryless careers. *Journal of Organizational Behavior*, 31: 647–666.

Guindon, M. H. and Smith, B. (2002) Emotional barriers to successful reemployment: Implications for counsellors. *Journal of Employment Counseling*, 39: 73–82.

Hakim, C. (2006) Women, careers and work-life preferences. *British Journal of Guidance and Counselling*, 34(3): 279–294.

Haynie, J. M. and Shepherd, D. (2011) Toward a theory of discontinuous career transition: Investigating career transitions necessitated by traumatic life events. *Journal of Applied Psychology*, 96(3): 501–524.

Hoobler, J. M., Lemmon, G. and Wayne, S. J. (2011) Women's underrepresentation in upper management: New insights on a persistent problem. *Organizational Dynamics*, 40: 151–156.

Houston, D. M. and Marks, G. (2003) The role of planning and workplace support in returning to work after maternity leave. *British Journal of Industrial Relations*, 41: 197–214.

Jahoda, M. (1982) *Employment and Unemployment*. Cambridge: Cambridge University Press.

Kanfer, R., Wanberg, C. R. and Kantrowitz, T. M. (2001) Job search and employment: A personality–motivational analysis and meta-analytic review. *Journal of Applied Psychology*, 86(5): 837–855.

Klaas, B. S., Brown, M. and Heneman III, H. G. (1998) The determinants of organizations' usage of employee dismissal: Evidence from Australia. *Journal of Labor Research*, 19(1): 149–164.

Kubler-Ross, E. (1969) *On Death and Dying*. New York: Macmillan.

Lyness, K. S. and Heilman, M. E. (2006) When fit is fundamental: Performance evaluations and promotions of upper-level female and male managers. *Journal of Applied Psychology*, 91(4): 777–785.

Maniero, L. A. and Sullivan, S. E. (2005) Kaleidoscope careers: An alternative explanation for the opt-out revolution. *Academy of Management Executive*, 19(1): 106–123.

Millward, L. J. (2006) The transition to motherhood in an organizational context: An interpretative phenomenological analysis. *Journal of Occupational and Organizational Psychology*, 3: 315–333.

ONS (2013) *Labour Market Statistics* retrieved from: http://www.ons.gov.uk/ons/rel/lms/labour-market-statistics/march-2013/statistical-bulletin.html

Patton, W. and McMahon, M. (2006) *Career Development and Systems Theory: Connecting Theory and Practice.* Rotterdam: Sense Publishers.

Poduval, J. and Poduval, M. (2009) Working mothers: How much Working, How much mothers, and where is the womanhood? *Mens Sana Monographs*, 7(1): 63–79.

Sullivan, S. E., Forret, M. L. and Maniero, L. A. (2007) No regrets? An investigation of the relationship between being laid off and experiencing career regrets. *Journal of Managerial Psychology*, 22(8): 787–804.

Ward, A., Sonnenfeld, J. A., Kimberly, J. R. (1995) In search of a kingdom: Determinants of career outcomes for chief executives who are fired. *Human Resource Management Journal*, 34(1): 117–139.

Part II

Career coaching approaches

Chapter 7

Career decision-making difficulties

Where do clients encounter problems?

There has been considerable research examining the mechanisms underpinning the way that we make decisions in life (some of which we covered in Chapter 3) but in comparison with many life decisions, career decision making has particular challenges. First, the number of alternative options is vast. There are 665 different groups identified in the UK's Standard Occupational Classifications (SOC 2010) and for each of them, there is a great range of possible variations, specialisms, courses, qualifications and employers. In making a career decision, we are narrowing tens of thousands of options down to one. This is not easy. Second, the amount of information available to us about each one is vast. We talk in Chapter 15 about some of the mechanisms that we have developed for making sense of the onslaught of labour market information that we face every day, but making informed and rational choices based on information gleaned from websites, books, marketing literature, friends, family, the media and our daily life is no mean feat. Third, decisions are based on such a wide range of factors that they cannot always be easily compared: it's hard to feel confident about your choice when comparing one job which is near to home, interesting and has great colleagues to another which is well paid, varied and well suited to your skills. Finally, there is inevitably some uncertainty in the decision. However much research you put into the process, you can never be completely sure that the apparently charming, intelligent and thoughtful person you met at interview will actually be a great boss, or that you will actually get on well with your clients, or indeed that the organization won't fold within a year. Viewed this way, it is no wonder that so many of us struggle to make confident choices.

Clients can get stuck at any point of the career decision-making process and each person's story is unique. There are, however, some broad themes and scenarios that we come across more often than others. It is useful as a career coach to have an understanding of some of these more common challenges that our clients face, in part so that we can more easily spot them in our clients' stories, but also as a useful structure for our own learning as we read about techniques to help support them.

Gati *et al.* (1996) conducted a large-scale quantitative study into the most common sticking points in clients' career decision-making processes and identified three broad themes and ten sub-themes that appear to cause people the most trouble. In this chapter I will present these ten common decision-making difficulties and some suggestions for coaching approaches and techniques that could be particularly useful.

The first group of issues is around lack of readiness. This can then in turn be split into people struggling with lack of motivation, indecisiveness and dysfunctional myths, all of which lend themselves to a coaching style of professional support.

1. **Lack of motivation.** People often need to make career decisions at a time that is not of their choosing – when their school or university courses finish, for example, when their work contracts come to an end, or perhaps when they face redundancy. Regardless of whether the individual feels ready to make a change, external forces may control their circumstances, and while clients can be aware intellectually that they need to make a decision, they may not feel much enthusiasm about the change. Some clients simply don't like change, feeling safer in the comfort zone of the familiar; others might feel that they are still getting a lot from their current position and are not ready to move on.

   Possible coaching approaches: Motivational interviewing (see Chapter 9) is a technique that builds on the humanistic techniques of reflective listening in order to help clients increase their intrinsic motivation to change.

2. **Indecisiveness.** Career decisions are important, and individuals can some-times be so torn between two or more options that they can't move forward. The decision may be 'do I stay or do I go?' or there might be two or more alternative options that your clients are considering.

   Possible coaching approaches: A person-centred approach can help clients to identify which of the options would best fit with their values and aspira-tions, and the GROW model can provide a useful framework for this kind of evaluation. Asking clients what advice their role models would give them can be revealing.

3. **Dysfunctional myths.** Clients can find themselves unable to act through assumptions or fears that are not always grounded in reality. The issue could be 'people like me don't get jobs like that', 'I'd never manage to do that kind of role' or 'I'm rubbish at interviews'.

   Possible coaching approaches: One of the most effective approaches for dysfunctional myths is cognitive behavioural coaching. This approach (see Chapter 12 for more details) enables clients to link their feelings, thoughts and behaviour and provides techniques for deliberately changing the thoughts, which then has an impact on behaviour.

The next series of career decision-making difficulties centres around lack of information, either about the self or about occupations and how to find and get the jobs individuals want.

4. **Lack of information about the process of career decision making.** This might include clients who don't realize that they need to fill in a UCAS form to get a place at university, who haven't considered an internship or whose horizons are limited to the occupational roles within their immediate family.

Possible coaching approaches: This is one situation where giving your clients some information can be useful. If you are in possession of a discrete piece of information that could help your clients make more realistic choices, then it is often in their best interests to communicate this piece of information directly. If you know that a first step to a career in television often begins with an internship, then sharing this with your client in your conversation could not only save your client a lot of time but also allow a more productive use of your meetings as you can focus the conversation on how your client could go about finding that work placement.

5. **Lack of information about the self.** Good career decisions often rely on clients having a real insight to their skills, interests, motivations and values. For many of us, developing an honest and in-depth understanding of ourselves is a lifetime's work, but for some clients – particularly perhaps younger people who may have had less life experience – the sketchy picture they have of themselves is not enough to allow them to feel confident about a career decision.

Possible coaching approaches: There is a great array of effective coaching approaches and techniques that can be helpful for getting clients to understand themselves better. Coaches could suggest online assessment tools that can stimulate discussions, such as the Strengths Finder (www.authentichappiness.com). Some of these can be done between sessions and can form the basis for a discussion; others, such as discussions about role models, can be done as exercises during the interventions. These and some others are explored in more detail in Chapter 14, on coaching tools.

6. **Lack of information about available options.** Help with generating options is one of the most common requests that career coaches receive. Clients may know that they are not in the right role, or perhaps may know what sorts of roles they would not be suited to, but are unclear about the kinds of options that are available to them.

Possible coaching approaches: It can be very tempting when presented with this kind of client dilemma to feel that you should be offering suggestions, but while offering one or two ideas can be genuinely useful, it is typically the case that with a gentle nudge or two, clients can come up with their own (usually better) ideas. Asking clients to present the ideas they have had on a 'mind map' (Buzan 2000) can often generate new ideas, and suggesting that they keep a career journal for a few weeks, in which they can scribble down any thoughts and ideas that occur to them, can also help. If your clients have identified their key character strengths (using the Strengths Finder noted above), you could use this as a means to structure their thoughts. Ask them to think of ten different occupations that utilize each of their top five strengths, and use this as a basis for a discussion.

7. **Lack of information about ways of obtaining information about jobs.**
We referred earlier to the challenges of processing the vast array of career
information available to us, and many clients find this a real sticking point.
Clients struggle both with knowing how to get the information they want and
with knowing whether a particular source of information is credible.
Possible coaching approaches: A client-centred questioning approach can
allow your clients to realize that they know perhaps more that they thought,
but this is one career coaching dilemma where some signposting from the
coach might provide a useful addition to their existing knowledge. Your
clients, for example, might not know about the Sector Skills Councils, which
provide a great range of impartial career information, or might not have
realized that colleges have open days or that they could ask to do some
work shadowing.

The last group of career decision-making difficulties is concentrated around
inconsistent information which can be due to unreliable sources of the information,
or conflicts – both internal and external.

8. **Inconsistent information due to unreliable sources.** Career information
comes to us from all sorts of different sources, can be very subjective and
changes rapidly. A few years ago, there was some talk in the media about
plumbing being the great career change to make if you wanted autonomy and
a decent wage packet. Fast forward a few years and so many people have
taken this advice that plumbers begin to face stiff competition and wages are
dropping. Does a teacher earn a lot of money? Well, that depends on your
perspective: compared to a social care worker, yes; compared to an investment
banker, no. Reading a university's web page about a given course, you might
imagine that all their graduates have gone on to highly fulfilling and well-
paid jobs; speaking to graduates from that very course, you might get a
different view.
Possible coaching approaches: A client-centred questioning approach is
usually the best and most straightforward kind of interaction to have with
clients in this situation. This approach can encourage your clients to reflect on
the information that they have encountered with a critical eye, make their own
judgements about what to believe and identify alternative sources to help
resolve the dilemmas.

9. **Inconsistent information due to internal conflicts:** We often find ourselves
listening to an inner dialogue, as our minds try to take account of all the different elements of a situation and the different aspects of our personalities and
our circumstances: 'I'm unhappy where I am but frightened to make a change',
'my head tells me to go for the banking job, my heart wants to teach'.
Sometimes these contradictions can be easily resolved, but on other occasions
individuals opt to see a career coach to help them make sense of them.
Possible coaching approaches: Person-centred coaching, one of the core
coaching approaches, is often the best way to help these clients to think
through the different arguments that may be running round their heads.

10. **Inconsistent information due to external conflicts.** Our career decisions will often have an impact on those closest to us; equally, those closest to us will often have an impact on our career decisions. Sometimes these interactions all line up in perfect harmony but it is not uncommon for clients to face a conflict between their own views and those of their significant others. They may, for example, feel pressure from their parents to make a different choice, or face concerns from a spouse about the impact their choice might have on the family.

Possible coaching approaches: Personal relationships are of course enormously complex, and as coaches we need to accept that sometimes these issues may be beyond the scope of a coaching session. For external conflicts that might be addressed within a coaching session, there are a few techniques that can be helpful. Transactional analysis (covered in more depth in Chapter 13) is a psychological approach that can help clients to see their relationships in a new light, and this can lead to relatively straightforward behavioural changes that can have a big impact. Role play is another tool that we can employ, helping clients to prepare for difficult conversations by playing the roles of both themselves and their significant other.

SEVERITY OF DIFFICULTIES

While the career decision-making difficulties listed above are commonly experienced by clients, they are of course not all equally difficult for them. The key factor determining the severity of the career decision-making difficulty is the length of time it is likely to take to solve the problem. This can be neatly illustrated in the difference between indecision (likely to be a short-term single issue) and indecisiveness (more likely to be a longer-term issue that needs to be addressed at a more basic personality level).

Career decision-making difficulties can also be analysed in terms of their causes and the consequences that might occur if they are not satisfactorily addressed.

Causes can be divided into those that stem from issues within the individual, such as lack of self-awareness, and those that stem from external issues, such as conflicts with others (Murdock and Fremont 1989). Career decision-making difficulties that arise as a result of internal issues are more difficult to resolve (Gati *et al.* 2010) than those caused by external factors because any solution is likely to involve a process aimed at creating and sustaining a significant change within the client, and this will take time and commitment. Causes of internal difficulties are either cognitive or emotional. Those with a cognitive source might include issues around the collection and processing of information (e.g. Gati and Tal 2008), and those with emotional roots might include personality traits such as indecisiveness or internal conflicts (Saka and Gati 2007). Perhaps not surprisingly, it is the difficulties arising from emotional causes that are the most challenging to address, as they are more likely to require long-term intervention such as counselling; the cognitive-driven difficulties can usually be tackled with information.

In terms of consequences, if a career decision-making difficulty is resolved, it could have three different types of outcome. It could prevent a decision from being made, halt the decision-making process before it reaches a conclusion, or result in a 'non-optimal' decision (Gati *et al.* 1996). Career difficulties leading to non-optimal decisions tend to be easier and quicker to sort out than those which might actually prevent the decision from being made. The characteristics of the specific situation will generally determine which of these categories a client's particular challenges fall into but broadly speaking, lack of motivation, general indecisiveness and internal conflicts are more likely to prevent a decision being made. A lack of information, or unreliable information about occupations, is more likely to lead to a non-optimal decision.

The framework presented here is a useful tool to help you understand where your clients are at the moment, and what kind of issues they need to resolve before they are likely to be able to move on. Many clients will struggle with more than one category and it is of course rather artificial to separate them into such distinct categories when we know that in real life, issues are interdependent and it is often the combination of issues that causes the problem. An individual might be perfectly capable of finding the information that they need to make their career decision, but if their situation involves a lack of information, a conflict of views with their partner, and a tendency to indecision, then the situation can become overwhelming and they may seek professional career coaching. Using this framework to unpack each of these issues can be a valuable first step in getting your clients to understand what is going on and this process in itself can make their challenges seem less onerous.

REFERENCES

Buzan, T. (2000) *The Mind Map Book.* London: Penguin.

Gati, I., Amir, T. and Landman, S. (2010) Career counsellors' perceptions of the severity of career decision-making difficulties. *British Journal of Guidance and Counselling*, 38(4): 393–408.

Gati, I., Krausz, M. and Osipow, S. H. (1996) A taxonomy of difficulties in career decision making. *Journal of Counseling Psychology*, 43: 510–526.

Gati, I. and Tal, S. (2008) Decision making models and career guidance. In J. A. Athanasou and R. Van Esbroek (eds), *International Handbook of Career Guidance*. Berlin: Springer, pp. 157–185.

Murdock, N. L. and Fremont, S. K. (1989) Attributional influences in counsellor decision making. *Journal of Counseling Psychology*, 36: 417–422.

Saka, N. and Gati, I. (2007) Emotional and personality-related aspects of persistent career decision-making difficulties. *Journal of Vocational Psychology*, 40: 340–358.

SOC (2010) Standard occupational classification: ONS retrieved from http://www.ons.gov.uk/ons/guide-method/classifications/current-standard-classifications/soc2010/index.html

Chapter 8

Humanistic coaching

There are many different styles of career coaching and, indeed, many different styles of good career coaching. I mentioned in Chapter 1 De Haan's (2008) playing field model, illustrating some of the most fundamental differences in approaches. The model proposes that coaching styles can be plotted on two continuums: one that runs from suggesting to exploring and one that runs from confronting to supporting.

Person-centred or 'humanistic' coaching (the terms are more or less interchangeable) is firmly situated in the exploring and supporting quadrant. This is the pure version of humanism, and while this might feel a bit extreme for many career coaches and their clients, its ethos and tenets should underpin most of the coaching sessions that you are ever involved with.

The goal of person-centred coaching is to help clients on their journey towards being 'fully functioning' people. In humanistic terms, this refers to someone who knows themselves and has a clear sense of their direction and how they can get

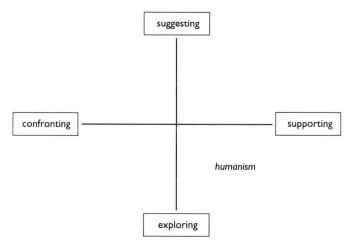

Figure 8.1
Adapted from De Haan 2008

there. A fully functioning person is able to be themselves and is not swayed by others' opinions, accepting themselves and others for what they are and taking responsibility for their own behaviour.

This chapter will introduce this important and influential approach. There are two fundamental assumptions underpinning humanism, namely the principle of self-determination and the self-actualizing tendency. This chapter will briefly explain these assumptions and then move on to exploring how you might integrate the principles and techniques into your career coaching practice.

ASSUMPTIONS

The principle of self-determination holds that individuals are best placed to make decisions about themselves and for themselves, as they are the only ones who will fully understand the context and implications of a decision. From the perspective of a career coach, you might feel that you understand your clients well, and may have spent considerable time thinking about their motivation and character. In truth, however, you will only ever get access to a thin 'slice' of them, who they are and the life they are living. Your clients, in contrast, are likely to have spent many hours considering the issue troubling them, and will have an understanding of the many different facets of their situation. Solutions and ideas that they generate are usually going to be better ones than any that you can come up with.

If we accept this humanistic assumption, then we should be extremely circumspect about our role in suggesting ideas and solving problems. Even if we think we have the perfect solution, it is only our *clients* who are in a position to judge whether or not it is a suitable way forward.

The second fundamental assumption is the self-actualizing tendency. This is the desire that exists in every one of us to make our lives better, and to grow and develop personally. Humanism describes this drive as a biological tendency rather than a moral imperative, meaning that it is simply something that we all feel and is part of the human condition. It is something that we do, rather than something that we ought to do. Although the tendency is present within us all, we do not always act on it. Our drive towards self-improvement and growth can be thwarted by a range of factors such as fear of failure, lack of opportunities, circumstances and a lack of self-awareness. Humanistic interventions aim to clear the path for the self-actualizing tendency to drive behaviour by holding up an 'intelligent mirror' to the clients, allowing them to hear their own thoughts and clarify their own views.

Sound familiar?

As you read through the book, some of these ideas will come up time and again. It is hard to overestimate the influence that humanism has had on counselling and derivative practices. Motivational interviewing (see

Chapter 10) is firmly grounded in the self-determination theory. The idea of a motivational interview is that you are trying to increase your clients' intrinsic motivation and that the most effective way to do this is by using humanistic techniques to allow clients to explore their own feelings about the change, and to encourage their self-actualizing tendency to flourish.

Another coaching approach covered in this book that is significantly influenced by a humanistic philosophy is positive psychology (Chapter 11). Positive psychology shares with humanism a belief in self-determinism and a focus on self-actualization and optimal functioning.

Chapter 13 on transactional analysis introduces us to Berne's idea of 'I'm ok; you're ok' as a model of healthy adult relationships. In this are echoes of the humanistic fully functioning person with acceptance of oneself and acceptance of others.

In fact, such has been the influence of the humanistic philosophy, you would be hard-pressed to find a career coaching theory that doesn't embrace a client-centred approach to some degree. Humanism offers a combination of straightforward techniques and dramatic results and can be applied to varying degrees in many different contexts, and it is these factors that have contributed to its widespread influence.

CORE CONDITIONS

Carl Rogers was one of the founding forefathers of the humanistic approach. Perhaps his most enduring theoretical contribution was the conceptualization of the five core conditions that he states are necessary and sufficient for change to take place within a therapeutic context. In other words (Rogers 1957), these five conditions all need to be present (necessary) for a one-to-one intervention to be successful, and if they are all present, change will inevitably happen (sufficient).

1. Two persons are in psychological contact

The first, and most basic, of the core conditions is that there need to be two people involved, and they need to be communicating with each other. So far, so good!

2. The client is in a state of incongruence

The 'incongruence' here is between the client's current state and their ideal state. There must be something that the client is looking for, or doesn't quite understand about themselves, which has brought them into this coaching relationship.

3. The coach is congruent in the relationship

'Congruence' refers here to a sense of authenticity. If the therapist or coach is having to act or pretend in the relationship, they are unlikely to be able to use their own experience to help them empathize fully, and this will diminish the power of the relationship.

4. The coach experiences unconditional positive regard (UPR) for the client

This condition is at the heart of client-centred, non-judgemental practice. Unconditional positive regard or UPR is an attitude that the therapist or coach must have towards their clients; it must be completely accepting of who they are and the decisions that they have made. Having UPR for your clients is not about approving of their actions per se, but approving of the clients themselves and not judging their actions. It entails believing that whatever they have done, whatever choices they have made and whatever consequences their actions have had, you, as coach, truly believe that they are fundamentally sound human beings.

Is it possible to increase your unconditional positive regard?

It may be a straightforward concept, but the practice of approaching every client with UPR is not easy. There are two elements that you can usefully reflect on to help develop your own UPR for clients.

First, you need to hone your self-awareness. You need to be sensitive to the kinds of things that are likely to make UPR challenging for you, and one place to start is to be clear about your own values, and aware of the ways in which other people might violate the principles that you hold dear. For example, if you are a feminist, you are likely to find dealing with hints of sexism tricky; if you are a socialist, you might struggle with capitalist bankers; if you are a committed atheist, you might find it more difficult to work with clients who are motivated to serve God. Your own experiences can also shape your judgements: if you grew up in a war zone, you might have strong feelings about people wanting to join the army; if you have a menagerie of pets at home you might struggle to work with someone who does tests on animals.

The next step is to let your natural empathy dominate. Values are determined by a whole range of factors, and if you can find out where your clients' views have come from, you usually stand a good chance of empathizing with them a little more. You don't need to agree with them to make the coaching relationship work, but you do need to feel some understanding for how they have ended up where they are.

And if those strategies still don't work?

Once in a while we all will find ourselves in a working relationship where our unconditional positive regard for a client is less than optimal. If or when this happens to you, you have a choice to make. You could make the decision to continue with the coaching relationship and hope that you can disguise your judgements to allow your client to gain something from the coaching. I am suggesting in this chapter the idea that UPR is crucial for change to occur in a coaching setting, but you might argue that its status as a 'necessary and sufficient' condition may depend to some extent on the topic at hand and the nature of the relationship. If you are working in an environment where you tend to see clients just once or twice and the focus of your conversations tends to be around job applications and CVs, then you might argue that UPR is less crucial than if you are working through some more deep-rooted issues of identity. In this setting you might decide that the relationship is good enough to do the job in hand.

If you feel that your opinions or judgements are getting in the way of your relationship, you might decide to have a conversation with your client during which you share some of your concerns. This, of course, risks ending the relationship and could also cause distress, as your client may feel judged and rejected. The conversation therefore needs to be conducted sensitively, perhaps stressing that any issues have arisen because of an incompatibility rather than due to a fault with either of you. If you can identify a colleague who might be able to serve the needs of your client better, then it might be helpful to see if you could refer them. The conversation won't always result in you and your client parting company. Your client may feel that they are getting enough from their sessions to make it worth continuing, and might appreciate your honesty. Your revelation might also spark off some interesting self-reflection in your client which can be helpful.

Some coaches tend to start their coaching relationships with a 'chemistry session'. This is an opportunity for the both parties to see whether or not they warm to each other, and for the coach, this could be a good time to assess your own UPR. If you feel that your client might be able to develop a more effective relationship with another coach, you now have a golden opportunity to raise the issue before the relationship goes too far.

5. The coach experiences an empathic understanding of the client's internal frame of reference and endeavours to communicate this experience to the client

This is all about empathy and active listening. Empathy involves putting yourself in your client's shoes and imagining – and to a degree actually *feeling* – what they are feeling. At the heart of empathy is an interplay of listening and self-awareness. You need to really listen to what your client is saying and then you need to be very aware of your own response, which should guide your questions or comments. Your internal response is likely to mirror your client's feelings to some extent. If you feel confused by their story, then it is possible that your client too feels confused, so asking them to explain it a little more can truly help them to understand their own views; if you are feeling sad at their story, then it is quite possible that it is something that has caused them some pain, so asking them to explore their feelings, or saying something very gentle like 'that sounds like it could have been very hard for you' can encourage them to talk some more about it. If you feel that there is a contradiction or a gap in the story, then you can ask them about it; if there is one word in their statement which stands out or which surprises you, then it is often really helpful to pick up on it: for example, 'you used the word "dread" when you talked about your Sunday night feelings. Can you tell me a little more about that?' Simply re-stating a single word with a questioning intonation ('dread?') can also encourage reflection and exploration in your client.

Levels of listening

Listening doesn't sound too hard. Most days we don't get through an hour without listening to someone or something, and it is something that we are born able to do. So what's all the fuss about? Hawkins and Smith (2006) shed some light on the differences between everyday listening and the kind of listening that is needed for a successful coaching conversation. They describe four different levels of listening:

Level 1: attending listening

This involves providing *time and space* in which others can talk. Speakers should be allowed to empty themselves of noise. At this level, listening is more about not talking yourself: providing a silence while others can express themselves.

Level 2: accurate listening

Here, we listen in order to *reflect back and paraphrase* content. Accurate listening involves paying some attention to what is being said, at least enough to be able to repeat some phrases back if pressed.

Level 3: empathetic listening

Here, we listen to the *words and feelings* being conveyed. At this level, the listener attends not just to the words but to their meaning, and makes some effort to understand the content and emotions expressed.

Level 4: generative empathetic listening

This is the kind of listening that we aspire to as coaches. A listener at this level can play back thoughts and feelings on the *periphery of awareness*. They understand not just what is said, but something beyond that, picking up on clues in the tone of voice and body language, what is left unsaid, and on information that is gleaned from their own empathetic response to the listener.

Hawkins and Smith suggest that in most of our daily conversations we interact at levels one or two. Good coaching relies on us getting up to level four.

6. This communication is achieved to a minimal degree

Rogers's final core condition is that the empathy is communicated at least a little. Your clients need to feel that you have to some degree understood them and where they are coming from.

HOW TO APPLY A HUMANISTIC APPROACH IN YOUR PRACTICE

The word used to describe this type of coaching is an 'approach'. It is not a framework or a series of techniques, but a much broader philosophy that underpins coaching practice. As such, there is no specific set of steps that you need to work through to run a humanistic career coaching session. Instead, there is another principle that can guide your humanistic interactions, and which can also help explain how humanism can be incorporated within other frameworks. That concept is non-directivity, and specifically two dimensions within this: principled non-directivity and instrumental non-directivity (Grant 2004). Principled non-directivity is a fundamental part of any humanistic approach. The idea here is that as a coach, you do not direct your clients to do anything. Principled non-directivity is the practical manifestation of the self-determinism principle: in theory, you believe that clients are best placed to make their own decisions; in practice, you allow them to do just that, while you resist any urge to make suggestions, find solutions or give ideas. You let your clients set the agenda, identify the issues and come up with their own action points.

Instrumental non-directivity concerns the process of the intervention. The clients here set the agenda, not just for the topic of conversation but for the process of the intervention. The role of the coach is to ask the clients what they want to discuss and then to stick with their train of thought, meandering with it wherever it goes.

Humanistic coaching in its purest form involves both instrumental and principled non-directivity; the clients decide on both the content and the process of the intervention. But a wholehearted adoption of the philosophy is not the only contribution that humanistic principles can make to our practice. Many coaches (myself included) adopt a hybrid approach, mixing principled non-directivity with instrumental directivity: the clients control the content and the coach controls the process. A coach might choose to use a humanistic approach within a GROW framework. You could, for example, propose the use of the model at the beginning of the session and then gently impose the framework as the conversation progresses, suggesting that the client might want to identify a goal for the session, and later steering the conversation through the stages until a clear way forward has been generated. The client does all the hard work of generating options and identifying solutions, but the coach ensures that a goal is set and achieved during the course of the session. A coach might also have a range of tools and techniques at their disposal, and might suggest some cognitive behavioural techniques, or some exercises that could be done either within the session or between sessions. The client would make the final decision about whether or not to actually do these exercises, but the coach might use their knowledge of coaching techniques to enable the client to find new ways of looking at their situation.

Key humanistic skills

We talked above about listening as the most important humanistic coaching skill, but listening is not always enough on its own to move your client's thoughts further forward. Other reflective skills, such as silence, summarising and paraphrasing, and the art of questioning, also have an important role to play.

Silence is a crucial humanistic skill. Its power lies in the fact that it is not common in everyday conversation, so its presence can spark off thoughts that are different from those generated in everyday conversation. But because it is not used much in the ordinary run of things, it is a technique that coaches need to practise and hone. Ordinary conversation involves a lot of overlaps: we finish each other's sentences and start to make our own next point as soon as we have grasped the essence of our companion's comment. The result is that our thinking is front-loaded: we do our thinking *before* we start to talk and rarely get a chance to reflect on what we ourselves have said. In a person-centred coaching session, the pace of conversation is usually a little slower. As the coach, you need not only to wait until your clients have finished what they were going to say, but to wait until they have had a chance to hear their thoughts out loud and consider how they feel about what they have said. This can take a few moments. Knowing how long to maintain the silence is a skill that you develop with practice, but you can pick up cues from your client's face. As they are thinking they will often look down, up, or into the middle distance; when they have reached the end of their thinking and are ready for a response from you, they may meet your eye again.

Summaries can be useful in a number of ways. First, they are a great way to get your clients to carry on talking. If your clients seem to dry up but you are not sure whether they have finished completely, you can summarize their story so far, (or the last part of it) and this will often encourage further thoughts. Then summaries can be useful to help your client structure their thoughts. If their story is complex or wide-ranging, a summary can provide a framework that helps them make sense of the narrative. A summary can be chronological or thematic, but either way can help to add 'subheadings' to their story. Finally, summaries can be used to show empathy. I mentioned above that communicating your empathy is one of Rogers's core conditions, and a summary can show your client that they have been listened to and understood.

The last key skill that we will look at here is that of questioning. The art here is knowing what to ask, when to ask it and how to express your question. The success of person-centred coaching relies on the relationship, so it is crucial that your questions enhance your clients' thoughts without sounding combative. That is not to say that you shouldn't challenge, but more that you should be very cautious about the words that you choose and the tone in which you say things. The skilful humanistic coach will ask questions or make statements that allow the client to challenge themselves, rather than asking challenging questions. There are some examples in the box below, but you can see that rather than asking 'why did you make that decision?' – which might sound a little provocative and judgemental – simply saying 'I was wondering about that decision' might result in the same sort of response, while managing to preserve the coaching relationship.

In general, questions should be used sparingly within a humanistic context. We talked above about the principled and instrumental non-directivity of a person-centred coaching session. Too many questions from the coach can serve to put the coach in charge. The dynamic of the interaction can shift to a question and answer session, and clients can be swept into a more passive and less empowered role. Questions are an important part of a humanistic session but as coaches we must be mindful of the implications behind our questions and ensure that they are not leading or condemnatory in any way. A question such as 'what have you done about this so far?' might be very suitable in some coaching contexts, but within a humanistic session could give the impression that the coach feels that the client ought to have done something about their issue already, and this perceived judgement could damage the relationship. Instead, questions should be used more to encourage the client to explore their thoughts further. The box below gives some examples of questions that might be appropriate within a person-centred career coaching session.

Useful humanistic phrases

Questions

- 'Tell me a bit more about that.'
- 'And how did that experience make you feel?'
- 'I was just wondering about that decision.'

- 'What impact did that have on you?'
- 'Now that you've shared some of your story with me, how does it sounds to you?'
- 'Now that you've heard your story out loud, how do you feel about it?'

Reflection

- 'It sounds as though that was hard for you.'
- 'Your whole body really came alive when you talked about that experience.'
- 'That was an interesting choice.'

Summaries

- 'Can I just check that I'm following things so far?'
- 'So it seems that there are two main issues here.'
- 'I wonder if it would be helpful if we just summed up where we've got to?'

The humanistic tradition has influenced coaching profoundly. You may feel that at its pure form with both instrumental and principled non-directivity, it lacks the direction and call to action that many clients benefit from, but the principles of self-determination and self-actualization are at the very heart of career coaching. The focus on encouraging clients to take responsibility for their own actions and think things through in a non-judgemental environment should be at the core of every career coaching intervention and the emphasis on the importance of the relationship provides an important dimension. Humanistic ideas can and should be incorporated in every career coaching session.

REFERENCES

De Haan, E. (2008) *Relational Coaching: Journeys towards mastering one-to-one learning.* Chichester: Wiley.

Grant, B. (2004) The imperative of ethical justification in psychotherapy: The special case of client-centred therapy. *Person-centred and Experiential Psychotherapies*, 3: 152–165.

Hawkins, P. and Smith, N. (2006) *Coaching, Mentoring and Organizational Consultancy.* Maidenhead: McGraw-Hill.

Rogers, C. R. (1957) The necessary and sufficient conditions of therapeutic personality change. *Journal of Consulting and Clinical Psychology*, 21: 95–103.

Chapter 9

The GROW model

A framework for interventions

We saw in the last chapter that the process associated with humanistic coaching is a non-directive one. When it comes to almost any other coaching intervention, however, the process will take the form of a more structure framework. The structure fulfils a number of important functions, the most crucial of which is that it helps to make sure that you make the most of your time together. A clear framework ensures that you know where you are hoping to get to by the end of the session and helps you map out the most direct route. It gives you a tool to manage the time and makes sure that you do not go off at a tangent or waste time on issues that are not pertinent.

There are myriad career and coaching frameworks that can provide a structure for one-to-one interventions. Some frameworks have been devised to address a particular type of issue with a particular approach. Motivational interviewing, for example, which we look at in the next chapter, has its own structure that has been tried and tested and found to be effective in specific situations. But many of the models, such as the Ali-Graham model (Ali and Graham 1996) and the LEAP framework (Whitten 2009) are variations on a theme. The most common structure involves some clear goal-setting at the beginning, a call to action at the end, and some exploring and analysing in the middle. The model that I have chosen to describe in this book is the GROW model (e.g. Whitmore 2002, Alexander 2006). It is arguably the best-known and most widely used coaching model. I wouldn't suggest that it is conceptually any more sophisticated than any other framework, but it is explained with such intuitive language and in such a straightforward way that it is perhaps the easiest to understand, remember and explain to your clients.

To share or not to share

The primary role of the model is to give you a structure that allows you to meet a realistic goal during the session. Whether you decide to share this process with your clients is down to your own professional preference, but explaining the model to them has some benefits. One of the great joys of the GROW model is that it is easy to explain, so if you do prefer to share it, it is not going to take too long or cause too much confusion. Explaining the process to your clients can help in two particular ways. First, it de-mystifies the process, which sets the tone for a relationship of equals and indicates from the outset that you are sharing the responsibility for the session: the clients must be active participants rather than passive recipients. Second, it makes it more straightforward for you to keep on track. If you have talked openly about the goal for the session but the conversation then veers away from that, a shared understanding of the process can make it a little easier to highlight the tangent to your client. You can then decide together whether to stick to the original goal or perhaps re-work it in the light of the exploration. It can make it easier for you to 'park' issues or suggestions that come up to return to later in the process: 'That sounds like a very practical solution – I might just make a note of it here, and then maybe we could come back to it when we get to the "Way Forward" stage of the session?' (See below.)

THEORETICAL ORIGINS

The origins of the GROW model are unclear and both Sir John Whitmore and Graham Alexander, two of coaching's great thinkers, have been cited as its originators. Since its launch in the early 1990s, however, its user-friendly simplicity has taken the coaching world by storm. The model's theoretical approach has its origins in behavioural coaching and behavioural psychology. According to behavioural psychologists, change can be encouraged by stimulus (a negative consequence of staying the same), reward (a positive consequence of changing), and reinforcement, which creates a habit and cements the links between the new behaviour and the consequent reward or stimulus. Two further elements to behavioural psychology, both germane to coaching and introduced by Bandura in the 1960s, are social learning and self-efficacy. Social learning theory holds that you can make behavioural changes by observing other people's stimulus, reward and reinforcement as well as experiencing your own. So, for example, you can learn how to behave at work by trying things out and seeing what you get praised for and what you get criticized for, but you can also look at colleagues, observing who gets promoted and who doesn't, and identifying what is distinct about their behaviour. Self-efficacy, which we will encounter a number of times in this book, is your perception of your own abilities, and this has been found to have more of an impact on your behaviour than your actual abilities. Self-efficacy has an impact on behavioural change in that you are more likely to make changes that you believe are within your capabilities. The final behavioural theory underpinning the GROW coaching model is goal-setting theory (e.g. Locke and Latham 1990). The process of setting yourself goals, and the specific nature of those goals, has quite an impact on behaviour. Having a goal that is explicit and clearly articulated is much more likely to lead to a change in your behaviour than one that is vague and unspecified. For a goal to have its optimum impact on behaviour, it also needs to be at the right level – challenging but achievable.

The GROW model then encourages clients to apply these behavioural principles to themselves. The model provides a structure through which they can set goals, identify and analyse stimuli and rewards, and specify and reinforce exactly which behavioural changes will reap the rewards that they seek. The model ensures that each of these elements is addressed and the coach ensures that clients fully, authentically and realistically explore the issues and has a role in nurturing self-efficacy.

In this chapter we will take the model stage-by-stage and explain what the stages mean and why each is important. We will also give some ideas for skills and questions that you can use to make the most of each one.

Stage One: Goal

In stage one, you work out together what clients want to achieve during the session. This stage can be a two-way process of negotiation, but it is crucial that it is the clients who are in charge of, and responsible for, the content of the goal. Your role is to ensure that the goal is specific and feels realistic and achievable during the time that you have. The goal is the bedrock of the session: without one, you are unlikely achieve much and even if you do, you won't be sure whether you have gone far enough or whether it was the right thing to achieve in the first place. Identifying a specific and realistic goal is not necessarily easy, but don't be tempted to move on until you have.

The goal stage is often separated into two, and sometimes even three levels. It can be helpful and encouraging to start the interaction by identifying your clients' broad career goals. As they talk about a dream or aspiration, your role is to listen enthusiastically and to respond positively. As the conversation starts to narrow down to a more specific goal for the session you will need to make sure that you completely understand their goal, so you might ask some questions to clarify their meaning. The session will be at its most productive if the goal is clear and if you share a clear understanding of what it is. It is also entirely reasonable for you to judge whether or not you think this feels like a realistic outcome for the session. In the coaching relationship, your clients are responsible for the content of the sessions, but it is your responsibility to manage the process, so while you should not judge or direct the topic, it is important that you make sure that the goal you end up with is one that you agree is realistic for the time frame and context in which you are working.

An example of the different levels of goal might be:

Dream: 'One day I'd like to have my own business.'
Mid-term goal: 'I need to get a job that's going to give me a really good business education and allow me to develop the right mix of skills.'
Today's goal: 'I'd like to get a clear list in my mind of the skills that I want to develop.'

In general, it is fair to say that it is relatively easy to get clients to talk about their bigger picture goals, but that narrowing clients down to something specific for the session can be more tricky. You should not be tempted to leave it before you feel confident that the goal is specific and realistic, but it can be useful to have a few different ways to ask the same question to avoid sounding pedantic.

Questions for the Goal stage

- 'How can I help you today?'
- 'What would you like us to talk about today?'
- 'What is the topic that you'd like to discuss today?'
- 'That sounds like a fantastic plan for you. Tell me what you would like to focus on today, that might help towards it.'
- 'When you get up to leave at the end of our session today, what would make you feel that it had been a really worthwhile session?'
- 'Where are you hoping to be by the end of the session?'

Stage Two: Reality

During this stage, you give your clients support by thoroughly understanding what is going on for them right now, and some of the humanistic skills we discussed in the previous chapter are suitable for this process. In the reality stage, you will mainly be asking open, exploratory questions, and listening reflectively, paraphrasing and using summaries. You might want to pick up on certain things your clients say, comment on how they sound or look while talking, or challenge them on what might sound like contradictory statements or self-limiting beliefs. The content of the section might focus on events, either current or in the recent past, or might focus more on the emotional side of how your clients have experienced the events.

This stage should last as long as you feel it needs to, to allow your clients to be really straight in their own mind about what has happened and how it has affected them; but it is your responsibility to manage the process and to make sure that the session doesn't go on longer than is productive. You should have the agreed goal for the session in your mind throughout, and if you think it is helpful, return to it together with your client to check that the conversation is relevant and feels productive. Having someone listen to your story with no agenda and no judgements is a rare privilege and it can be tempting for clients to want to extend this stage. If you feel that they continue to gain insights from the conversation and you can still see a clear link between the conversation and the agreed goal, then a full reality stage can be productive. If the conversation begins to go off course, repeat itself or to start to feel indulgent, then it is time to revisit the goal and move on to the next stage of the model.

Occasionally, the exploration during the reality stage illustrates that the agreed goal is not the best one to discuss in that particular session. If this appears to be happening, it might be a good idea to stop the flow of the conversation and discuss this with your clients. You could explain how things are developing from your perspective, and ask them how they feel about that. It might be that your clients decide to stick with the original goal, in which case you can continue the session in a more relevant direction, or it may be that it has become clear to them that there is a more appropriate goal that they could discuss at that stage.

Questions for the Reality stage

- 'So tell me a little about what's going on at the moment?'
- 'That sounds like a very difficult conversation that you had. How were you feeling?'
- 'Tell me about Sunday nights. How do you feel about the week ahead?'
- 'Could you talk to me about something you've done at work that has gone well'
- 'How would you like it to be?'
- 'What's important to you in a job?'
- 'What has been the best job you've ever been in?'
- 'What is it about you that made that project such a success?'
- 'How do you feel when you describe your job to new acquaintances?'
- 'What kind of role did you imagine you would be in?'

Two techniques that can be particularly valuable during this phase are visualization and drawing. We'll look at the nuts and bolts of these tools in Chapter 14 on coaching tools, but both can be used to help clients who are finding it difficult to identify or articulate the reality of their situation. Both are mechanisms for tapping into the unconscious mind, and can be very revealing for clients as they work through them and as they discuss the exercises afterwards.

Stage Three: Options

In the third stage of the session, your conversation looks forward to what options are available to your clients. The stage tends to be split into two parts. In the first part you work together to generate options, thinking in a broad, non-judgemental and creative way about all the different possible options that might be open to them. In the second part, you take your newly created list of options and apply some analysis, evaluating the various options in terms of how desirable or realistic they are for your clients. In the first part, you try to come up with as many options as possible and in the second, you narrow it down to something more manageable.

Suggestions

One temptation during the first part of the options stage is to offer a few suggestions. You might feel that you have a good idea of something that may genuinely help your clients, or you may feel under some kind of pressure (either from within yourself, or from your clients) to contribute something tangible to the discussion. If you find that you are struggling not to give your tuppence-worth, there are three things to bear in mind. First, your clients' suggestions will probably be better than yours. Theirs will take into account the whole story, the background, the emotions, the personalities, the history of their relationships and all manner of details that you don't know about. Their ideas are much more likely to suit them than yours are. Second, they are ten times more likely to put a plan into action if they've come up with it themselves than if you've 'told' them what to do. Third, giving suggestions risks showing a lack of respect for your clients: they have been wrestling with this problem for some time and have spent some considerable time thinking about it. You, on the other hand, are very much a newcomer to the issue and to think that you can wade in after half an hour and provide better solutions than them can seem patronizing. It also doesn't suggest a great deal of respect for their intellectual capacities and problem-solving abilities.

I would not go so far as to say that you should *never* make a suggestion, but I am advocating that you make suggestions late in the process and that you offer them tentatively.

The options stage might start with asking your clients to talk about any ideas they have had so far. Try at this stage not to be too analytical about the ideas. The goal here is to generate a good number of options – six has been shown (Iyengar and Lepper 2000) to be around about the optimum number: it allows individuals to feel that they have a meaningful choice but does not overwhelm them with information. When they seem to have run out of ideas, you can ask them 'what else' could they do, and you could repeat this phrase a number of times to see if any other suggestions are forthcoming. One coaching technique that can be effective in this phase is the use of silence: as the silence grows uncomfortable for your clients, their discomfort may push their unconscious into suggesting an idea, and this could be one that they've never quite articulated before.

If asking directly about options does not generate enough, then there are plenty of other techniques at the coach's disposal. Some of the most common and straightforward might include mind maps (Buzan 2000), drawing a picture of the future, visualizations and using role models to generate ideas. These are covered in more depth in Chapter 14.

Questions for generating options

- 'So what have you thought about so far?'
- 'What else could you do?'
- 'Any more ideas?'
- 'What strategies have you tried in the past?'
- 'How do you think you could generate some more ideas?'
- 'What other advice have you been given?'
- 'What would your role model suggest?'
- 'Which strategies have you seen other people use successfully?'
- 'If you knew you couldn't fail, what would you do?'
- 'If all jobs paid the same, what would you do?'

The aim of the second part of the options phase is to narrow down the options to a handful of the best, so the conversation at this stage focuses on identifying which ones are the most appropriate. Your role is to help your clients work out which ones are best for them, and it can be useful to start off by asking them how they would like to evaluate the options. The two broad approaches to evaluating options are a logical approach and an instinctive approach. Decisions combining both approaches generally result in the most satisfactory outcomes (Singh and Greenhaus 2004), so it can be helpful to encourage your clients to think in both ways. A standard logical approach might involve devising a list of pros and cons, or giving each option a score on certain key qualities and then adding up the scores. Approaches based more on gut instinct include writing each option on a piece of paper and asking your clients to pull one out of a hat; as they pull a piece of paper out, ask them what they are hoping it says. Asking them which option their role models would advise can provide a channel to their unconscious ideas, and suggesting that they visualize a future where they have made one or other decision can give clues to their gut responses.

Questions for evaluating options

- 'How would you like to evaluate these options?'
- 'Are there any here which you'd like to eliminate straight away?'
- 'Shall we identify the pros and cons of each?'
- 'Can you tell me what your heart and your head are advising you to do?'
- 'Who do you most admire and what would they advise?'

Stage Four: The 'Way Forward'

The aim of this phase of the intervention then is to enable your clients to identify some specific steps that they can take to help them towards meeting their goals. Coaching is about change and movement, and a clear plan at the end of the session can help to motivate your clients into putting their ideas into action.

Action points need to be owned by the clients and they need to be specific and challenging but realistic. Let's take each of these in turn. The most important factor here is that the action points should be the clients'. You may have made some marvellous suggestions throughout the session and have some very clear ideas about what you think clients need to do, but if they don't generate the action point themselves, they are very unlikely to do anything about it.

The steps must be specific. It is worth really pushing your clients towards this: the more specific the goal, the more likely they are to achieve it (Locke and Latham 1990). You can ask your clients to specify exactly who they are going to speak to, when they think they might have the conversation and what exactly they want to find out.

Goal-setting theory (Locke and Latham 1990) tells us that the goals that are most likely to lead to the most positive outcomes must be challenging but realistic. If they are not challenging, then at best the clients will achieve less than they could and at worst, may feel that it has been a pointless exercise. Similarly, if the action points are unrealistic, the clients will not achieve them and this may have an adverse impact on their self-belief. In this stage of the GROW model, you need to work with your clients to make sure that the goals they have set will take them as far as they can go, but are still achievable within the time frame and the clients' context.

As with all stages of the GROW process, your clients take responsibility for the content while you take responsibility for the process. Your clients must set their own goals, but you have a role in helping to make sure that the goals are as motivating as possible. It can be useful to ask your client to identify any barriers that they might face when putting their plans into action. You can then have a useful discussion around strategies for overcoming the obstacles. You might also want to ask them how inspired they feel about the different action points, perhaps using a rating scale to help identify and articulate exactly where their motivation levels are: this can lead the clients to think about whether there is anything they can do to increase their commitment to change.

Questions for the 'Way Forward'

- 'So we've talked about a lot of ideas today. What are you going to go away and do?'
- 'What do you think is going to be the most effective way to achieve this?'
- 'How realistic is this for you?'
- 'What's a realistic time frame to get this done?'

- 'Can you think of anything that might get in the way of you doing this?'
- 'What or who could help you to overcome these barriers?'
- 'On a scale of one to ten, how motivated do you feel about putting this plan into action?'
- 'How could we move you from a 7 to an 8?'
- 'What can I do to help you to motivate yourself?'

The GROW model is a marvel of effective simplicity. Its straightforward framework makes it easy to learn, remember and share, yet it can be used in a wide range of contexts to explore subjects to a significant depth. You can use it on its own or can incorporate other approaches, tools or techniques within it. It is applicable in most contexts, and is a model that you can encourage clients to use on their own to help structure their thinking about all sorts of issues. It is not the only coaching model that I would recommend but it is the one I use most often, and it rarely lets me down.

REFERENCES

Alexander, G. (2006) Behavioural coaching. In J. Passmore (ed.), *Excellence in Coaching*. London: Kogan Page.

Ali, L. and Graham, B. (1996) *The Counselling Approach to Careers Guidance*. London: Routledge.

Buzan, T. (2000) *The Mind Map Book*. London: Penguin.

Iyengar, S. S. and Lepper, M. (2000) When choice is demotivating: Can one desire too much of a good thing? *Journal of Personality and Social Psychology*, 76: 995–1006.

Locke, E. A. and Latham, G. P. (1990) *A Theory of Goal-setting and Task Performance*. Englewood Cliffs, NJ: Prentice Hall.

Singh, R. and Greenhaus J. H. (2004) The relation between career decision-making strategies and person–job fit: A study of job changers. *Journal of Vocational Behavior*, 64: 198–221.

Whitmore, J. (2002) *Coaching for Performance*. London: Nicholas Brealey.

Whitten, H. (2009) *Cognitive Behavioural Coaching Techniques for Dummies*. Chichester: Wiley.

Chapter 10

Motivational interviewing

Career coaching is always about a change, or at least the possibility of one. Some aspects of this change, such as the decision to take the plunge and the exact timing of it, are often in the control of your client, but this is not always the case. Clients facing redundancy, or long-term unemployed clients coming up against the benefits system, can feel anything from ambivalence to overt hostility about an imminent forced change, and even young people or students coming to the end of a course can be less than entirely comfortable about the timing of the career choice that they are facing.

Motivational interviewing (Miller 1983) is a technique grounded in the principles of humanistic counselling that helps individuals to become more intrinsically motivated to change. In their taxonomy of career decision-making difficulties that we looked at in detail in Chapter 7, Gati *et al.* (1996) highlighted 'lack of readiness to change' as one of the key reasons why clients chose to seek support with their career decision making, and motivational interviewing is one technique that can help them to make the first move.

I introduced the transtheoretical model of change (Prochaska and DiClemente 1984), and Barclay *et al.*'s (2011) adaptation of this model to career changes in Chapter 5, when we were looking at planned career changes. I summarize the stages briefly below, but do turn back to pages 55–56 for a refresher if you feel that would be helpful.

1. **Pre-contemplative**. Clients experience discouragement and dissatisfaction but are not sure why.
2. **Contemplative**. Clients experience growing discouragement and thoughts of future career paths; there is ambivalence to change.
3. **Preparation**. Clients experience increased motivation to change and thoughts, ideas and plans emerge.
4. **Action**. Clients redefine themselves. They look for and establish themselves in a new role.
5. **Maintenance**. The career move is complete. Clients embed into the new role and developing relationships.

(Adapted from Barclay *et al.* 2011)

In the examples I cited earlier – i.e. clients facing redundancy or the long-term unemployed being forced back to work – clients may need help moving from the pre-contemplation to the contemplation stages, but in fact people can encounter problems at any stage. Motivational interviewing is an approach or a set of techniques that have been shown to have quite dramatic results in moving clients from one stage of change to the next and in increasing clients' motivation to change.

Motivational interviewing was first developed to help clients with addictions to drugs, alcohol and smoking, but more recently has been applied to topics of well-being and its impact within the coaching arena is being increasingly well documented.

I mentioned earlier that motivational interviewing was a process geared towards increasing clients' intrinsic motivation. In this sense it differs from the more persuasive techniques of behavioural coaching that try to encourage change by rewarding particular behaviour externally through, for example, increased pay or status. Motivational interviewing, by contrast, encourages change by simply increasing the clients' desire for the outcomes of the change for their own sake. The theory can be explained using two ideas. First, the reflective process of motivational interviewing enables practitioners to decrease clients' resistance to a change and to talk in more positive terms about the change and the benefits of change. Second, the amount of time clients spend talking about the benefits of change correlates with their chances of changing their behaviour after the motivational interview.

We are going to look now at the central tenets of the approach and then later in the chapter we will cover some practical techniques that can be used in a career coaching context. We will end the chapter with an exploration of some of the research that examines whether, how and to what extent the technique actually works.

KEY TENETS

A collaborative relationship between coach and client

Motivational interviewing is grounded in a humanistic philosophy (Rogers 1959). Specifically, its success relies on a non-judgemental relationship of equals in which the principal role of the coach is to reflect the words and meanings of clients in order to allow them to better understand their own thoughts and opinions.

Change usually involves some ambivalence

Motivational interviewing accepts that while people in general do want to improve their own lives (this is known as the 'self-actualizing' tendency in humanistic theory), ambivalence is also a natural part of the change process and for every impetus to change there is a desire at some level to keep the status quo. Core to motivational interviewing is an acknowledgement of this ambivalence. Clients who have been unemployed for some time might feel very positive about the idea of earning some more money, having a greater sense of purpose to the day and regaining some of the identity and prestige associated with regular employment. But that may not be the whole story. On top of this pull towards work, there may be a corresponding push away from the change. Clients may have developed a comfortable routine since becoming unemployed, with a social life during the day with other friends who are also not in work. They may feel more relaxed without demands placed on them and hate the idea of returning to the stress of the workplace, and they may feel frightened at the risk of not succeeding in a new job.

In contrast to many approaches that might focus on persuading clients that life really would be better if they were in work, motivational interviewing accepts the ambivalence. The role of the coach is to acknowledge and explore the client's resistance and to encourage clients to fully explore their own thoughts, and listen to their own 'inner voice' (Rogers 1980).

Developing discrepancy

The motivational interview process focuses initially on identifying and exploring discrepancies within clients' thoughts, feelings and ideas. The psychological concept underpinning this focus is that of cognitive dissonance, identified in 1957 by Festinger. Cognitive dissonance theory argues that our brains are uncomfortable holding two apparently contradictory thoughts simultaneously. In these situations, the brain does what it can to resolve this contradiction by changing a view, changing some behaviour or finding an explanation that allows both concepts to sit comfortably together. So, for example, my own self-concept as a gregarious extravert is cast into doubt by my choice to refuse an invitation to a party in favour of a night in, in front of the TV. My mind is uncomfortable with the following two bits of contradictory evidence and needs to find a resolution:

1. I'm a sociable person: I'm the kind of person who accepts party invitations.
2. I'm not a sociable person: I'm the kind of person who chooses a television programme over a party.

The resolution could be that I change my plans, so that my behaviour fits in with my self-concept. I could change my decision and go to the party or shift my self-concept to fit my behaviour, perhaps starting to think of myself as less gregarious than I had previously imagined. Alternatively I could *reinterpret* the behaviour to fit my self-concept; for example, I might start to convince myself that the reason I can't go to the party is because I have a cold coming, and am too ill to go out. Which of these solutions I pick will depend on how important or desirable the self-concept is to me, and how easy I imagine I would find it to make the change.

Cognitive dissonance is one of the building blocks of motivational interviewing, but it needs to be combined with a realization or understanding within clients that the behavioural change is attractive or will lead to an attractive outcome. If you can get clients to identify a discrepancy between their behaviour and their values, their current self and their ideal self, or their goals and actions, then you heighten awareness of some cognitive dissonance. If you can combine this cognitive dissonance with an increase in their views of the desirability of the person they could be or the life they could lead if they made the change, that combination will make them want to change. The cognitive dissonance will make them feel uncomfortable with the status quo, and the increased desirability they now place on one particular course of action will encourage them to move in that direction.

One theoretical extension to this that has been widely backed up by empirical research (e.g. Bem 1967) is that people believe what they hear themselves saying. Linked to the theory of cognitive dissonance, our brains are quite uncomfortable with the idea of a discrepancy between what our minds are thinking and what our mouths are saying, so will find some way to resolve this discrepancy, even if it entails a shift of opinion. This 'change talk', as it is known, can be important in motivational interviewing as expressing their desire for a change increases a client's intrinsic motivation towards that change. If you ask your clients to come up with a reason to leave their employer organization, for example, or get back into work, then however slight or insignificant that reason, it can get their brain to think that this is something that they want. Miller and Rollnick's (1991) research further explored this idea and showed that people are also more likely to take it a stage further and put a plan into action if they have heard themselves justifying it.

Self-efficacy

The final prerequisite for successful motivational interview is a belief by the coach that clients have the ability to change, but that they lack the self-efficacy that would allow them to feel confident enough to do so. We have encountered the notion of self-efficacy before in this book, and will return to it again later on – it has an impact on many elements of the career choice process. First conceptualized by Bandura in the 1970s (Bandura and Adams 1977), self-efficacy refers to the confidence one has about one's own ability to do a specific thing. In this case, the coach needs to believe that the client can change but that he or she might just need some help to believe that they can.

These, then, are the central assumptions that underpin motivational interviewing. Let's move on now to looking at how it can be used in practice within a career coaching context.

MOTIVATIONAL INTERVIEWING IN PRACTICE

The motivational interview tends to have two distinct phases, each with a range of associated techniques that practitioners can use to help. Phase one is focused on increasing motivation, while phase two identifies specific action points for the client to complete in order to move towards their goals.

In the first phase, the coach uses the active listening techniques of humanistic counseling to get clients to explore and better understand their own ambivalence to change. The phase is dominated by the humanistic coaching skills of open questions, affirmations, reflections and summaries, all supported by active listening skills and clear empathy.

Coach: 'So tell me a bit about how you are feeling about the redundancy.' *open question*

Client: 'Just devastated. I had put my heart and soul into the role and I can't believe that I'm out on my ear after less than a year.'

Coach: 'So you're feeling really low about it.' *empathy* 'It sounds as though you had worked really hard in the role.' *affirmation*

Client: 'Yes, I loved my job and I really wanted to make it work.'

Coach: 'From what you're saying, it was a job that you cared about, and being made redundant after you'd put so much into it has hurt you a lot.' *summary.* 'It sounds in many ways as though you were happy there, but I wonder, were there any things about the job that were less than perfect?' *moving to explore ambivalence*

Client: 'I suppose I didn't always get on terribly well with my line manager.'

During this phase, the coach should encourage the client to identify their motivation for change, articulate their desires, needs and reasons for change, and explore their ability to make the change. Introducing high levels of this 'change talk' into a motivational interview has been shown to link with the motivation to make changes.

Coach: 'So we've talked about some of the things that you most enjoyed about your old job. Let's move on now to thinking in more detail about the change that you are facing. Perhaps you could start by telling me a little about why you might be thinking about looking for other work?'

Client: 'Well, I suppose fundamentally, I have to. If I don't, I'll be out of a job, and I can't afford not to work.' (***need to change***)

Coach: 'I wonder what else there is? When we were talking earlier, you did mention a few things that weren't quite right in your current role.'

Client: 'Yes, I do have a difficult relationship with my line manager, and that has caused a few problems.'

Coach: 'So tell me more about what it could be like if you found a really good new job?'

Client: 'Well, it would be fantastic to find something closer to home. My current commute is ok, but I'd love to be able to cycle or even walk to work.' (*desire to change*)

Coach: 'What would be so good about that?'

Client: 'Well, first of all, I'd save an hour or so a day, which would be great. And then it would be lovely to get my daily exercise done as part of a routine – not needing any extra motivation or time. And then it would be a real relief to be relatively near the kids' school if they're sick, or if I need to see their teachers.' (*building up motivation*)

One useful technique that you can use in this phase is the rating scale. This can be deployed in a range of interventions (see for example the section on solution-focused coaching in Chapter 11), but here is used in quite a specific way. The coach asks clients to rate how they feel about the change on a scale of one to ten, explaining that one is 100 per cent against it and ten is 100 per cent for it. In nearly every instance, clients will give a score of two or above, and that is all that you're looking for. This provides some evidence that there is at least a small glimmer of positivity associated with the change, and gives the coach a starting point for a conversation about reasons to change. The coach should then ask clients to explain why they have given it a rating of, say, four (or whatever score was given), and no lower. What factors were they thinking about when they decided not to give it a three or a two? The coach should encourage clients to explore these issues in-depth – remembering that the more they talk about the positives of the change, the more motivated they will feel about it. The next phase – which could be done straightaway, or which the coach could return to later in the session – is to ask clients what they would need to do to move their rating up a notch, from a four to a five. It is important here that clients are asked to think about a small change only. This will feel more realistic and more manageable to the clients and will help to maintain the relationship between the coach and client, as the coach is demonstrating that they understand where the clients are right now.

Coach: 'So if I asked you on a scale of one to ten how you felt about the idea of getting a job, where would you put yourself?'

Client: 'I'm really unenthusiastic about it. I think I might give myself a three.'

Coach: 'OK, so you would put yourself at about a three. I wonder if you could tell me why you gave yourself a three, and not a two, or even a one?'

Client: 'Well, although I've made a nice life for myself as things are, I do sometimes think that it would be nice to have some more money. It would be nice not to have to think hard about every penny.'

Coach: 'So you sometimes feel that you'd like to have a bit more money? Can you tell me how that would change things for you?'

There are two reflecting techniques that coaches can use in this phase: amplified reactions, and reframing. Amplified reactions can be used to give clients something to argue against. Here the coach exaggerates their reflection of clients' comments to suggest a more extreme outcome than they may have implied. This can highlight a discrepancy between their behaviour and their self-concept that can help to increase motivation to change:

Client: 'I really don't want to apply for that job because I'd never get it.'
Coach: 'So you see yourself as someone who can't cope with failure?'

As a coach, you need to be cautious and gentle when using this technique. Too strong a response or too critical a tone, and clients may quickly feel defensive.

The second reflecting technique that can be very effective in a motivational interview is that of reframing. Reframing can allow clients to view their behaviour in a different way, and this can be a helpful method of encouraging self-efficacy and increasing confidence.

Client: 'I've applied for dozens of jobs and have had no success.'
Coach: 'It sounds as though you're really motivated to succeed with this job hunt.'
OR
Client: 'I didn't manage to get that job application finished in time for the closing date.'
Coach: 'It's great to want to get it right before you send it off.'

That gives you some idea of the sorts of things that could be covered in the first phase of the motivational interview. By the end of this phase, clients should be aware of some cognitive dissonance that may be making them feel uncomfortable with their current situation, and should have spent some time talking about all the possible positives that might be associated with the necessary behavioural change. Their desire to make the change at this stage may have increased, but the chances of them actually making the change will be significantly higher only if you take them on to the second phase of the motivational interview. Here, you allow clients to identify what steps they need to take to actually make the change happen and it follows a process that is more familiar to us. In this phase, the coach leads the client through a more traditional coaching process of setting goals, identifying options and agreeing action points. In addition to the more typical skills and techniques used by a coach for these purposes, during this phase in a motivational interview, the coach would make sure that they included summaries of the key elements that have been identified as most motivating the client during phase one.

THE EVIDENCE FOR MOTIVATIONAL INTERVIEWING

The impact of motivational interviewing is well documented, but seems to be not very well understood: we know that is works, but we don't know why or how. Meta-analyses (e.g. Hettema *et al.* 2005) have revealed quite dramatic effects in a range of health and well-being settings but within these figures are hidden some complexities. Let's look now at a few of the more intriguing findings.

1. Motivational interviewing can have quite an impact in a very short space of time – even one session can lead to significant behaviour changes. But the effects appear to lessen gradually over the course of the following 12 months unless the motivational interview input is part of a broader support programme. For example, if a motivational interviewing intervention is the first session within a six-week career coaching programme, the impact of the motivational interview would be greater than if the client were to have a single session that focuses just on motivation. The message for our practice is that motivational interviewing can have a real impact, but works best in conjunction with other tools rather than as a technique used in isolation.

2. Cultural differences too seem to moderate the impact of motivational interviewing, with different effect sizes seen in different cultural groups. Cultures whose interactions naturally tend to be more reflective, such as Native American cultures, show larger effect sizes from motivational interviewing interventions, suggesting that this reflective technique works better when it is a 'culturally congruent intervention' (Hettema *et al.* 2005: 105).

3. Although the approach can be applied to clients at any stage of the change cycle, Heather *et al.* (1996) found that it is at its most effective with clients who are angry and resistant to change, rather than with those who are already committed to change and ready for action.

4. The key, it seems, to predicting how successful a motivational interview will be lies in the strength of commitment to change demonstrated in the last few minutes of the session. Amrhein *et al.* (2003) analysed the language the clients used during their sessions and identified that language which indicated high levels of motivation to change (desire, needs and reasons) did not predict a subsequent change in behaviour. This kind of language did, however, lead to increased commitment to change, and it was this that correlated with a change in behaviour after the session. These findings underpin the two phases of the motivational interview, as the practitioner initially drives to increase motivation and then goes on to use this increased motivation to encourage clients to express their commitment to change and specify the steps they are intending to take.

5. One final piece of evidence concerns the way that practitioners can best learn to be experts in motivational interviewing techniques. The traditional notions of good practice in training seem not to apply when training motivational

interviewing practitioners, and although researchers have not yet come up with a plausible reason for this, the evidence is pretty clear. Miller and Mount (2001) found that practitioners who attended a two-day intensive training course felt a reasonable degree of confidence in their own abilities but that their interventions had little effect on their clients' behaviour. In addition, practitioners who stuck faithfully to the procedures outlined in the training manuals were found to conduct sessions that had limited impact (Miller *et al.* 2003). The training technique that does seem to work is what Miller calls a 'learning to learn' approach, which involves teaching practitioners the underlying principles and then encouraging them to learn from their clients and use their clients' responses to shape the session. Miller *et al.* (2004) found that the most successful training programmes included an ongoing mechanism for reflective practice, such as consultations with an expert practitioner.

Case study

Jo had been made redundant a year before. She came to see a career coach because she had applied for what seemed like dozens of jobs and hadn't had any success. Through the initial conversations with the career coach, it emerged that although the redundancy had been finalized 12 months earlier, she had spent most of the previous year doing bits and pieces of short-term and part-time work for her former employer.

Jo was feeling very low about the whole thing. She was demoralized about her job hunt, still full of anger and bitterness towards her old employers and her self-esteem was rock bottom. Jo came to realize that some of her lack of job-hunting success was the product of how she was feeling. Her low self-esteem was preventing her from applying for some interesting positions, and was clouding each application form that she wrote and each interview that she had. She also saw that she was lacking enthusiasm for anything: she had no idea what she wanted to do, and never got excited about any of the jobs she saw advertised.

The career coach talked to Jo about the concept of career decision-making readiness, and Jo saw that her utter lack of motivation was preventing her from moving forward. Until she was able to move on emotionally from her last job, this would hold her back.

At the next session, the career coach introduced the notion of motivational interviewing and Jo agreed to try it. They talked first about the good parts of the old job, and Jo identified her amazing colleagues and how great it was to be in a job that was able to fit around her family, allowing her to spend two days at home with her little girl each week. They moved on then to talking about the aspects of the job that weren't quite so good, and as she got talking, Jo remembered a whole host of things that frustrated her. She had been in the role for seven years and it had just stopped stimulating her. There were no opportunities for promotion and the role seemed to be getting progressively narrow. She had stopped learning. She was asked when she would have wanted to leave the organization if the decision had been entirely hers, and Jo admitted that she had been looking for other jobs for two years before the redundancy.

The coach then asked Jo to imagine two futures: one where she managed to find a new job with great colleagues, flexible working arrangements *and* more stimulation, and one where she had stayed on in her old organization. The two pictures were quite different, and the coach asked Jo to focus on the differences – both the differences in her life and the differences in her emotions, and to explain them in more detail.

They moved on then to talking more specifically about Jo's motivation for change. The coach asked Jo to rate, on a scale of one to ten, how motivated she felt about looking for a new job. Jo said that she might say five – which she said was already two points higher than it would have been at the start of the session. They discussed in more detail the reason that Jo had chosen a five rather than a four or a three, and Jo explored some of the reasons, desires and needs behind this score. The coach then asked what it would take to get it up to a six, and Jo thought that the next step for her motivation would be to get a clearer idea of the sort of job she might want. It was agreed that they would focus the next session on trying to get some clarity around a specific job goal, but also discussed some ideas that Jo could work on during the next week to start the process. They discussed how motivated Jo was to start on those particular tasks, and she said that she actually felt quite excited about the process now. The coach asked Jo to articulate what she found exciting, and to imagine for a minute how she was going to get started and how she might feel when she'd finished.

Jo left the session saying that she felt more positive than she'd been for months.

The case study above is an example of using motivational interviewing as a framework to help move someone on to the next phase of the change cycle. Motivating people to change is not always as straightforward as this may have sounded. In this instance the client actually had a lot of reasons for wanting to change, so the ambivalence, when it was exposed was pretty one-sided. It is also worth pointing out that this kind of process will not always move forward steadily. It would be quite common for someone in Jo's situation to feel very positive at the end of the session, only to lose motivation the moment they leave the room. The specific tasks and the visualization at the end could both help to keep the momentum going, but generating the motivation to change is not always easy.

We've talked in this chapter about the motivational interview as a framework to structure a whole session, but it can be seen as a set of principles that can be applied in different ways. Motivational interviewing can, for example, be used in bite-sized chunks. It could be that the career coach in the case study might suggest a short motivational interviewing intervention at the beginning of each subsequent session; alternatively, a coach could use some motivational interview questioning within the framework of a GROW session. And I think it can be useful for coaches in many settings to remember the principle that you believe what you hear yourself saying.

REFERENCES

Amrhein, P. C., Miller, W. R., Yahne, C. E., Palmer, M. and Fulcher, L. (2003) Client commitment language during motivational interviewing predicts drug use outcomes. *Journal of Consultant Clinical Psychology*, 71: 862–878.

Bandura, A. and Adams, N. E. (1977) Analysis of self-efficacy theory of behavioral change. *Cognitive Therapy and Research*, 1: 287–308.

Barclay, S., Stoltz, K. and Chung, Y. (2011) Voluntary midlife career change: Integrating the transtheoretical model and the life-span, life-space approach. *The Career Development Quarterly*, 59(5): 386–399.

Bem, D. J. (1967) Self-perception: An alternative interpretation of cognitive dissonance phenomena. *Psychology Review*, 74: 183–200.

Festinger, L. (1957) *A Theory of Cognitive Dissonance*. Stanford, CA: Stanford University Press.

Gati, I., Krausz, M. and Osipow, S. H. (1996) A taxonomy of difficulties in career decision making. *Journal of Counseling Psychology*, 43(4): 510–526.

Heather N., Rollnick, S., Bell, A. and Richmond, R. (1996) Effects of brief counselling among heavy drinkers identified on general hospital wards. *Drug Alcohol Review*, 15: 29–38.

Hettema, J., Steele, J. and Miller, W. R. (2005) Motivational interviewing. *Annual Review of Clinical Psychology*, 1: 91–111.

Miller, W. R. (1983) Motivational interviewing with problem drinkers. *Behavioral Psychotherapy*, 11: 147–172.

Miller, W. R. and Mount, K. A. (2001) A small study of training in motivational interviewing: Does one workshop change clinical and client behavior? *Behavioral Clinical Psychotherapy*, 29: 457–471.

Miller, W. R. and Rollnick, S. (1991) *Motivational Interviewing: Preparing People to Change Addictive Behavior*. New York: Guilford Press.

Miller, W. R., Yahne, C. E., Moyers, T. B., Martinez, J. and Pirritano, M. (2004) A randomized trial of methods to help clinicians learn motivational interviewing. *Journal of Consultant Clinical Psychology*, 72: 1050–1062.

Miller, W. R., Yahne, C. E. and Tonigan, J. S. (2003) Motivational interviewing in drug abuse services: A randomized trial. *Journal of Consultant Clinical Psychology*, 71: 754–763.

Prochaska, J. O. and DiClemente, C. C. (1984) *The Transtheoretical Approach: Crossing Traditional Boundaries of Therapy*. Homewood, IL: Dow Jones-Irwin.

Rogers, C. R. (1959) A theory of therapy, personality and interpersonal relationships as developed in the client-centred framework. In E. Koch (ed.), *Psychology: A Study of Science – Formulations of the Person and the Social Context*. New York: McGraw-Hill.

Rogers, C. R. (1980) *A Way of Being*. Boston. MA: Houghton-Mifflin.

Chapter 11

Positive approaches

The 'coaching' brand is a positive one. Its image is aspirational and action-oriented, and coaches are seen as people who encourage and 'stretch' their clients (Yates 2011). This doesn't mean that we are unrealistic or unempathetic about the realities of peoples' lives, but it does mean that some of the new theories emerging from positive psychology and related disciplines seem to sit well with a coaching approach.

This chapter will focus on three separate coaching approaches: strengths-based coaching, appreciative inquiry and solution-focused coaching. The three approaches have quite distinct origins: strengths-based coaching derives from positive psychology; solution-focused coaching from family therapy; and appreciative inquiry from organizational development. But despite their different histories, the three approaches have a lot in common and can be usefully understood and even used together.

Many theoretical approaches within the broad church of 'helping' therapies are intent on working out why things have gone wrong, what the problems are and how clients or their situations can be fixed. These three positive approaches all start with a non-pathological assumption: individuals are good and can be great. (In the more traditional pathological or medical model, individuals are viewed as sick and need to get better.) The focus of these positive interactions is on identifying what works or what is going well, and enhancing that, rather than working out what is going wrong and fixing it.

Beyond this shared philosophy, each of the three positive approaches has its own underlying assumptions and some specific techniques and tools, and can be used separately or integrated into a broader positive philosophy. We will take each one in turn.

STRENGTHS COACHING

The idea of getting people to look at their skills with a view to trying to find a job that suits them is nothing new or revolutionary in the career world. Strengths coaching develops this basic concept, both broadening it (to include a wider range of qualities) and restricting it (with a focus on strengths and not on weaknesses) to make it more useful, systematic and motivating.

The notion of strengths coaching has its origins in the positive psychology movement. This is a relatively new branch of psychology that has gained a great deal of support and influence in its brief life as a result of the dramatic results that have been seen through its simple interventions. The founders of positive psychology are Seligman and Csikszentmihalyi (2000), and their approach re-frames the concept of psychology from a deficit model looking to identify problems and heal the sick, to a discipline that aims to make the healthy thrive.

Seligman and Peterson identified 24 strengths which stem from six virtues that seem to be consistently held in high regard across the world (Seligman *et al.* 2005): wisdom, courage, humanity, justice, temperance and transcendence. Three or four distinct strengths have been associated with each of these virtues; for example, the strengths associated with humanity are kindness, love and social intelligence, while those associated with temperance are forgiveness, modesty and prudence. The strengths are identified on the basis of 13 quite specific criteria, such as their moral value, whether they diminish others, and if it is possible to identify specific paragons who embody them strikingly. Seligman and Peterson have worked their ideas into a self-awareness tool that can be self-administered through their website (www.authentichappiness.com) and interpreted either independently or together with a professional to help clients work out how their strengths profile can be used in their lives.

Peterson and Seligman's research (Peterson and Seligman 2004) suggests that the strengths they have identified are pretty universal across cultures but that clients from different cultures may not be equally comfortable when talking about their own strengths. They point in particular to the 'British reserve' which can make UK clients feel as though they are bragging when they discuss their strengths. Coaches need to be sensitive to their clients' attitude towards this and might allay any awkwardness by acknowledging the feelings and explaining the process: 'I know it can be difficult to talk about your own strengths sometimes. But trying to identify a suitable career area can be much easier if we both have a clear sense of what you're good at.'

A strengths approach to coaching differs from more traditional techniques to enhancing self-awareness.

Self-awareness in traditional career guidance is often approached with an open, client-centred question; the practitioner might ask the client 'what sorts of things are you good at?' or 'what would you say were your particular skills or strengths?'. This has the advantage of giving the client the opportunity to define and identify the strengths themselves, but also has a disadvantage in that it assumes a client has a comprehensive internal 'list' of what we mean by strengths. The values in action – inventory of skills (VIA–IS) is an inventory of strengths that Seligman and Peterson have devised, based on a decade of research in this field. It provides a ready-made and thoroughly researched list which ensures that the client has considered a comprehensive range of strengths. The danger with using such a list is that it risks putting the client into a passive role and setting the coach up as expert. This needs to be handled carefully, therefore, with the coach actively involving the client in the interpretation process. For example, you could ask questions such as:

- 'Can you tell me about some of the key strengths that emerged for you?'
- 'What did you mean by "leadership" when you responded?'
- 'So having identified this list of strengths, what do you think would be the best use of it now?'

Traditional self-awareness tools focus both on strengths and weakness. The strengths inventory, and coaching conversations around the subject, look only at strengths. There are two positive consequences to this focus. First, it is much more motivating for clients. Conversations about things we do well have been shown to increase motivation and self-efficacy and clients are more likely to actually put plans into action following a positive conversation than after one focusing on their weaknesses. Second, it is more relevant. People tend to opt for career choices that play to their strengths rather than ones where they need to learn to overcome weaknesses.

The conceptualization of strengths used within positive psychology defines them more broadly than in traditional self-awareness tools, and covers a wider range of concepts than are usually associated with the kinds of skills audits that might be undertaken in a traditional career intervention. In addition to traditional concepts such as leadership and creativity, the VIA–IS covers strengths that we might be more likely to think of as values, such as integrity and open-mindedness, as well as other concepts (such as humour and spirituality) that wouldn't normally be included in this kind of conversation or tool. There is increasing evidence that values and meaning are some of the most important factors in determining job satisfaction, so this broader interpretation of qualities may have important implications for career choice.

Positive psychology has given us a number of other innovative tools and techniques. In Seligman et al.'s 2005 paper, the authors examine the effectiveness of some of these tools and identify a few very straightforward tools that we can share with our clients, all of which have been shown to have a significant effect on individuals' happiness six months after the individuals had used them for a week.

One of these techniques is the 'Three Good Things in Life'. Every night for a week, your clients should write down three things that went well during the day. Clients need to specify why the thing went well and what their particular involvement was. It does not need to be a life-changing or dramatic incident. The event might be as simple as that they had a really tasty sandwich for lunch, and their role in this was that they chose it.

In another technique, clients must first identify their 'signature strength', and are asked to use that strength in a new and different way every day for a week. If, for example, your signature strength is your love of learning, you could decide to watch a factual television programme one day, visit a museum in your lunch hour the next, and research a particular topic on the internet the day after.

These exercise can be particularly useful when working with clients who are feeling particularly down about their situation. Issues such as negative feelings about your current job, fears for the futures or lower self-esteem following some time out of work can all have an impact on how ready you are to make a change. Exercises such as these can be used to lift clients' spirits and allow them increase their positive feelings, meaning they can focus on their future.

APPRECIATIVE INQUIRY

The essence of appreciative inquiry (AI) is to identify what works and to do more of it. The approach is almost at odds with the idea of problem-solving, holding that identifying the problem – and then finding and implementing a solution – will not reap the same rewards as a focus on enhancing the things that are already working. The approach was developed by David Cooperrider (Cooperrider 2000) in Cleveland in the United States. Working as an organizational development specialist, he was brought into under-performing organizations to identify what was wrong and to put it right. Cooperrider was struck by how much was going well within these struggling organizations, and how enthusiastic and positive employees were when they had the chance to talk about the projects that they enjoyed and the processes that worked smoothly. He developed the AI approach as a way to harness the good work and positive spirit that you can find in any organization.

The approach has, at its heart, five key principles (Lehner and Hight 2006):

1. Constructionist principle. The meaning of an organization is a construct developed by the individuals in the organization through their interactions with each other and with the wider world.

2. Simultaneity principle. You start changing as soon as you start thinking about changing.

3. Poetic principle. As with a poem, everyone who is involved with an organization has their own interpretation of what's going on. AI encourages storytelling as a way of making meaning.

4. Anticipatory principle. It is the idea and image of the future that guides our present actions. Imagining a positive future makes it more likely to happen.

5. Positive principle. People want to improve their lives and are likely to feel positive about thinking about and making changes.

The AI model makes use of a four-stage process, which although originally intended for use within organizations, can be used effectively in a one-to-one coaching or a group setting. The four stages are: Discover, Dream, Design and Destiny or Deliver.

Discover

In the 'discover' stage, the discussion focuses on what has worked well in the past. The content of this stage will, of course, be determined by the issue the clients have brought to the session, but for those who are struggling to make a decision, you might talk about positive decisions that they have made in the past; if they are wondering what kind of role they might enjoy, you might focus on what aspects of jobs they have enjoyed in the past.

Dream

In the dream stage, the conversation moves to looking to the future. During this phase, you encourage your clients to think about possible ideas or strategies that might help them to reach their goals. As indicated by the word 'dream', you should encourage your clients to be creative here and think about a wide range of possibilities, even if they sound rather fanciful. A spot of blue-sky thinking can free up clients to be bold in their suggestions and even a totally unrealistic idea can eventually lead to an innovative but practical solution.

Design

In the third stage of the model, clients start to focus in on the ideas that seem to them most attractive or most realistic. You might want to suggest looking in quite a rational way at the pros and cons of different options: you could ask them what their gut instinct is telling them or make use of a ratings scale to help them to weigh one option against another. This may also be a good time to try to identify any gaps in their knowledge that could usefully be filled before a final decision is reached.

Destiny

The intervention draws to a conclusion with the Destiny phase. Also sometimes referred to as the 'Deliver' phase, this is the stage of the model that allows clients to make specific plans for the next steps. Your role here is to allow clients to identify specific and realistic action points that will lead them towards their goal.

You will no doubt have noticed the similarities here between the AI intervention model and the GROW model. The Discover stage resonates with the Realities stage; the Dream and Design stages could both be covered in the Options stage of the GROW model and the Destiny stage would cover similar ground to the Will stage within the GROW framework. The AI framework does not particularly focus on the need for a specific goal at the beginning of the process but neither does it preclude setting one, and indeed some interpretations of AI promote the idea of setting a goal before starting the process. We do know from the research into goal-setting theory (e.g. Locke and Latham 1990) that an appropriate and specific goal has a considerable impact on motivation, so identifying one before starting the AI session can be beneficial. The real difference between the two models, however, is the exclusive focus on the positive within AI that does not need to be there in a traditional GROW session. This is evident through the very words that have been selected to structure the intervention, such as 'discover' and 'dream', which both have positive and creative overtones.

SOLUTION-FOCUSED COACHING

Solution-focused coaching derived from solution-focused therapy, which was first proposed by de Shazer (de Shazer 1985) based on his work with the family therapy movement in Wisconsin in the early 1980s. De Shazer and his colleagues noticed that with some clients, the more they talked about their problems, the more backward-looking they became. They identified that a focus on 'what's gone wrong' is usually irrelevant, invariably time-consuming and sometimes downright obstructive in helping clients find a positive way through. The therapists started to reframe their sessions to focus on the solutions rather than the problems, and found that sessions framed in this way proved effective for many clients. Solution-focused therapy is known as a 'brief' therapy, but it is worth noting (before the budget-holders get too excited) that what they mean by this is more to do with the good use of time, rather than the overall amount of time – the implication is that every moment in a solution-focused session is a productive one.

A solution-focused approach can be particularly appropriate to use with some career coaching clients, as they will often access career support when they are feeling especially low – perhaps following a job loss, or when things are not going well at work. For this reason, it is not uncommon for clients to become entrenched in their problems, and as Bezanson (2004: 184) comments, 'possibilities are not often in the forefront of the client's mind' by the time they see a career coach. A coaching model which turns the traditional approach on its head, focusing exclusively on possibilities, can be enormously empowering and uplifting.

Many of the key tenets of solution-focused therapy are very similar to assumptions widely accepted within coaching more broadly, which is perhaps why this particular brand of therapy has been so easily assimilated into the coaching profession. These include the idea that clients are resourceful and have their own solutions, interventions should include goal-setting and action planning, and that an emphasis should be placed on working within a non-pathological framework. Other core beliefs of solution-focused coaching, though, are more specific to this approach, such as the idea that change can happen quickly, and the assumption (shared with cognitive behavioural coaching) that things themselves are not the problem, but rather the way we think about them. And it is this last assumption that leads on to the two main goals of solution-focused coaching: changing the viewing and changing the doing (O'Hanlon and Beadle, 1996).

Changing the viewing

In changing the viewing, the coach helps clients to see their problem in a new way. This will often make the problem seem less daunting and less overwhelming, and can make clients feel that it is something that they can cope with, leaving them some energy and time left over to start making plans for a better future. This can happen through shifting their thoughts away from dwelling on the problems and instead onto re-focusing their awareness on solutions.

Coaches support clients to change their viewing by using a range of techniques. Some, such as reflective listening, open questions and judicious use of silence will be familiar to all coaches. But solution-focused coaching adds some specific new techniques to our repertoires.

Scaling

I introduced the notion of the rating scale in the previous chapter. Scaling is a staple of the solution-focused coach's toolkit, but in this context is used slightly differently from its typical application in motivational interviewing. In a solution-focused approach, the question is used to achieve a range of different ends; for example, to ascertain where clients are in relation to their current goal, to help clarify their goals, to identify progress and to articulate small steps towards a goal.

Scaling question examples

Where is your client in relation to their goal:
'If at one you are at rock bottom – no solution in sight – and at ten everything is completely solved, where are you right now?'

Clarifying a goal:
'So you want your job satisfaction to score around an eight for you. Tell me a bit more about that. What does an eight look like and how would you know you were at an eight?'

Identifying progress:
'You say that you have reached around a four so far. Tell me how you've managed that.'

Articulating small steps towards the goal:
'You are at four now. What would it take to get you up to a four and a half?'

The miracle question

This is a widely used and effective way to help clients clarify their goals. The question can be asked in a number of different ways, so you can phrase it and contextualize it to make it relevant to your clients, but the essential question will be the same. It runs along these lines:

> Imagine that during the night a miracle happens, and when you wake up in the morning, your problem has gone away. What's the first sign you get that things are different?

Alternative scenarios might include asking your clients to imagine themselves in the future, gazing into a crystal ball, or watching two videos of themselves – one with the problem as it stands and one with the problem solved.

The coach can then follow this up with more specific questions as appropriate to the client situation such as 'can you tell me more about what you would be doing in this job?'; 'how will you know that you are doing well in this new role?'.

The miracle question encourages clients to focus entirely on the future, and gives their imagination licence to indulge in blue-sky thinking and unlimited possibilities.

Reframing

A direct way to change the viewing, reframing encourages clients to see their situation from a different perspective or a fresh angle. The coach can help this process using a number of specific techniques such as compliments, highlighting exceptions, refocusing on goals and turning problems into solutions.

Reframing examples (Cavanagh and Grant 2010)

Compliments:

Client: 'It's far too expensive.'

Coach: 'It's great that you are concerned with sticking to your budget. How can we make it more affordable?'

Exceptions:

Client: 'I really hate my work.'

Coach: 'It sounds very unpleasant: can you tell me about the parts of the job that are less awful for you?'

Goals:

Client: 'I really want to improve my leadership skills.'

Coach: 'So what does good leadership mean for you?'

Problems to solutions:

Client: 'I feel completely lost.'

Coach : 'So you'd like to get back a sense of direction and control.'

Changing the doing

Changing the viewing is important, both to enable change to happen and to give clients the belief that change could happen; but on its own it is not enough. The second key goal of solution-focused coaching is changing the doing, and the aim here is to build on what has worked in the past. The coach and the client have a very collaborative relationship and work to find solutions together. In fact, Lipchik (1997) who was at the forefront of the development of this approach, uses the term 'collaborating profession' to describe the coach, firmly emphasizing that the relationship is one of equals who share a goal and look for solutions together.

During this phase of the interview, the coach might suggest exploring relevant episodes from clients' experiences that have worked well, to see what they can learn about the future from the past: 'Tell me about a time when you were happy at work; what made it good?'; 'it sounds as though the decision to take that job was a good one. Tell me how you made that decision.'

Identifying exceptions can be another productive discussion to have in this phase, and one of the key assumptions of solution-focused coaching is that there are always exceptions. If clients feel that their work performance hasn't always been optimal, you might want to ask 'what are the things that you *have* done well at work?'. Similarly, if they feel that they can't identify any realistic career options, you could ask 'let's just try to think of one example of something you could do'.

Problems themselves can sometimes be turned on their heads to identify solutions (Jackson and McKergow 2007). You could work with clients to help them identify their dream job by identifying the opposite conditions to all those which frustrate them in their current role: 'so you hate the competitive atmosphere at work; you're looking for a collaborative environment?' Or if they can't identify any attractive career options, you could ask them about the roles they know they would *not* want to do and then see what you could infer from those choices.

A positive philosophy sits comfortably with career coaching. Coaching has been described as 'an ideal vehicle through which the science of positive psychology can be applied' (Kauffman *et al.* 2010: 159), and the shared focus on supporting people to strive for growth makes career coaching a natural home for positive approaches to career decision making and career development. As career-coaching professionals, we are not unrealistic or impractical, but a good coach will always believe in their client and will believe that there is a positive solution. We have in this chapter presented three different positive approaches: positive psychology, appreciative inquiry and solution focused coaching. You can choose to use the ideas in this chapter in a number of different ways – adopting one approach, blending all three or incorporating some individual tools and ideas into your practice. But whichever approach you choose to adopt, positive coaching provides some effective, concrete tools, and its positive and future orientation helps clients to focus on their strengths and solutions with greater motivation and optimism.

REFERENCES

Bezanson, B. J. (2004) The application of solution-focused work in employment counseling. *Journal of Employment Counseling*, 41: 183–191.

Cavanagh, M. J. and Grant, A. M. (2010) The solution-focused approach to coaching. In E. Cox, T. Bachkirova and D. Clutterbuck (eds), *The Complete Handbook of Coaching*. London: SAGE Publications.

Cooperrider, D. L. (2000) Positive image: positive action: The affirmative basis of organizing. In D. L. Cooperrider, P. F. Sorenson, D. Witney and T. F. Yaeger (eds), *Appreciative Inquiry: Rethinking Human Organization Toward a Positive Theory of Change*. Champaign, IL: Stipes Publishing, pp. 28–53.

De Shazer, S. (1985) *Keys to Solution in Brief Therapy*. New York: Norton.

Jackson, P. and McKergow, M. (2007) *The Solutions Focus: Making Coaching and Change Simple*, 2nd ed. London: Nicholas Brealey.

Kauffmann, C., Boniwell, I. and Silberman, J. (2010) The positive approach to coaching. In E. Cox, T. Bachirova and D. Clutterbuck (eds.), *The Complete Handbook of Coaching*. London: Sage.

Lehner, R. and Hight, D. L. (2006) Appreciative inquiry and student affairs: A positive approach to change. *The College Student Affairs Journal*, 25(2): 141–151.

Lipchik, E. (1997) My story about solution-focused brief therapist/client relationship. *Journal of Systemic Therapies*, 16: 88–99.

Locke, E. A. and Latham, G. P. (1990) *A Theory of Goal-setting and Task Performance.* Englewood Cliffs, NJ: Prentice Hall.

O'Hanlon, B. and Beadle, S. (1996) *A Field Guide to Possibility Land: Possible Therapy Methods.* London: BT Press.

Peterson, C. and Seligman, M. E. P. (2004) *Character Strengths and Virtues: A Handbook and Classification.* Oxford: Oxford University Press.

Rath, T. and Harter, J. (2010) *Well Being: The Five Essential Elements.* New York: Gallup Press.

Seligman, M. E. P. and Csikszentmihalyi, M. (2000) Positive psychology: an introduction. *American Psychologist*, 55(1): 5–14.

Seligman, M. E. P., Steen, T. A., Park, N. and Peterson, C. (2005) Positive psychology progress: Empirical validation of interventions. *American Psychologist*, 50(5): 410–421.

Yates, J. (2011) Career Coaching: New Direction for the Profession? *Constructing the Future,* VI. Stourbridge: Institute of Career Guidance.

Chapter 12

Cognitive behavioural coaching

Adapted from the world of therapy, where it was developed as an approach that deals with dysfunctional beliefs, cognitive behavioural coaching (CBC) is one of the most widely used forms of coaching. It can be used to great effect with the self-limiting beliefs that so often prevent our clients from pursuing the paths they dream of or taking advantage of the opportunities that present themselves.

The concepts are not new. Epictetus (55–135AD) could be said to have started the ball rolling nearly 2000 years ago, noting that 'Men are disturbed, not by the things that happen, but by their opinion of the things that happen', and Shakespeare sums it up with Hamlet's line 'there is nothing either good or bad but thinking makes it so' (*Hamlet*, Act 2, scene 2, 250–1). Bringing our inspirational intellectuals a little more up to date, the two forefathers of modern cognitive behavioural therapy are Ellis and Beck, who combined ideas from their different theoretical backgrounds (Ellis specialized in rational emotive behaviour, and Beck in cognitive therapy) to develop cognitive behavioural therapy.

In essence, the underpinning tenet of CBC is that it is not events themselves that upset us, but our response to them. Our response is not simple, however. CBC holds that we will react to an event with our feelings, our thoughts and our behaviour. Each of these will have an impact on the other two, but while it is pretty difficult to change behaviour or feelings in isolation, changing thoughts can sometimes be rather more manageable and if we manage to do this in a significant and sustained way, there will be an attendant knock-on effect on our feelings and behaviour.

When it comes to faulty thinking, we often commit one of two errors. We either overestimate the probability of some negative consequence ('I haven't polished my shoes. The interviewers are bound to notice), or we overestimate how bad the consequences will be ('if I don't get the job, my career is over'). It is our job as career coaches to listen out for examples of what might be faulty thinking and to help our clients work out whether or not their views are realistic and rational.

The first thing, therefore, is to listen out for possible thinking errors. The most common types are shown in Table 12.1 on page 128.

A CBC process

I have been rejected for a job I applied for *(event)*. I feel hurt and humiliated *(feelings)*. I think I'm a failure and not up to jobs at this level *(thoughts)*. I decide that I'm not going to apply for a job like this the next time one comes up *(behaviour)*.

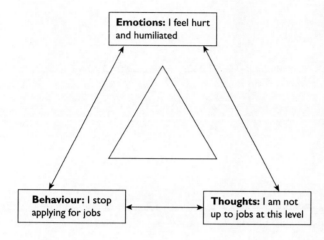

Figure 12.1

But while it is hard to make myself not feel hurt, and I am unlikely to throw myself, heart and soul into another application in this state of mind, I might be able to argue myself out of thinking that I am just not up to it. For example:

- I could think about whether I genuinely gave my best performance on the day;
- I could wonder whether the successful candidate had a pre-existing relationship with one of the panel members – perhaps they were an internal candidate;
- I could remind myself that interviews are not an exact science, and the interviewers might conceivably have made a mistake;
- I could consider the possibility that I might have come a close second;
- I could think about any possible flaws in my performance and come up with an action plan to help sort them out.

These thoughts might help me reframe the experience: I didn't get that job, but that doesn't mean I'm not capable of getting one just like it in the future.

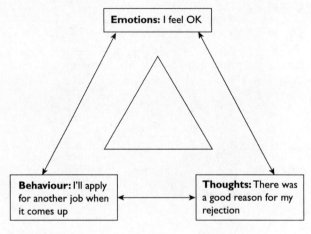

Figure 12.2

Within cognitive behavioural coaching, it is important to remember that these thinking 'errors' may actually be entirely accurate. It could indeed be the case that it genuinely *was* all your client's fault, or that they have actually never got a job they have gone for. Our role is to listen out for comments that could indicate these errors and then to explore with our clients whether or not there is a realistic and rational basis for their concerns.

Coaching, therapy and boundaries

I have talked so far in this chapter about cognitive behavioural coaching, but the approach and most of the research on it stems from a therapeutic context. The differences between cognitive behavioural therapy (CBT) and cognitive behavioural coaching are not explicitly articulated in the literature. Reading the CBC literature, you would be hard pressed to identify any theoretical distinctions between CBC and CBT, but the examples and case studies explain the context. In terms of practical application, the differences seem to lie more in the nature of the clients and their situations rather than in how the techniques are applied. As professional and ethical coaches, we need to be mindful of our boundaries. Coaches are not therapists and it is important that we don't get carried away with enthusiasm about our new skills, and start to over-reach ourselves. If you are working with a client whose thinking errors appear to have wider significance in their lives, then it might be appropriate to have a discussion with them about whether they might consider seeing a counsellor or therapist to ensure that they are being given the support they need from the right professional source.

TOOLS FOR THE COGNITIVE BEHAVIOURAL COACH

PITs and PETs

When it comes to faulty thinking, one technique that cognitive behavioural coaches can use is to encourage clients to replace their Performance Inhibiting Thoughts (PITs) with Performance Enhancing Thoughts (PETs). PITs are examples of thinking errors that we repeat to ourselves and which make us feel less confident and less capable than we really are. The technique is to encourage your clients to work out specifically what their PITs are, and then ask them what thoughts they would prefer to have, identifying which ones would be likely to make them feel positive and increase their self-efficacy. Their task then is to notice each time the PIT pops into their minds and then consciously and deliberately replace it with their new PET. This technique takes some practice but if they can stick with it, it can be remarkably effective. Your clients, for example, might realize that they keep thinking 'I'm never going to get that job', and might see that this thought is linked with feelings of inadequacy, and behaviour such as not bothering to prepare thoroughly for the interview. You could ask them what positive thought they would prefer to be thinking and they might suggest 'I am good enough to get this job'. The feelings associated with this PET are more likely to be confidence and determination, and the consequent behaviour might be more rigorous interview preparation.

Cognitive behavioural questions

Below are some examples of the kinds of questions you might ask if you felt that your clients might be displaying some thinking errors.

- 'How would you feel about someone else who was in your position? Would you judge them as harshly as you are judging yourself?'
- 'You say you're awful at that. Let's think about a scale running between excellent at 10 and awful at 1. Where would you put yourself?'
- 'What's your evidence for thinking that?'
- 'What would your colleagues say about you? Would they agree with your rating/description of yourself?'
- 'Let's think up a list of all the other possible explanations.'
- 'How likely is that to happen?'
- 'When you say you "must" do that, what does "must" mean? What would happen if you didn't?'

The ABCDEF Model

The classic intervention framework in CBC is the ABCDEF model. Ellis (1962) proposed the ABC model, where A is the activating event, B is the beliefs

Table 12.1

Thinking error	What it means	What the client might say	Possible consequence
All or nothing thinking	This is likely to be seen in a perfectionist who thinks that if something is worth doing, it's worth doing absolutely perfectly; and if it is not possible to do it that well, then there is no point in trying.	'There was no point even sending off for the details of that job because there is no way I would have had time to get it done by the deadline.'	They reject perfectly good opportunities because they have unrealistic expectations of how well they need to perform.
Magnification	The individual feels that the blame lies entirely on their shoulders.	'It was all my fault. If only I had spent a bit more time at the office, I wouldn't have been made redundant.'	Lowered self-efficacy, which could lead to setting lower goals in future.
Minimization	The individual doesn't seem to take credit for their achievements.	'It was nothing really – there was a great team working on it.'	Wasting an opportunity to enhance self-efficacy which is extremely useful for goal-setting, rising to a challenge and getting jobs.
Personalization	The individual feels personally responsible.	'They obviously just didn't like me.'	If the individual blames themselves as a person, they are not in a position to do very much to improve their performance another time.
Labelling	Stereotyping groups of people.	'People like me don't get jobs like that.'	Risks writing off opportunities
Focusing on the negative	Giving undue weight to a small negative experience.	'I never get jobs I go for.'	Results in lowered self-efficacy and could lead to a defeatist approach: 'there's no point in taking advantage of that opportunity because it will never come good for me.'

(or thoughts) and C is the consequences in terms of emotions, behaviour and physiology. Ellis added the D and E stages a few years later to transfer his theoretical model to a practical tool, incorporating two processes that can help individuals to respond more helpfully to the event. The D is the process of disputing – identifying and challenging any faulty thinking – and the E is the effective new approach, the stage in the process where the individual specifically identifies new ways of thinking that are likely to lead to more positive outcomes. Finally Palmer (2002) added the F stage, which represents the future focus. Here, the individual looks forward; they consider a broader range of goals and might spend time working out how to sustain their new effective behaviours in the longer term.

ABCDEF model

Activating event:
I've failed to get the promotion I went for.

Beliefs:
I'm just not cut out for this industry. I'll never get any further up the career ladder.

Consequences:
Emotional – I feel a failure; I feel humiliated.
Behavioural – I am now looking for a complete change in career direction.

Disputing:
Actually, plenty of people go for several interviews before they get a promotion. Perhaps I didn't fail; I just wasn't quite right for that role at that time. I haven't been working at this level for very long, and the person who actually got the job was significantly more experienced than I am.

Effective new approach:
Perhaps I need to think about the kind of experience that would be useful to gain before I try again. It could be helpful to work in a different kind of setting for a while to get a broader outlook.

Future focus:
I'm going to look for jobs at the same level that I'm on at the moment but in different organizations. That way I'll be able to broaden my experience, gain some new skills, and be in a better position to apply for a more senior job in a year's time.

Inference chaining

This is a very effective technique for getting clients to explore how bad something might be. We often make decisions based on a general sense that something bad will happen if we behave in a certain way, but we don't often push ourselves to identify what exactly that thing might be, and how bad it might get. Socratic questioning, a technique based on the teaching style of the Greek philosopher and teacher Socrates, enables clients to think through the consequences of a negative outcome right to the final stage. Having clarified in their own minds exactly what might happen, people are then in a position to make a reasoned judgement about whether to take the risk. More often than not, the worst case scenario actually doesn't seem as bad as all that.

At its most basic level, the technique involves the coach asking 'so if you did that, what would happen?' and then repeating 'and then what would happen?' until the client reaches the end of the series of consequences. The coach might then ask the client to reflect on these consequences and to consider how likely are they to happen and how bad would it be if they did.

A client, for example, might be feeling very anxious about the idea of giving up a salaried job to set up their own business, a long-held ambition.

> **Coach:** So what's holding you back?
> **Client:** Well, I suppose it's the fear that it might not work.
> **Coach:** And what would happen if it didn't work?
> **Client:** Well, I'd have to sell the business.
> **Coach:** And what would happen then?
> **Client:** I'd probably lose quite a lot of money.
> **Coach:** And what would happen then?
> **Client:** I might need to remortgage my house or even move to somewhere smaller.
> **Coach:** And what would happen then?
> **Client:** I'd have to look around for a job.
> **Coach:** And what would happen then?
> **Client:** I'd probably end up working back in this firm.
> **Coach:** And what would happen then?
> **Client:** Well, I'd be really embarrassed that I'd failed.
> **Coach:** And what would happen then?
> **Client:** I guess I'd probably get over that.
> **Coach:** And what would happen then?
> **Client:** I suppose at least I would know that I'd given it a go. I wouldn't always be wondering.

This technique is particularly useful when working with clients whose fear is holding them back, whether it's fear of rejection if they cold-call a potential employer, fear of failure if they apply for a job, or fear of humiliation if they go along to a networking event. The technique won't always result in them taking the plunge, but will help ensure that whatever decision they take is based on a realistic analysis of the consequences.

Mastery imagery

The use of imagery and visualizations is widely applied in CBC. One specific variation that is particularly relevant to the career context is mastery imagery. The technique helps individuals with performance anxiety and is suitable for clients who have an upcoming event that is causing them concern. It entails asking them to imagine the event as a great success, and to focus on imagining it in minute detail. The theoretical concept underpinning this technique is the idea that if you can imagine something very vividly, you can trick your brain into thinking that it actually happened. If that image is a positive one, you receive similar confidence-boosting feelings that you would have done had it been real.

This tool works particularly well for job selection, in particular presentations, psychometric tests and interviews.

Visualizing mastery

If clients have job interviews coming up, you could suggest that they try a vizualization. Ask them to close their eyes and tell them that you are going to get them to think about the interview, but tell them to imagine that it goes brilliantly from start to finish. You might say something like this:

> Imagine yourself arriving at the building. Think about what you are wearing, from top to toe, and think through how you might be feeling: perhaps you are a little nervous, but enthusiastic and excited about the opportunity to talk about your experiences; you might be feeling confident and sure of yourself, and you feel well rested and alert. Imagine introducing yourself at reception and waiting outside the interview room. You are called in by the chair of the panel. Imagine the room, the furniture and the people on the interview panel. What are *their* thoughts at this stage? They have perhaps read your CV and are already impressed. They're looking forward to finding out a bit more about you. They watch you walk in through the door, shake everyone's hands and greet them all. They notice your confidence and presence.
>
> The interview goes well. You can think of plenty to say to each question – the examples are all in the forefront of your mind. Your words flow fluently. The rapport is great – the panel are listening intently – lots of nodding, lots of scribbling notes. Before you know it, the interview is over. You shake hands, smile confidently and leave the room. How are you feeling? Confident? Pleased with yourself? Excited at the thought of working there? What are the panel doing, behind that closed door? And what are they thinking?
>
> Now, think of a word that you can associate with this scene. A word that will allow you to conjure up this image and these feelings each time you say it.

You might suggest that they recreate this scene in their minds in the days leading up to the interview, and each time uses the trigger word to help conjure up the images in their minds. On the day of the interview itself, suggest that they simply say the trigger word to themselves as they arrive.

Case study

Jon had made several career changes in his 15 working years. He'd started in the leisure and tourism industry, worked in events, done some web design, been a freelance copy writer and tried (without much success) to publish a novel. Prompted by a particularly vile day in the office, he came to see a career coach to talk about what he could do next. He really wanted to get out of his current industry, but just wasn't sure what would suit him. It became clear in his first session with the career coach that there was an idea that Jon had been thinking about on and off for more than a decade, which was to train as a paramedic. He had clearly given it a lot of thought and Jon's face lit up as he talked about the role. It seemed perfect. He'd be doing something that mattered; he'd have a tangible skill; the days would be varied and unpredictable; he'd be working in a team and making the world a better place. He could afford the training and was desperate to leave his current job. He left the session enthusiastic to find out more. But the weeks went by and Jon didn't do anything about it. It emerged through a session with his career coach that he had very little confidence in his own ability to make decisions. Using the ABCDEF CBC model, Jon identified the thoughts, feelings and physiological reactions he had to the idea of making and implementing his career idea, and began to understand the link between these and his reluctance to take a chance. He worked out that although he got quite excited at the idea of being a paramedic, as soon as he started thinking about the steps he would need to take – leaving his job and starting a new training course – he started to panic. He felt frightened and convinced that something would go wrong – either he would not enjoy it, or he wouldn't be very good at it. He identified his thoughts and realized that he believed that he was a bad decision maker, as so many of his previous decisions hadn't gone well. His coach helped him to think about some of the many good decisions that he made both with his career and in his personal life, and he began to regain a little confidence in his decision-making ability. The coach then used some inference chaining to help Jon establish, realistically and rationally, how bad it would be if he did make a mistake. This process reassured Jon that even if the worst came to the worst, things wouldn't be all that bad.

Armed with increased career decision making self-efficacy and reduced fear of the consequences, Jon applied to train as a paramedic.

Cognitive behavioural coaching can be used as the basis of a whole coaching session, or can be incorporated within a more conventional GROW session. If you feel that the faulty thinking you can see in your clients is really preventing them from moving forward, then you might suggest spending one or more sessions working through the issues. If the faulty thinking is perhaps limiting performance rather than preventing progress, you and your clients might feel that a shorter session within the GROW model might be more appropriate.

Thinking errors can emerge from all different angles within the career coaching process. Most often, you will find yourself using CBC techniques to help with job search, and in particular with increasing self-confidence for interview skills, but there can also be some very valuable work to be done around aspirations and goal-setting.

As with most techniques in this book, CBC is not a quick fix. For it to be most effective, it needs to be repeated and practised until it becomes a habit. Identifying clients who might benefit from CBC will become second nature as warning bells will start to ring in your mind whenever a client uses language that may indicate a thinking error. With practice, both on your part and the part of your clients, it can become a valuable coaching tool.

REFERENCES

Beck, A. (1976) *Cognitive Therapy and the Emotional Disorders.* New York: International Universities Press.

Ellis, A. (1962) *Reason and Emotion in Psychotherapy.* New York: Lyle Stuart.

Palmer, S. (2002) Cognitive and organizational models of stress that are suitable for use within workplace stress management/prevention coaching, training and counselling settings. *Rational Emotive Behaviour Therapist*, 10(1): 15–21.

Palmer, S. and Szymanska, K. (2007) Cognitive behavioural coaching: An integrated coach. In S. Palmer and A. Whybrow (eds), *Handbook of Coaching Psychology*. London: Routledge.

Chapter 13

Transactional analysis

Developed by Eric Berne in the early 1960s, transactional analysis (TA) is a theory that helps us to understand human communication. Berne was trained in the psychodynamic theory of relationships but was keen to find a model that could be easily explained and easily understood. His great achievement to this end has led to TA being sometimes dismissed as something quite superficial, but at its extended level it is a complex and comprehensive model.

TA can be used within career coaching in two different ways. It can be a model through which the coach can understand and analyse the coach/client relationship, thereby enhancing the interaction within the session. Alternatively it can be used as a tool to share with the client, to help them work on their challenging relationships outside the coaching sessions.

We saw in Chapter 3 when looking at career decision making that our nearest and dearest have a huge impact on our career decision making. For the most part this impact is a positive one, but of course it won't always improve things and it certainly doesn't always make the process straightforward. One of the most common issues that clients bring to career coaching sessions is what Gati, Krausz, and Osipow (1996) term 'external conflict'. Scenarios that might sound familiar to a career coach would include a client's loved ones fearing that the client is making a poor decision for his or her future – 'I want to study art, but my parents won't let me'; a client's loved ones fearing the impact that the client's decision may have on them, themselves – 'I want to leave my job and re-train but my wife hates the idea of me giving up my salary'; or the client's concerns about the impact their choice may have on others –'I want to resign but my line manager will struggle without me and is putting enormous pressure on me to stay'. In many of these situations, a greater understanding and empathy can help the interactions to move on and TA is one useful framework for this.

In this chapter, I will first present an overview of the key concepts of TA and then explore the different ways that it can be incorporated within career coaching practice, using the idea of perceptual positions in particular.

THE CONCEPTS

A transaction is an entity in itself

In the phrase 'transactional analysis' is embedded one of the underlying tenets of the philosophy, which is that a conversation (or transaction) is an independent entity, existing outside each of the individuals involved. The transaction is a construct based on the words used, the meanings implied and the meanings inferred. The TA model is a way of looking at the interaction from all angles. It broadens an interaction from 'he said . . . she said' to 'what he meant . . . what she hoped he would understand . . . what he actually understood . . . what motives he attributed to her . . .' and more.

I'm ok . . . you're ok . . .

A healthy interaction, according to the TA framework, needs to assume 'I'm ok' and 'you're ok'. The individual needs to value themselves and their contribution to the interaction ('I'm ok') and needs to value their conversation partner and their contribution ('you're ok'). The presences of these underlying assumptions will make communication more clear, straightforward and productive.

From this, we can then identify four communication states:

I'm not ok, you're ok	I'm ok, you're ok
I'm not ok, you're not ok	I'm ok, you're not ok

If an individual's feelings within an interaction are situated in the bottom-right hand quadrant ('I'm ok, you're not ok'), then they are feeling in a 'one up' position. They feel confident of their own position, but don't value the contribution of the other. Their dominant feeling is one of anger, and their instinct is to stop the interaction as soon as possible.

If the individual is in the top-left quadrant ('I'm not ok, you're ok'), then they feel in a 'one down' position, feeling helpless and seeing themselves as inferior to their conversation partner. This leads to the sense that they are not in control of the interaction and their instinct is to run away.

The most challenging of the communication states is the bottom-left quadrant ('I'm not ok, you're not ok'), where the individual neither values themselves nor their conversation partner. They feel that the conversation is hopeless and that there is no chance that it will get anywhere.

This model can be used with clients to raise their awareness of what is happening in their interactions, either with you, their career coach, or with others in their lives. While clients aren't usually in a position to change how their conversation partners behave, the model can help to explain why conversations aren't working, and can be used as the basis of discussions that may lead to clients changing their own behaviour.

Ego states

Berne proposes that within an interaction, there are three 'ego states' that we can each be in, or choose to be in: child, adult and parent. We can and all do communicate from each of the three states at different times, but although each has its place in effective communication, it is only from the adult ego state that change can happen.

a.   **Parent.** There are two sides to the parent ego state – the nurturing parent and the critical parent – and both are thought to be based on our childhood obser-vations of our own parents or other authority figures. The critical parent tells you not to do something, points out flaws and highlights problems. The nurturing parent reassures you, comforts you and showers you with praise.
b.   **Child.** The child ego state also has two sides. The free child is spontaneous and does just as it pleases, with no thought to consequences. This child can be creative and fun, or rebellious and naughty, but always responds instinctively and emotionally. The adapted child sets out to please, is rule-bound and behaves in the way they think they ought to.
c.   **Adult.** The adult ego state has only one side, which is the rational and respon-sible state. In the adult ego state, we make decisions objectively and logically, and take responsibility for our actions.

Although adult-to-adult ego state conversation is the most likely to lead to positive change, it's not always easy to maintain. Conversations will meander quite naturally through different combinations of ego states, and some relationships can seem stuck in one particular style of interaction. Moving from one state to another tends to be an automatic process, driven both by your own feelings about the transaction, and the specific comments and ego states of your partner. A comment from a child ego state ('I just don't want to do it!' or 'have I done the right thing?') is likely to engender a parent ego state response ('well, you'll just have to' or 'yes of course you have') and we tend not to be aware of or in control of these changes.

The various combinations of ego states all have their place in day-to-day conversation, but for a change to take place, the individuals need to be in the adult ego state. And it can take a good deal of self awareness, confidence and empathy to stick with the adult ego state when your conversation partner is (albeit unconsciously) trying to force you into parent or child.

Using TA ego states in career coaching

I've introduced TA as an approach to help clients to more productive conversations with their loved ones, but it can be a valuable concept to help your own inter-actions with your clients. I'll deal with its role in the practitioner/client relationship first and then move on to some examples of how it can be used to help with the client/other relationships.

As noted above, for change to take place within an interaction, the conversation needs to be between adult ego states and for most coaching interactions, this is important. Although we, as coaches, do what we can to establish the coach/client relationship as one of equals, the nature of the financial transaction and the professional status of the coach can lead to clients looking on the coach as both expert and problem solver. This can lend itself to a child/parent interaction with the client in the subordinate role, taking limited responsibility for their actions, solutions and the coaching process. This tendency for clients to lean towards an expectation of a parent/child interaction can then be compounded by the emotional state that our clients can find themselves in when facing redundancy or searching for a professional identity. These situations can make clients feel vulnerable and they may take refuge in a child ego state, seeking a nurturing parent in the coach.

If you become aware that a parent/child interaction is developing, you can react in two ways. In the first instance, you can respond to the client's parent or child ego state from your adult ego state, which will encourage the client to do the same (see below). This will often be all that is needed to return to the adult/adult interaction, from which change can take place. But if the client persists in their child or parent ego state, or keeps returning to it, then a more direct approach will be needed; it might be helpful to share your perceptions of the conversation, perhaps within the TA framework, directly with your client.

Responding to your client's 'child' comments from an 'adult' state can be enough to steer the conversation back to the more productive adult/adult transaction:

Client as 'child': 'It is going to be alright, isn't it? I will find a job eventually, won't I?'

Coach as 'parent' (more natural conversational response): 'Of course it will; you will find a job, and everything will be ok.'

Coach as 'adult' (more appropriate coaching response): 'It sounds as though you're really struggling with the uncertainties of your current situation.'

Client moving in to adult state: 'Yes you're right, and I am finding it really tough.'

Sometimes this won't be enough and the coach might decide to discuss ego states with the client:

Client as 'child': 'It is going to be alright, isn't it? I will find a job eventually, won't I?'

Coach: 'I keep feeling that I want to reassure you and tell you that everything is going to be alright. Is that what you are wanting me to do?'

Client: 'That's interesting. Yes, I suppose I am looking for someone to make me believe that everything is going to get better.'

Coach: 'There is a framework called transactional analysis that might help us to understand what's going on here. Would it be ok if I shared it with you?'

I said earlier that in most coaching conversations the adult/adult transaction is the most useful, but there are exceptions. One of the key characteristics of the free child is its creativity and within career coaching sessions this can be a very useful state for generating options. If your client is trying to come up with ideas of solutions, then shifting the transaction to child/child states can be a useful way to get the creative juices flowing.

Perceptual positions

One other way to use TA with clients is through a technique called 'perceptual positions'. This draws on the notion of totality, taken from Gestalt psychology, which holds that experiences can be understood only within their environment: in order to understand what has happened, we need to understand the context in which it took place. As far as transactions are concerned, a single comment taken from a conversation makes sense only if you understand something about the relationship between the two participants, and what has already been said.

Perceptual positions is a tool that uses empathy to help clients better understand their interactions with others, making use of different physical spaces to allow clients to unlock their unconscious understanding of their partner's thinking and feeling.

The classic interpretation of the technique requires three chairs set out in a triangle within a room. One is the place of your client (position one), one is the place of their conversational partner or the 'other' (position two) and the third (position three) is the place of the interested but objective observer.

First, ask your client to identify a conversation that they have found or might find challenging. It is usually more productive to get your client to reflect on a real conversation that has actually taken place, but it can also be effective to ask them to imagine an anticipated conversation. You then ask them to sit in position one and to tell you about the conversation from their own perspective. You can ask them to describe what they said, what they meant by it, and what impact they hoped it would have on their partner. Then ask them what their partner said, what your client thought they meant, and how it made them feel. When you feel that you have explored the conversation from this perspective fully, you change tack. It can be helpful at this stage to have a short break from the topic, briefly discussing something else or pausing to get a cup of tea, before then asking your client to sit down in position two. You ask your client to re-live the conversation from the perspective of the partner, asking them to answer all the same questions but role playing the part of the 'other'. After another short break, you ask your client to sit in position three, and describe the interaction again but this time from the point of view of an interested but impartial observer.

The technique can be greatly revealing and used in conjunction with the ego states, can allow the client to empathize more with the feelings and motivations of their partner and to view the interaction from an 'adult' ego state, perhaps identifying some unproductive parent/child transactions within the conversation.

Following this three-way analysis of the conversation, the coach and client can usefully spend some time exploring ways in which the client could change the direction of the conversation, for example, by thinking about techniques for sticking to responses from their adult ego state, or by showing more empathy with the feelings experienced by their 'other'.

Case study

Sam had gained a place on a prestigious graduate training scheme in the HR department of a large department store chain when she graduated eight years ago. She had been with the company ever since and had moved up the corporate ladder, earning promotions and salary increases as she went. She came to see a career coach as she was increasingly dissatisfied and stressed in her current role, but didn't understand why or how to move forward.

Sam grew up in a very achievement-oriented environment. Her father was a successful business man, she attended a results-focused boarding school, and her older sister had gone on to be an investment banker. With support from her career coach, she identified that her own definition of 'success' was at odds with her family's. She eventually reached the decision that she wanted to re-train as a primary school teacher and although she was quite comfortable with her own choice, it was important to her to have the support of her parents in this decision. She felt sure that they wouldn't understand, however.

By using perceptual positions to 'play out' an anticipated conversation with her father, Sam came to a greater understanding of both her own position and her father's. She realized that her own main concern was that her parents would think of her as a failure, and this in part stemmed from her own automatic thoughts that perpetuated the idea that you would opt for a teaching job only if you had failed to make it in the corporate sector. The exercise also allowed her to understand her father's view better. She realized that regardless of his own understanding of the concept of 'success', the pressure he put on his children to achieve in high-prestige roles was born out of a desire for them to be happy – it was just that he thought that happiness lay in financial security. Sam saw that if she was able to explain to him that her current role was making her unhappy and how a role as a teacher could meet her needs more effectively, she might be better able to get her father to understand her choice. She also acknowledged through the exercise that her transactions with her father are often adaptive child/ critical parent interactions, and that her desire to please her father is not always healthy: in fact, it has led her to make some unfulfilling decisions over the years.

During the coaching process, Sam and her coach worked on some techniques to reframe her own view of 'success'. They also role-played some imagined conversations with her father to give her some practice of responding to 'critical parent' comments from her adult ego state.

The possible applications of TA are very wide. Once you feel comfortable with some of the key elements and models, you may find yourself using it to understand many of your everyday transactions. The simple and accessible models and language mask a profound and comprehensive theory that has wide-ranging implications. The approach and techniques can also be shared with clients to allow them to understand any important but difficult relationships that may be holding them back. For career coaching practice, it can be of great benefit to your relationships with your clients. If you can identify what is not quite working in your coach/client conversations, you can do something about putting them right.

REFERENCES

Berne, E. (1962) Classification of positions. *Transactional Analysis Bulletin*, 1(3): 23.
Berne, E. (1963) *The Structure and Dynamics of Organizations and Groups*. New York: Grove Press.
Gati, I., Krausz, M. and Osipow, S. H. (1996) A taxonomy of difficulties in career decision making. *Journal of Counseling Psychology*, 43: 510–526.

Chapter 14

Coaching tools

One of the most firmly held principles in coaching is that clients have the answers. In practice, though, clients will often seek career support when they don't realize that they know the answer, or when they can't access it. Our job in these cases is to help our clients connect with the insights, ideas and solutions that are kept under lock and key in the depths of their unconscious minds.

Various coaching tools have been developed or adopted from other disciplines to help clients do just that. They will not all be useful for each client in every situation, but it is great to have them within your coaching repertoire to draw on where appropriate.

Clients may vary in their enthusiasm for trying these tools. Some will see these activities as just what they came to you for and will embrace them all as ways to increase their self-awareness and generate options. Others may be more wary. A bad experience in art class at school may have left them anxious about anything visually creative; a client with dyslexia may feel daunted at having to write anything down. As a career coach, you need to be sensitive to these kinds of concerns and imaginative about how you respond to them: a client who doesn't like to write, for example, may be happy to make an audio recording; someone who hates drawing may be much more comfortable making a collage. But don't be put off. Clients come to see us because they are looking for some extra help. If we allow them to stay in their comfort zones throughout the sessions then we are at risk of letting them down by not stretching their thinking or expanding their horizons. Exercises can be at their most powerful when they are pushing boundaries: an artistic client might enjoy a drawing exercise, but they may well have already conceptualized their situation visually so putting their ideas down in this way may generate nothing new. By contrast, a client who hasn't drawn a picture since they were 14 might gain some real insights by trying something that feels so alien.

After the exercise itself (which could take place either as part of the session itself, or by the client on their own in between sessions) comes the debrief. This can be the most important part of the process and may take some time. Your role during the debrief is to encourage your client to talk about their experience of the exercise and to help them make links between that and their current situation or dilemma. You might ask how they felt about doing the exercise, how easy they found it and what it all means. You can ask about what they have included and what they have omitted. And you can then ask them how this relates to their current situation and future goals.

The exercises I am including in this chapter are of course only a few of the many available to you. I have included some suggestions for further reading at the end, but would encourage you to devise your own strategies. For each of the suggestions I have included here, I have explained how you can use the exercise with clients, but these are not sacred methodologies. Do feel free to interpret these ideas, come up with your own variations and make them your own.

I have also included suggestions for the kinds of clients and scenarios that they might be particularly applicable to but most can be used in a wide range of contexts with just a small amount of tweaking.

1. Family genogram

A straightforward and visual way to enable clients to reflect on some of the influences on their career thinking.

How: Ask your clients to put together a family tree of the occupations of the key members of their family. The scope of the tree should go as wide as needed to incorporate the client's major family influences; for some, that could mean parents only, but for others might include siblings, grandparents, uncles, aunts and cousins. The tree could be limited to just occupations and educational levels, or could extend to whatever issues feel relevant to the client's current career issue, for example, salaries, occupational prestige or satisfaction levels.

Debrief: Ask your clients to talk about the different people and the influences that they've had on your client's choices and values. Identify themes, patterns and contrasts.

Useful for: Enhancing self awareness; external conflicts with family; internal conflicts of values.

2. Drawing

One of the most widely used coaching tools, this is a remarkably effective way to help clients make sense of their feelings.

How: Provide a pen and paper for your clients and suggest that they draw a representation of how things are for them right now. Make it clear that it doesn't have to be a 'picture' as such: clients might use shapes and lines, or draw metaphors, but it needs to be something that represents how they are feeling about things at the moment.

Debrief: Ask your clients to explain what they've drawn and how it makes them feel. You might want to ask about the details in the picture, the use of space, the size and position of the parts of the drawing and differences between the various elements of the picture – differences in size, position or levels of detail.

Case Study

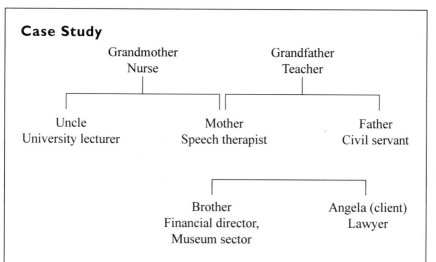

The striking theme that Angela was able to see clearly when she'd drawn her family genogram was the strong culture of public service that ran throughout Angela's family. Angela was the only member of her close family to work for the private sector, and as a corporate lawyer, Angela's role felt to her quite different from those chosen by the rest of her family. Although the facts of the various occupations were of course nothing new to Angela, she hadn't quite seen the pattern in such stark terms before. A more in-depth exploration of the topic allowed Angela to understand some of her own fears and anxieties about her own role and ambitions.

Variations: You could ask your clients then to draw a picture of how they would like their life to be right now, or how they would like their life to be, say, five or ten years down the line.

Useful for: Clients who are struggling to understand, make sense of or articulate the emotions associated with their current situation. The contrast between their image of things as they are now and things as they might be can help with goal-setting and with increasing motivation.

Case study

Sarah was in a job that in many ways suited her down to the ground: it was interesting, rewarding and, crucially for her, fitted in neatly with her family. The only thing that let it down was the enormous and seemingly endless volume of work. She came to see a career coach to get some help with making a decision about what to do. She felt that she ought to just get on with it and remember how lucky she was to have such a great job. But still she wasn't quite happy.

> The career coach asked her to draw a picture to represent how she was feeling about things now. Sarah, who hadn't picked up a drawing pencil since school, was sceptical, but trusted the coach and so gave it a go. The image she drew was a powerful one. It was a picture of her curled up in a tight ball at the foot of a big oak tree, with driving rain pouring down all around her. She started to cry as she explained what it all meant to her, highlighting the fear, the isolation, how utterly overwhelmed she felt and how she just wanted it all to go away.
>
> Reflecting afterwards, Sarah said that she felt that the drawing had given her a window into her emotions, and had allowed her to accept her own feelings, and that this had made her feel that she was right to want to change things.

3. Collage

This is a technique adapted from art therapy and can be used in group settings or as part of one-to-one coaching interventions. (With the latter, it is often useful to ask your client to complete this task in-between sessions, as it can take some time.)

How: Ask your clients to prepare a collage that represents their life as it is at the moment. They can use images from newspapers or magazines, photographs, drawings, coloured paper, words, bits of fabric – anything, in fact, that they feel says something about their life as they currently experience it. Encourage your clients to think about the size of the images, how they arrange them on the page, and to think about all aspects of their lives.

Debrief: Ask your clients to talk about their collage and to explain their choice of images, what they mean and how they have arranged them. Find out how they feel about the different parts of the collage, and whether there is anything missing. Do offer reflections of your own about the collage as you may have noticed things that the client was unaware of, and try to identify themes.

Variations: Suggest that your clients might like to make a collage of their life as they would like it to be, either right now, or in, say, five years' time. You can then ask them to compare the differences and use that as a starting point for a discussion about goals.

You could suggest that they make a digital collage, using images from the web, and cutting and pasting them onto a Word document online. Clients tend to report (Loader 2009) that this is harder to do as they are having to generate each thought as they type it in to a search engine, rather than reacting to images they see in magazines. That said, they also find that they need to think harder to compose the collage, and that can be helpful.

Useful for: Clients who are struggling to make sense of their current situation or who need some extra support in identifying their future goals. This technique can be used effectively with clients who find it hard to articulate their feelings, and can be particularly revealing for clients who tend to think with words rather than pictures.

Case study

Karen came to see a career coach in her early 40s knowing that she wasn't in the right job, but not knowing where she wanted to go to. She brought a collage of her life as it was at then, and one of her life as she wanted it to be in ten years' time. The process of putting the two collages together raised a number of interesting issues for her. First, while she found it easy to come up with lots of ideas and images for her current life, she found it difficult to picture a desirable future for herself. She just didn't know what kind of future she wanted, and it dawned on her that this lack of clear aspiration was making her current decision very difficult. Second, she noticed that many of the images she used in her 'future' collage were identical to those she had used in her 'current' collage. This reminded her about some of the positives of her present situation, and highlighted how much of her day-to-day life she loved and wanted to keep.

In discussion with the career coach, more themes emerged. The coach pointed out that there were two images of cars – one on the open road in the US, and one in a traffic jam in London. Karen hadn't noticed these parallel images and the contrast led to a productive discussion about the different associations. Karen's career decision-making self-efficacy seem low as she talked about her inability to make good decisions. The career coach was able to use some of the positive images on the collages to allow Karen to remember some of the good choices she had made, and how she made them. Finally, the images that Karen had used allowed the career coach to explore some of her emotions. The coach asked Karen how she felt when she was, for example, on that ski slope, or on those stairs leading up to her office.

The collage enabled Karen to clarify her thinking and gave rise to some constructive discussions with the coach about her current reality and her future goals.

---

4. Role models

Exercises using role models can be used in a variety of ways in a career coaching setting and are a surprisingly direct way to access your client's unconscious thoughts about their values. A typical role model will be someone whom they admire and aspire to be but to whom they can also relate in some way. This gives an interesting insight to their ideas of possible, future selves.

How: Ask your clients to identify three or four role models: they could be people they know, famous people they've heard of, or even fictitious characters from literature or television. Ask the clients to identify what it is they admire about each role model. Then ask them to articulate in what ways they are similar and in what ways they are different from that person. It can be helpful for the subsequent discussion for your clients to put these thoughts down on paper in the form of a mind map.

Debrief: Ask your clients to identify some themes from their analysis of the role models and the similarities and differences they have identified and share with them any threads you have picked up on. Discuss how these themes might relate to your clients' current career dilemmas and how they fit in both with your client's current life and their future aspirations.

Variations: If your clients need some support with making a particular decision, you could invite them to consider what advice their role models might give them, and explore whether they think this is good advice or not.

Case study

Jason was struggling to work out what he wanted from life. He was in a job he disliked and knew that he wanted to get out, but when his career coach started to ask him what kind of life he envisaged in the future, he couldn't find anything concrete to say. His coach suggested that identifying one or two role models might enable him to see the kind of future he wanted. This resulted in the surprising revelation that he didn't *have* any role models; he genuinely could not think of anyone he knew whose life he wanted. This really helped Jason to understand why he was finding it so hard to work out what he wanted from the future. With the help of his career coach, he began to piece together a composite role model: taking some elements from one person and some from another. Gradually he began to build up a picture of a future that appealed to him. The exercise allowed him to understand why he had been finding the decision so hard, and gave him a starting point for identifying future goals.

---

5. Visualizations

We looked at these techniques in Chapter 12, but they can help to find an alternative route into the client's unconscious thoughts and opinions in a variety of contexts. One group of clients who often benefit from visualizations are those who are finding it difficult to articulate their career aims and to set goals.

How: Ask your clients to close their eyes, relax and imagine themselves five years from now. Next, gently and gradually ask them to start to put the scene together. Get them to think about how they are getting to work, what the building is like and what they are wearing. Then as they go into the building, who do they meet and speak to, and what kind of environment is it? Ask them to work out what is happening, what are they doing and what are other people doing. You can also ask them to look back from their future, asking their future self what steps they took to get there.

Debrief: The nature of the debrief will depend on what you are trying to achieve with the exercise (see the variations below), but you might want to ask your client to think about the images that they conjured up, what they meant to them and how they made them feel.

Variations: The exact nature of the image that you ask your clients to conjure up will depend on the aim of the exercise.

1. Overcoming self-limiting beliefs. As we saw in Chapter 12, visualization can be used to help clients overcome self-limiting beliefs and assist them with coming across well at interviews or during presentations. Here, the coach might ask them to visualize performing at their absolute best in the upcoming situation.
2. Goal-setting. 'The miracle question' is often used in solution-focused coaching (see Chapter 11) to help clients identify goals. The coach asks clients to imagine that they wake up one morning to find that during the night, a miracle has happened and their problem has gone away. The clients are asked to say what is the first thing that they notice that demonstrates the problem has been solved.
3. Decision making. Visualization can be used to help clients decide between different options. If clients are deciding between, for example, staying in their current role and getting a job elsewhere, you could ask them to do two separate visualizations: one of their work life two years down the line if they stay, and one if they leave. You could pause between the two and get them to identify the highs and lows of that particular option, or even give it a rating on a scale of one to ten. Then ask them to provide the same kind of analysis after the second visualization, and this can be the basis for a discussion about the two routes.

Useful for: These techniques are often best used when you have developed a good relationship with your client, as relaxation is key to their success.

Case study

John had a job interview coming up. He had been in his current role for nearly ten years and hadn't had a selection interview for over a decade. His confidence was low and he was feeling very unsure of his ability to come across well.

As part of his career coaching programme, the coach suggested that he might like to try a visualization. His coach asked him to imagine himself in he job interview, performing at his absolute best. The scene played out in his mind's eye. He was wearing a suit, well-ironed shirt and polished shoes. He entered the room confidently, walking tall and with purpose, and held out his hand with a smile. It felt exciting and full of possibilities. The interviewers were impressed with his presence and greeted him warmly. They were looking forward to hearing what he had to say. John broke the ice by asking them if they'd managed to get a break for lunch and after some comfortable chit-chat, the interview started. John was sitting up, leaning into the room and talking with a confident and enthusiastic tone. He was using his hands to emphasize his points and easily communicated his passion for the work. The examples were flowing well and as he watched the interviewers nod and scribble furious notes, he felt that there was clearly a meeting of minds. It felt more like a comfortable conversation than a formal job interview. John left the room and the interviewers looked at each other, nodded and smiled. The job was his.

John played this scene over in his mind every evening in the days running up to the interview itself and used the trigger word 'confidence' to recreate the scene and the feelings that it engendered in him.

John felt that the visualization enhanced his confidence and contributed to his strong performance at interview.

6. Writing a letter to yourself

In contrast to some of the more visually creative tools discussed above, this tool is all about words. It's an imaginative way to get your clients to see their current situation from a different angle.

How: Ask your clients to write themselves a letter. The letter is from their future self, ten years down the line, to their current self. Their future self should simply give their view on the client's present situation, providing a longer-term perspective. It might include some advice on what to do, how to handle the situation and how to view things right now. It might be a call to action, a reminder of the positives of their current situation or some encouragement to keep going.

Debrief: Ask your clients to read the letter out to you, and then ask them to identify the themes and key messages. Encourage them to analyse why their future self has chosen that perspective or that particular piece of advice.

Variations: You can vary the stage from which the future letter should be written (e.g. one year, two years, five years hence), and you could specify the issue that the letter should focus on. Rather than a letter, the written document could be a legacy or eulogy given at the end of a life, or the speech given at your retirement party.

Useful for: Clients who can't see the wood for the trees, as they struggle to get a realistic perspective on their current situation.

Case study

Katherine was feeling that her career had stalled. She had always seen herself as a high flyer but progress now seemed to have dwindled. There had been a couple of promotion opportunities that she hadn't been able to take when she'd been on maternity leave, and now she had two young children, she felt constantly pulled in two directions. To make a real success of herself at work, she needed to spend more time working, but this was inevitably at the expense of time spent interacting with her children. It was really important for her to be a good mother, but she felt frustrated that she didn't have the time to do more career-wise.

Katherine's career coach suggested that she should write herself a letter from her 51-year-old self to her 41-year-old self, giving a perspective on her current situation and some advice about how best to handle it. The thrust of Katherine's letter was that she should relax about her work situation. The future Katherine reminded the current Katherine that her children wouldn't be young for long and that she was sure that she would regret it if she wasted their precious early years stuck behind a computer. She had done well in her career and now had a reasonably senior, relatively well-paid job that, crucially, allowed her to spend time with her children.

In discussion with the career coach, Katherine reported that while the essence of the letter didn't entirely surprise her, she was struck by the clarity of the message.

7. Metaphors

The world of career communication is peppered with the use of metaphors. We talk about career ladders, the career path, square pegs in round holes and the rat race. We highlighted in Chapter 2 the way that metaphors can be used to understand career theories. Here, we find value in using metaphors as a useful tool for work with clients. Metaphorical thinking provides a useful mechanism through which we can sum up a complex, multi-layered situation in a single image. Metaphors help us to see things in different ways, as particular elements take centre stage while others play a supporting role or wait in the wings. As well as conveying the facts about the past and present, they reveal intentions and aspirations for the future and incorporate analysis, judgement and emotional response.

How: Ask your clients to come up with a metaphor that represents their career history. They might want to describe their metaphor with words, or to draw it.

Debrief: When your clients have explained the metaphor to you in some detail, ask them about their emotional response to it: how do they feel about the metaphor and what they feel it says about them and their experiences, and what might it indicate about their future? Ask them to talk about whether they feel their metaphor is an optimistic one and whether it indicates control and confidence.

Variations: If your clients' issues are intricately bound up with their close relationships, you could ask them to imagine what metaphors their loved ones would use to describe their career path. If your clients find it difficult to generate a metaphor from scratch, you could use a tried-and-tested career metaphor and ask them to describe their own experiences in terms of it. For example, you could say, 'if you were to see your career as a journey, tell me a bit about the kind of journey it has been'; or 'if the perfect career were a square peg in a square hole, tell me about the "fit" of your career'.

Useful for: Uncovering new insights into a well-told story.

Case study

Ted came to see the career coach with lots of different minor issues, but no clear sense of what was really troubling him underneath. The coach asked Ted to describe his current work life using a metaphor. Nothing immediately sprang to mind for him, so the coach talked in general terms about metaphors linked with journeys, with building, with fit and with the theatre. Ted immediately thought of a Formula One race. The coach asked him how this symbolized things for him right now, and he talked about the idea of rushing round and round in circles, being far too fast and furious to notice anything, make any conscious choice about the direction or to spot any alternative routes. Ted said that he felt that his work life at the moment was just too full, and even though many of the elements were interesting and fulfilling in themselves, he was so busy that he simply needed to get his head down and get on with work. The coach asked him to imagine a journey where things were different, and the image that popped into Ted's mind was of cycling at a leisurely pace round the French countryside on a tandem. The contrast of the two images helped Ted to understand not only where he was right now, but how he would like things to change in the future.

---

8. Story boarding

Linking in with the narrative ideas of story-telling, story boarding is a way to encourage clients to create a narrative using the idea of a sequence of boxes showing separate scenes as they might appear in a comic strip or graphic novel. In mixing pictures and words, this tool may have unconscious associations with childhood that could help the clients find a new way of looking at their situation. It is also particularly useful for encouraging clients to identify the specific steps or sub-goals that they need to meet in order to fulfil their overall goals.

How: Divide a piece of paper into eight or so squares. Ask your clients to draw a sketch of their current situation in the first square, on the top left of the paper, and their goal in the last square, on the bottom right. Then ask them what needs to go in the squares in-between. It may be that eight squares are not enough for your clients' story, in which case you can add more in; conversely, simply cross out empty squares if eight are too many.

Debrief: When your clients have identified the steps they need to take to reach their goal, gently challenge them to see whether there are any more steps that might be helpful to identify. You might then want to have a discussion around action planning – asking your clients to think about what barriers there might be to achieving these goals, and what support they might need to assist them. It could also be useful to use a rating scale to initiate a discussion around their levels of motivation and whether there is anything that they could do to further increase their commitment to act.

Variations: Use Post-it notes instead of drawing squares on the paper. This allows your clients to play around with the order of the goals and can be useful as they identify sub-goals during the course of the conversation.

Useful for: Clients who need a little extra support in identifying the specific steps they need to take in order to reach their goal.

Case study

Jack was feeling overwhelmed. He was coming to the end of his undergraduate degree and was applying for jobs for when he graduated. He planned to take some time out over the summer holidays and travel around South-East Asia but he needed to earn some money to fund the trip, and had no clear plan for what or how to do this. He felt that he had far too much to do and that all of it was urgent. Jack's career coach gave him a pile of Post-it notes and a large piece of paper, and Jack started off by drawing a picture of each of his goals. Then, taking each in turn, he drew on separate bits of paper each step he needed to take in order to achieve the goals: each piece of coursework, each application form and upcoming interview, and every element of preparation for his trip abroad. He then started to put them all in order in a single timeline, with dates where appropriate.

The final version was long and Jack knew that the next few months would be busy, but it was at least clear and Jack said that he felt a sense of relief at having clarified exactly what needed to be done and when.

I mentioned in Chapter 1 that the use of tools is one thing that distinguishes career coaching from other types of career support. There are dozens of tools that you can find out about from books or the internet that you can use or adapt to the needs of your particular client group. The chances are that a handful will emerge as your favourites, and they will be the ones you find are most consistently effective in your interactions with your clients. But having a wide range of tools and techniques at your disposal will mean that you are able to tailor your coaching interventions to the specific needs of each individual client and ultimately you will be more effective as a practitioner. New ideas are emerging constantly from practitioners and scholars in the career coaching world, and constantly updating your repertoire will help to keep your practice fresh and ensure that you are do the very best for your clients.

FURTHER READING

Heppner, M. J., O'Brien, K. M., Hinkelman, J. M. and Humphrey, C. F. (1994) Shifting the paradigm: The use of creativity in career counseling. *Journal of Career Development*, 21(2): 77–86.

Inkson, K. and Amundson, N. E. (2002) Career metaphors and their application in theory and counseling practice. *Journal of Employment Counseling*, 39(3): 98–108.

Jones, G. and Gorell, R. (2012) *50 Top Tools for Coaching*. London: Kogan Page.

Loader, T. (2009) Careers Collage. *Australian Career Practitioner*, Summer: 16–17.

McMahon, G. and Archer, A. (2010) *101 Coaching Strategies and Techniques*. Hove: Routledge.

Rowan, S. (2011) *Brilliant Career Coach*. Harlow: Pearson.

Part III

Coaching into the world of work

Chapter 15

The world of work

Traditionally within the careers professions distinctions are made between various types of information about the world of work. There is occupational knowledge (what you actually do in particular jobs, what qualifications you need, what you might earn), labour market information (facts and figures about employment trends, what industries are in decline, what regions in the country have high unemployment) and labour market intelligence (an interpretation of these facts). These classifications were devised by careers information professionals to help them structure their libraries and their own research, but were of little benefit to clients. For individuals trying to make sense of the complexities of the world of work, it doesn't really matter how the information is classified; we just want to know whether the job would suit us and if (and how) we would get it. So for the purposes of this chapter, I am eschewing these distinctions and favouring a structure that better reflects the interests of the practitioner and client.

The chapter begins with a debate about *how much* a career coach should know about the world of work, and then in section two moves on to look at *what* we should know, focusing on the kind of information that clients tell us they want, information that we know can have an impact on job satisfaction, and information that can help clients actually get the jobs they apply for. In the third part of the chapter, we will examine some of the research that shows us how people process information and try to make sense of the enormous amount of job-related data that is fed to them. The final section suggests some ways that a coach can help clients to navigate it most effectively and the chapter concludes with a list of websites to help you with your own research.

HOW MUCH SHOULD A CAREER COACH KNOW?

There are different schools of thought surrounding this question. There are career coaches who firmly believe that having a good overview of the labour market, occupational information and local employers is a fundamental part of what they do. Their experience leads them to feel that clients expect a degree of knowledge from them and that they would be doing them a great disservice if they couldn't answer their information queries. You will then find practitioners at every point in the scale, right down to those who feel that there is no place for careers information within a career coaching session, and that a coach who feels the need to inform their client is at best a bad coach, and at worst risks undermining their client's decisions. My own view is that a degree of knowledge can help to make sure that important areas are covered, that clients have confronted the realities of the options they are considering, and that Plan Bs are considered where appropriate. But information should be used sparingly, cautiously and infrequently.

My reason for advocating this caution is that a coaching relationship based on comprehensive labour market information is neither possible nor desirable. Let me expand on this.

1. No one knows everything about the labour market. According to the government categorization, the Standard Occupational Classification (2010), there are 665 groups of occupations; each occupation will have a number of different pathways, routes and specializations and each different employer may have their own versions of what the job entails and how to get there. In addition, a 'full' knowledge would need you to keep up to date with regional, national and international trends, and have a clear idea of future directions and new developments in industries. You will *never* have a complete grasp of all the details of the world of work. Your picture will only ever be partial, so if you set yourself up as a font of all knowledge you will either mislead clients by presenting only the bits of information that you know, or you will lose credibility when clients realize that your expertise is not comprehensive.
2. It is very hard to be objective about information. When it's shared, information is inevitably interpreted, so what you say to your clients will be biased: you will choose what to focus on, how to express it and the tone with which you say it.
3. The philosophy behind coaching is rooted in empowering and enabling, not doing things on behalf of our clients. If we give our clients a piece of information, it may help them in that particular situation, but we have not enhanced their self-efficacy in their own ability to research or encouraged them to develop skills that might help them in the future.
4. Given that the information needed is almost always available within a few clicks on the internet, it doesn't feel like a very good use of resources for a client to spend their time with their coach absorbing information. There are particular skills that a coach can bring to a one-to-one intervention that they would find hard to get anywhere else. Factual information is not one of them.

Do note that I am not suggesting that you don't need to know about the world of work. The issue here is about how, and how much, you share with your clients. Information can and should play a significant role in your interventions but it needs to be used judiciously.

So having made the case that information is important but needs to be handled with care, let's turn now to considering the nature of information that can be of most use to us.

WHAT SHOULD A COACH KNOW?

I have split my analysis of the most useful kinds of information into three groups, looking at the information that clients say they want, information that may influence their future job satisfaction, and information that will help them actually get jobs.

What do clients want?

Clients value information, but rather than seeing career coaches as information givers, they are often more interested in being given routes to access the information for themselves. In a survey for the Warwick Institute for Employment Research (Bimrose and Barnes, 2006), researchers found that 98 per cent of clients who rated their careers intervention as useful reported that the interaction focused, in part, on the labour market but for most, the information given was in the form of signposts to useful websites rather than the careers information itself.

Looking more specifically at the kind of information that is valued, Offer (2000) found that clients in particular are interested in the kind of information that can tell them how likely they are to get a job in a particular field, and how they can maximize those chances. To help clients identify their own chances of getting a given job, they want to know the competition they face, the availability of jobs in particular geographical regions and their chances of success. They also want to know about entry routes, the value of qualifications and the selection and recruitment methods most commonly used in the particular field.

One final finding from Bimrose and Barnes's study (2006) is their observation that people are increasingly interested in information not just about the occupation itself, but about the kind of people who do it and the lifestyles with which they tend to be associated. We talked in Chapter 3 about Brower and Nurius's (1993) concept of the 'niche', which is our individual stereotype of the life lived by holders of certain jobs, and the influence that this has on the career decision-making process. It is interesting to see that client demand is beginning to reflect this.

What information factors contribute to job satisfaction?

One of the useful links that you as a professional can help your client to make, is that between job information and job satisfaction.

A more in-depth exploration of the topic can be found in Chapter 4, but it is useful to refresh our minds about the work factors that can lead to job satisfaction: task variety, colleagues, working conditions, workload, autonomy and educational opportunities.

It can be useful to share the link between these factors and job satisfaction with your clients. If they are trying to choose between two different roles, you might want to talk to them about, for example, the literature that suggests that task variety is a key factor in job satisfaction. You can then use this as the starting point for a discussion about what kind of variety would best suit them, and which of these roles they might find most varied. As with all the research presented in this book, the evidence on job satisfaction concerns trends and likelihoods rather than certainties. Just because there is empirical evidence to show that task variety is linked to job satisfaction, it doesn't mean that this will inevitably be the case for your clients. As noted above, you should also always bear in mind that the notion of task variety is a subjective one: not everyone will share the same opinion of what is a varied job.

These aren't always easy things to find out about: websites will not generally cover many of these issues and to a great degree, these factors are organization-, if not department-specific, so it is nigh on impossible to find out accurately through the usual channels of careers information. But given the impact they can have on a role, they can be a starting point to a valuable conversation.

What is particularly striking about the two sections above is that the lists of career information are different. The information that clients are asking us for is quite distinct from the information that could give them a clue as to how satisfied they are likely to be in their jobs.

Information that can help clients to a more fruitful job hunt

Our clients are, more often than not, ultimately looking to get a job as a result of their coaching sessions, so it is useful to consider the career and occupational information that might help your clients to 'play' the labour market or make themselves more attractive than other applicants.

An understanding of future trends within the economy as a whole and within a particular industry can allow clients to anticipate changes in the job market and to shift their job search strategies accordingly. For example, there is within the fashion industry a suggestion that print designs are becoming increasingly important. Armed with this knowledge, a budding designer might decide to fill her portfolio with designs for fabric, which might be more likely to impress an employer.

An awareness of the job shortage areas within our labour market can also give clients an idea of the specific roles that might be less competitive. It might help an up-and-coming doctor interested in working with children to know that while consultant jobs in paediatric medicine rarely come up and are hotly contested, paediatric surgery is far less competitive.

If a client is interested in re-training or upskilling, a knowledge of the specific technical skills or qualifications that are most desirable can be useful. A client might be able to gain a competitive edge by knowing that, for example, out of the hundreds of journalism courses in the country, there are two which are, by far, the most admired within the profession.

We've spent some time now looking at the sort of information that can be useful to our clients both during the career decision-making process and the job hunting phase. We will move on now to the more complex issue of how we make sense of it all.

HOW DO WE PROCESS CAREERS INFORMATION?

Making sense of careers information is an enormous challenge. We are bombarded with information about jobs, occupations, industries and the economy from all different kinds of angles on a daily basis. Every time we contact a call centre, book a doctor's appointment or buy a stamp, we are feeding, expanding and confusing our understanding of the world of work and we need somehow to put this all together to form a coherent picture that allows us to start to evaluate and make decisions.

Proponents of a trait and factor approach to career choice and a conscious rational approach to decision making would want us to build up an accurate, complete and in-depth picture of the world of work before we start to make any decisions, but this is clearly beyond even the most virtuous of us. So how does it actually work in practice? Bimrose and Barnes (2006: 7) suggest that career decisions are 'based not on careful information searches or on strictly rational processes of deciding, but on a mixture of facts, feelings, ideas and images, forming the perceptions of what is available and how "good" the available options are', which feels like a much more accurate picture of how we build up our mental picture of the world of work in real life.

I have some examples here which illustrate the complexities of our information-processing systems. This is not a comprehensive account of the cognitive processes that go on but will remind us that learning about the world of work is not a straightforward process.

Sauerman (2005) explains how the context in which we learn about occupations influences the judgements we make. People reach different conclusions when evaluating a single option in isolation than they do when evaluating two or more options. You might, for example, give teaching quite a high score on the dimension of 'helping others' when evaluated on its own, but when rated alongside humanitarian aid worker and palliative nursing, its rating is likely to go down.

Occupational information tends to be gleaned from a variety of sources, which will often provide different information, presented in different ways. When comparing occupations (or other options), therefore, you will often not have comparable information. You may, for example, know the starting salaries for all jobs you're considering, but only the levels of autonomy for one, and the typical hours worked for another. Houston *et al.* (2000) showed that factors which you can compare directly are given more weight in your mental calculations than others, regardless of how important the factors are to you. So in this example, even though autonomy might be the single most important factor to you, the conclusions you would draw from your research would be based principally on the starting salaries, because those are the elements you can compare.

Gati and Tikotzki (1989) summarize some of the unconscious heuristics (or rules of thumb) that we have developed to deal with the sheer volume of information available today. One strategy is to focus in on a subset of occupations, making a swift, only partially informed decision to look at jobs in, say, the media before starting to do some more in-depth research in order to decide between TV production and advertising. Alternatively, we go for a single factor and research that widely – for example, jobs with high starting salaries which could lead us to a choice between law and banking. We can become overwhelmed with choices, however, and as information increases, our awareness goes down. When the information goes beyond what we can manage, we will restrict the processing that we do to avoid cognitive stress. The theoretical underpinning of these ideas is provided by cognitive load theory, which gives some great food for thought about the whole arena of information processing.

We don't always evaluate the information that we get with the cold, critical eye of a research scientist. 'Hot' information, which comes from people you know, is much more appealing to us than 'cold' information, which comes from more formal sources such as government websites and career books (Greenbank and Hepworth 2008). This tendency is traditionally something that has been associated with people from working-class backgrounds, but it now seems clear that this effect is shown across all groups. So in career terms, we're much more likely to base our view of how easy it is to make a success of a new business venture on Uncle Bob's thriving company than on the BIS website's claim that 90 per cent of new businesses fold within two years. Compounding this effect, people also have been shown to trust anecdotes, stories and images more than they trust facts.

Then there is the impact of goal direction motivation. Brownstein (2003) has written widely on the topic, describing it as a process that we think is well reasoned but actually is biased to serve a particular purpose. We talked in Chapter 3 about our gut instinct, and here, with information processing, we see again how our unconscious reason can delude our conscious minds. Our unconscious can make an early choice and then force our conscious minds to find information to support this preference. We end up processing information selectively – highlighting and focusing in on information that justifies our decision. Goals also bias the evaluation of research: we believe research that supports our preference but critically question studies that call our choice into question. If, for example, your unconscious has decided that a career as an actor is the one to pursue, you will find that you pay attention to every story you hear about individuals who make a success of an acting career against all the odds, and that you downplay the statistics and anecdotes that you come across to the contrary.

Young people

In most parts of the career decision-making process, there is little distinction between the processes and experiences of different groups of clients. Whether you're 16, 36 or 66, your decision-making processes and the sorts of tools coaches can use to support you are pretty similar. One area where there are significant differences, however, is in our understanding of the world of work.

Bimrose and Barnes (2006) showed that young people conceptualize three types of jobs:

1. Lottery jobs. These are the high-profile, high-status jobs such as pop stars or footballers that young people are exposed to widely in the media. Young people tend to have a relatively accurate perception of their own chances of making a career in this way, understanding the role of chance and the improbable odds.
2. High-status jobs. These jobs share the high status of the lottery jobs, but in this case, it is high-level qualifications that are needed rather than luck. Jobs in this category include medicine and law.
3. Customary jobs. These are the occupations that the young people are directly exposed to, such as jobs of family members.

Young people's view of the world of work is more or less entirely determined by their own experiences. With older clients, there is more often an understanding that a 'wider' world of work exists beyond their own experience and they can be keen to enhance their own knowledge, but young people tend to be more confident that they know all that there is. Jobs are either visible (ones they've had personal access to) or invisible (those they haven't come across) and each job also has visible and invisible parts: a teacher's visible duties, for example, would include standing in front of class, but their lesson planning and Ofsted paperwork would be invisible. One great contribution that a career coach can make to younger clients is to raise awareness that the visible jobs and the visible tasks are not the only ones that exist.

As well as having a certain amount of confidence that they are aware of all existing jobs, it seems that although they have less experience and knowledge of the world of work, young people's views are fairly well entrenched. The process of actively researching careers information does make them better informed but doesn't tend to make them think more broadly. When presented with new information about careers, they have been shown to attend only to the information that is linked to their already chosen career. They will end up with a fuller picture about that particular career option, but are less likely to have added any alternatives to their shortlist of occupational choices.

New information is overlaid on old information rather than replacing it. One interesting study (cited in Bimrose *et al.* 2005) evaluated the impact of a careers event that aimed to change young people's perceptions of engineering. The pupils had previously conceptualized engineering as 'a dirty job' and the event organizers wanted to encourage them to think about the intellectual complexities of the profession. The upshot was that the careers event led the young people to think of engineering as a dirty job that needed maths and physics.

The situation for all kinds of career decision makers trying to make sense of the world of work is not straightforward. The structure of traditional careers education presupposed that we learned about the labour market in a logical and objective way, and that the main function of a careers library was to provide all the information that might be needed and then sit back and allow clients to read and process it in isolation. The research quoted above suggests that actually analysing and evaluating careers information is an extraordinarily complex process, and that through a better understanding of how it all works, a coach can considerably enhance a client's information analysis.

HOW TO USE THESE IDEAS IN YOUR PRACTICE

Using information to guide your input during the intervention

A valuable – arguably the most valuable – way to apply your knowledge of the world of work is to use it to help you structure your intervention. Your expertise can help you to know when and how far to challenge your client; it can allow you to push where you need to push and leave things when there is no need to pursue; and it can help you decide whether it is likely to be useful to a client to think about alternatives, do further research or spend more time honing their skills. And you can do all this without telling your client a single thing.

Your client might present to you wondering about making a career for themselves in what you know is a industry very much on the decline. You, of course, are not in a position to predict what is going to happen to the industry, whether or not this client might make a very satisfactory career in its dying embers, or indeed use a brief career in it as a springboard for something different but equally satisfying. Then again, you might feel that it could be helpful to your client to make their decision with their eyes fully open to the situation and to the future. As a coach, you might choose to ask the client about the research they have done in this field, and what their understanding is of the industry at the moment, and whether they know anything about the trends for the future. Naturally these are questions that you might well ask any client about any field, but if you are in possession of this kind of labour market insight, you will probably stick with this line of questioning a little longer and perhaps be a little firmer than you might with a client whose industry of choice is growing and thriving.

Case study

John was really keen to break into advertising. He and his coach were both very aware that this was a highly competitive area, and that jobs were always hotly contested. John showed the coach his CV, which was well written, relevant and neatly laid out. It was not, however, creative. The coach had recently been talking to a recruiter within the advertising industry and was aware that creativity was a highly valued attribute. He had been told stories of the kinds of CVs that made it through to the shortlist: the winning ones all had something that made them stand out, and the recruiters had made it clear that they would be more likely to be attracted by a CV that was a little out of the ordinary. The coach used this information to help direct her questioning. She asked John what impression he thought his standard layout would give, and asked him to compare that to the ideal image that the recruiter might have in mind.

At this stage, John might have made the decision to stick with his original layout, or to experiment with something that better reflected his creative side. But the coach's knowledge allowed her to ask the question that encouraged him to think it through.

Giving information directly

At the beginning of the chapter, I gave my reasons for advocating restraint whenever you are tempted to give information directly, but there are exceptions and it *can* sometimes be valuable to share information with clients. Here are the three types of information that I most commonly give my clients.

Websites or other resources

The internet allows us all to access at the touch of a button or two all the information that we could ever possibly want, but it also provides two key challenges. First, how you find your way to the websites that are going to be of most use to you; second, how to ensure that the information you are reading is of good quality. Clients can therefore appreciate some suggested websites: ones that you have used, or been recommended and that you feel confident are accurate and up to date. There are also books, articles, and events that you might know about that could provide your clients with useful information, and in sharing resources rather than sharing information directly, you can preserve the relationship of equals that is so important to the coaching process.

Entry level pre-requisites

If clients are talking about a specific career area and you know that it requires, for example, particular A levels or a degree, it can be helpful to share this with your client to make sure that they factor this in to their thinking early on. A two-hour coaching session focusing on primary teaching, setting goals, identifying steps and increasing motivation might be seen as a disappointing waste of time when the clients discover later down the line that the maths GCSE (that they feel that they could never, never get) is a pre-requisite for teacher training.

Job ideas

This is more controversial and takes delicate handling. The challenge here is that if you are not very careful, you can set yourself up as the expert job idea generator, which both detracts from the client-centred heart of the coaching relationship and may encourage the client to give more weight to your suggestions that perhaps they warrant. But sometimes it can be helpful to clients if your suggestions are made tentatively and prefaced appropriately. Finally, as a career coach you will sometimes find out about very niche, obscure, unusual jobs or courses that your clients may simply not be aware of such as a fashion forecaster, or a search engine optimization consultant.

STRATEGIES FOR SHARING INFORMATION WITH CLIENTS

There are a few important things to bear in mind when sharing information with clients.

The first challenge is maintaining a good coaching relationship if much of the session is spent informing your client. The client-centred bedrock of coaching assumes that the client has the answer and is the expert. If you say too much, this can shift the balance to 'coach as expert', which can lead to the client taking a more passive role in the relationship.

Second, you should always bear in mind that people cannot process a lot of information at once. Our brains can cope with only about seven different items at one time (Miller's 1956 'magic number seven') and beyond that, information gets forgotten or confused. The amount of information that you communicate to your client therefore needs to be limited. It can be quite effective for you to provide the information in written form or encourage your client to write it down themselves, but it is always a good idea to genuinely prioritize what you tell them in the hope that your message sticks.

Finally, it's better if the client can generate the information themselves. Confucius's maxim 'I hear and I forget' is a good one to keep in the back of your mind when you're tempted to share your wisdom. If you can use appropriate questions, make good use of silence and employ some coaching tools, more often than not you get your client to find their own answer.

Coaches sometimes like to ask permission before making a suggestion: 'A couple of ideas have popped into my mind while we've been talking. I wonder if you would mind if I shared them with you?' This has the benefit of maintaining the sense of the client being in control. Sometimes there is a very good reason why a client hasn't mentioned an apparently obvious choice and it can be useful to ask about this: ' "teaching" is a job that would seem to meet all your requirements but it's not one that you have mentioned. I wonder why that is?' Or you can be explicit with your caveats: 'you would obviously be the best judge of whether these might fit the bill, but I wondered if you would be interested in adding teaching to your list of ideas?'

Sources of information

I have thought carefully about whether to include this section. I have a few concerns, the first of which is that this information will date. Careers information changes constantly, and information over two years old is generally thought to be worse than no information. Second, this is my list, not yours. The kind of information you find useful and which sources you trust and find accessible is terribly personal; *I* find these sites useful, but they may just not work for you. Third, and very much in the 'enabling' spirit of coaching, I think you can learn a lot by trawling through websites and a short cut, although attractive at the time, may not help you to build up your own bank of knowledge.

On the more positive side, however, practitioners may find the information useful. So in the spirit of any short cuts being a good thing, I am going to tentatively give you some ideas of places to start, with the caveats that this is not exhaustive and is very much my list of what works for me.

The information here is all web-based, but the links will often recommend books and journals. The authors of the websites I cite here tend to have fixed guidelines to work to when putting the text together. The result is that the information is likely to be factual and accurate, but perhaps not terribly personal and anecdotal. Book authors (and this of course will vary from book to book) tend to be able to inject a little more personality into their writing, so you can sometimes get a more readable and real version of the role from a printed volume. Journals then cover the industry from a different angle, providing up-to-date news about industry trends, employers and individuals, and will often provide details of events and vacancies.

Occupational and sector information

One solid place to start is with the Sector Skills Councils. Every industry within the UK is allocated to a Sector Skills Council, which are government-funded portals whose remit includes providing labour market information. As such they are reliable, objective and comprehensive.

Another useful group of websites are the professional bodies. These are organizations funded by members to support their professional needs, and one of their usual roles is to promote the particular profession or sector to potential new recruits. Their information tends to be accurate and up to date but they do, of course, have an agenda which you need to bear in mind when reading their pages. A full list of professional bodies can be found easily on Wikipedia: http:// en.wikipedia.org/ wiki/List_of_professional_associations_in_the_United_Kingdom

Vacancies

There are hundreds of job vacancy websites, focusing on different regions, different industries, different target audiences and with different agendas. The best known include Worktrain (www.worktrain.gov.uk), Monster Jobs (www. monster.co.uk), Fish4 (http://fish4.co.uk/jobs/index.jsp), The *Guardian* jobs section (http://jobs.guardian.co.uk), Doctorjob.com (www.doctorjob.com) and Gumtree (www.gumtree.com).

For comprehensive and objective information on graduate jobs, associated vacancy bulletins, and a vocational interests matching questionnaire, the Pro-spects website is a good resource (www.prospects.ac.uk). The Association of Graduate Recruiters (www.agr.org.uk) has some useful information on trends and developments for the organizations who run graduate training schemes, including information on shortage areas and skills.

Further study . . . or not

For those choosing university courses, Unistats (http://unistats.direct.gov.uk/) is a government-funded website that allows you to compare universities and courses on the basis of various criteria such as employability statistics, number of tutor contact hours, and so on. The PUSH guide (www.push.co.uk) does something similar, but with rather more personality.

For a whole range of different kinds of course, including evening classes and FE courses, the Hot Courses website is easy to navigate (www.hotcourses.com).

Not Going to Uni (http://www.notgoingtouni.co.uk) does pretty much what it says on the tin, providing a really useful range of information about gap years, apprenticeship, jobs and events.

Facts and figures

The NOMIS site (www.nomisweb.co.uk) is a good place to find out about local labour market information. The data is supplied by the civil service Office of National Statistics but while it is robust, it is in a raw form and you will have to do the analysis yourself. The Department for Business, Innovation and Skills (www.bis.gov.uk) can give you access to information, data and support around a wide range of employment issues, including legal matters and advice on starting up your own business. The Office for National Statistics (www.ons.gov.uk) provides a wealth of reports and articles about the labour force, from all different angles, including age, race, gender and salary.

Social media

Resources such as blogs and Facebook or LinkedIn groups can be a great way to inject some reality and life into your understanding of a career. They can provide a 'warts and all' version of a job, which can be valuable, but when you're reading them it's vital to remember that this is just one person's subjective experience and there will be no one out there assessing them for accuracy or generalizability. For this reason, it is an area that I shall leave to you to research, and I suggest that you leave it to your clients in turn.

REFERENCES

Bimrose, J., Barnes, S. A., Green, A., Orton, M. and Davies, R. (2005) *Enhancement of the National Resource Service: Local Labour Market Information (LLMI)*. Warwick: Institute for Employment Research, pp. 3–5.

Bimrose, J. and Barnes, S. A. (2006) Is career guidance effective? Evidence from a longitudinal study in England. *Australian Journal of Career Development*, 15(2): 19–25.

Brower, A. M. and Nurius, P. S. (1993) *Social Cognition and Individual Change*. London: SAGE Publications.

Brownstein, A. L. (2003). Biased predecision processing. *Psychological Bulletin*, 129(4): 545–568.

Frey, D. (1982) Different levels of cognitive dissonance, information seeking, and information avoidance. *Journal of Personality and Social Psychology*, 43(6): 1175–1183.

Gati, I. and Tikotzki, Y. (1989) Strategies for collection and processing of occupational information in making career decisions. *Journal of Counseling Psychology*, 36: 430–439.

Greenbank, P. and Hepworth, S. (2008) *Working Class Students and the Career Decision-Making Process: A qualitative study.* (Report for the Higher Education Careers Service Unit.) Manchester: HECSU.

Houston, D. A., Sherrill-Mittleman, D. and Weeks, M. (2000) The enhancement of feature salience in dichotomous choice dilemmas. In E. U. Weber, J. Baron and G. Loomes (eds), *Conflict and Trade-offs in Decision Making*. Cambridge: Cambridge University Press, pp. 65–85.

Miller, G. A. (1956) The magical number seven plus or minus two: some limits on our capacity for processing information. *Psychological Review*, 63: 81–97.

Office for National Statistics. (2010) *Standard Occupational Classification 2010*. London: ONS.

Offer, M. (2000) The discourse of the labour market. In B. Gothard, P. Mignot, M. Offer and M. Ruff (eds), *Careers Guidance in Context*. London: SAGE Publications, pp. 78–79.

Sauermann, H. (2005) Vocational choice: A decision-making process. *Journal of Vocational Behavior*, 66: 273–303.

Chapter 16

Job search strategies

When it comes to a strategy for job hunting, the received wisdom from career practitioners is generally that people should put more time in to looking for more jobs in more ways (for example, Nelson Bolles 2012). There is, of course, a lot of common sense in this advice but in this chapter we are going to look beyond our instinct to examine the empirical evidence. We will introduce the topic by looking at three different ways to conceptualize job hunting strategies and then go on to look at what determines the specific types of strategy that individuals adopt. In the second section, we will examine which job seeking strategies are the most effective and end with some ideas for incorporating this information into practice.

WHAT DIFFERENT JOB SEARCH STRATEGIES ARE THERE?

People have classified job hunting in many different ways.

The first framework we will look at here describes the different chronological phases of the job hunt. Blau (1993 and 1994) splits the typical job search into three separate phases through which job seekers progress in sequence. In the preparatory phase, the individual gathers information and identifies potential leads. This takes them to the second phase, in which specific jobs and organizations that might be of interest are identified. In the third stage, the individual is engaged in active job search and choice, which comprises activities such as sending CVs, responding to adverts and attending job interviews. Saks and Ashforth (2000) add a fourth dimension of career planning which would precede these three. They describe this initial stage as 'setting career goals and formulating strategies for realizing those goals' (2000: 647).

Stevens and Turban (2001) provide our second conceptualization, identifying three styles of job hunting: focused, exploratory and haphazard. An individual involved in either a focused or an exploratory job hunt will have high standards and will be looking for a job that suits them well and leads to a high degree of job satisfaction. A focused job hunt will also be goal-directed, with the individual having a clear sense of where they are heading. An exploratory job hunt will have no clear goal but will involve finding out about a wide range of options, and will respond to the opportunities and ideas that emerge through the process. A haphazard job hunt has no specified goal, and no aim other than to get the first possible job.

Two other key concepts here are those of job search intensity and job search effort. Job search intensity refers to how many approaches you make during your job hunt – how many jobs you apply for, how many CVs you send off and so forth. Job search effort refers to how much time you spend on your job search altogether. Although these sound similar, they are distinct concepts. You could, for example, have high job search intensity and low job search effort if you sent off a hundred identical CVs to the names on a list you've been given, but high effort and low intensity if you spent days crafting a perfect CV to send to one particular employer.

Individuals opt for one strategy over another for a range of reasons. Personality plays a great part, with extraversion (Kanfer *et al.* 2001), conscientiousness and a proactive personality (Brown *et al.* 2006) all being linked with job search effort, job search intensity and a tendency to use networking as a job search strategy. Conscientiousness is also more likely to lead to an emphasis on the planning stage of the process (Crossley and Highhouse 2005) and a focused job hunting strategy. Kanfer *et al.* (2001) found that one of the best predictors of job search behaviour was the individual's social context: the more social support you have, the more effort you are likely to put into your job hunt.

Having looked briefly at some of the concepts underpinning the job search process itself, let's move on to the key question and explore the evidence for the kind of job search strategy that is most likely to lead to success.

WHICH JOB SEARCH STRATEGIES ARE BEST?

The research paints a complicated and patchy picture of the elements that lead to a successful job hunt. Figure 16.1 summarizes the research into the factors that increase your chances of more job offers or that seem to lead to a higher quality job.

But what exactly is meant by a 'successful' job hunt? At the most straightforward level, you could simply say that a successful job hunt is one that results in a job, so you could opt for what the literature refers to as 'employment status' as your definition. You could extend it a little to look at the strategies that result in the most job offers, or that result in the quickest route to a job offer. And then one stage after that would be to look at the quality of the job you get – either in terms of objective success such as salary or seniority, or by the subjective measures of job satisfaction.

We will look now at the evidence that show links between different kinds of job search and different kinds of outcomes.

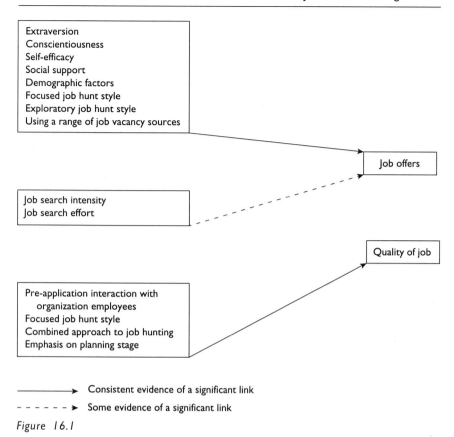

Extraversion
Conscientiousness
Self-efficacy
Social support
Demographic factors
Focused job hunt style
Exploratory job hunt style
Using a range of job vacancy sources

Job search intensity
Job search effort

Pre-application interaction with
   organization employees
Focused job hunt style
Combined approach to job hunting
Emphasis on planning stage

Job offers

Quality of job

Consistent evidence of a significant link

Some evidence of a significant link

Figure 16.1

The process

There has been considerable attention paid to the links between job search intensity and effort, and job search outcomes. Common sense would lead you to think that both intensity and effort should be linked to better employment outcomes, but the research paints a relatively complex picture.

Some research suggests that although the scattergun job search (i.e. more approaches to more companies) gets you more interviews and job offers (Saks 2006), it is the amount of effort you put in to each approach that leads to an offer that you actually want to accept (Kanfer *et al.* 2001). Based on this, clients might be well advised to apply for fewer jobs, but to spend more time on each one. The evidence isn't entirely consistent, however, and some studies (e.g. Šverko *et al.* 2008) suggest that demographic factors such as education, age and employment duration have much more impact than the amount and type of effort people devote to their job hunt. One or two studies (e.g. Song *et al.* 2006) have even found a *negative* relationship between job search intensity and the speed of re-employment, which might indicate the counter-intuitive idea that a leisurely job search is a better approach .

So if the evidence does perhaps suggest that putting in more effort to a job hunt isn't necessarily the best way to improve your chances, what alternative strategies can we offer our clients?

There are five individual factors that appear to have a significant impact on job search outcomes (Kanfer *et al.* 2001). First, there are the personality traits of extraversion and conscientiousness. Extraversion is a job hunting bonus for a number of reasons, as individuals with high levels of this trait tend to have advantages at both identifying opportunities (because they are more actively engaged with a wider network) and getting through job interviews (Chapter 18, which covers interview coaching, explains this in more detail). Conscientiousness tends to lead individuals to plan, pay attention to detail and work thoroughly and thoughtfully, all of which can have quite an impact on the success of a job search or application.

Using this information with your clients

Although it is arguably impossible to change our underlying personality traits, it is quite within our powers to change how we behave. An understanding of our traits and the impact that our instinctive behaviour may have can allow us to make decisions about how we want to behave. Clients who score low on conscientiousness may find it more difficult to approach their job hunt in a careful and considered way, but they are perfectly capable of changing their behaviour if they so wish. You, as their career coach, can talk to them about the kinds of behavioural patterns that are more likely to lead to a job offer and encourage them to explore whether they would like to make a change in the light of this new information.

On top of these two personality factors, there are other individual factors that have been shown to have an impact on your chances of getting a job. Significant social support is one such. It has been shown that being surrounded by family and friends who support your decision, show an interest in the process and can be there for you when the rejection letters come through really makes a difference, not just to how you feel about your job hunt, but to how quick and how successful it can be. The two last individual factors are self-esteem and job search self-efficacy. Although related ideas, the self-esteem is a broader concept, referring to how you feel about yourself generally, while job search self-efficacy indicates how confident you are specifically about your ability to find a job. Both have quite an impact on how successful your job hunt is; individuals with high self-esteem tend to have shorter job hunts, and those with the highest job search self-efficacy tend to have the highest number of job offers (Kanfer *et al.* 2001).

Another variable that has been shown to have an impact on the outcomes of the job hunt is the job search style that you adopt. Job hunting that follows a logical and considered path, such as the focused or exploratory strategies of Stevens and Turban (2001), is likely to result in a larger number of job offers than an intuitive or haphazard style. But if your goal is to land a job that provides ongoing job satisfaction, then it's wise to combine job search styles, mixing a goal-directed focus with some intuition and exploration (Koen *et al.* 2010). This recommendation to combine styles echoes that given in Chapter 3 when we explored career decision-making processes.

Following on from this, there are some other factors that have been shown to have an impact on whether your job search leads to a job that suits you. Making links with the organization before you apply seems to correlate positively with a better person–organization fit, so it can be of great benefit to your clients to engage in some informal communication, whether with the recruiters or other employees within the organization, before preparing their application (Rynes 1991).

Finally, there is some information about which stages of the job search process are most crucial when it comes to long-term job satisfaction. It seems (Saks and Ashforth 2000) that if you research your job area thoroughly, you are more likely to end up feeling confident that you're applying for a job that will suit you well. However, the effort put into researching does not correlate with how well suited you actually feel once you're in post. The job search behaviour that is going to increase your chances of finding a job that suits you and makes you happy longer term is putting extra effort into the career planning stage – setting goals and identifying strategies. This is a really useful piece of evidence to share with your clients, and suggests that some goal-orientated coaching early on in the job search process can have a positive and more enduring impact.

Sources of vacancies

Much attention has been paid to networking as a source of job information in the last decade or so. Networking has been found to be an effective way to get job offers, but not necessarily the best way to find the right job. It has been shown to increase the likelihood of finding a job but only in that it increases the amount of effort that you're putting in to a job search. It does not add incrementally over other strategies, so improves your chances only if you do it in addition to your existing methods, rather than instead of them (Wanberg *et al.* 2000), although there is a suggestion that it comes into its own when the employment climate is more challenging, so could be particularly useful for clients in the current employment market.

Saks (2006) looked at the relative impact of using formal or informal sources of information. This piece of research found some evidence that basing your job search on informal sources is more likely to lead to jobs (and indeed to well-paid jobs), but that formal sources are more likely to lead to a job that is a good person–environment fit. This could suggest that in job hunting through your networks, you tend to apply for whatever jobs happen to come up, whereas when you are job hunting through more formal sources you will be rather more selective about what you apply for. Van Hoye and Lievens (2009) provided some evidence that relates to this, showing a correlation between the amount of time you spend networking and the number of job offers you get, but also a negative relationship between the amount of time you spend networking and the employment outcomes of both employment status (actually being in work) and job–organization fit, which is an indication of how suitable the job is. According to this evidence, then, networking leads to numerous offers of inappropriate jobs: jobs that people don't accept, or that people accept but find they are not well suited to when they start.

But the research isn't entirely consistent. Griffeth *et al.* (1997) showed that employees who were recruited via word of mouth tended to be good news for the employer, demonstrating more organizational commitment and being less likely to leave than those recruited from more traditional sources. As organizational commitment and low turnover are two factors linked to higher levels of job satisfaction, we might infer that there is a link between finding your job through networking and being happy in it, which is at odds with van Hoye's findings. Zottoli and Wanous (2000) provide a plausible explanation for this, and suggest that both the employer and the candidate will use the informal conversations as a way to pre-screen and only the most apparently suitable candidates will go forward. A further explanation for the positive outcomes of word-of-mouth recruitment is that the referring existing employee is likely to act as a mentor to the new recruit, easing their way into the organization.

Van Hoye also explored the kind of network that is most likely to be effective and found, perhaps predictably, that the bigger your network and the closer the ties within it, the more time you are likely to spend networking. More surprisingly, he found that the kind of network that has been shown to be the most effective in terms of leading to a suitable job is a network that is joined by *weak* ties. The theory here is that within a network of strong ties, everyone will tend to know everyone else, so you end up with a narrower pool of potential opportunities. Weak ties would tend to indicate a network that stretches out in different directions and is more likely to give you access to a wider pool of job opportunities. This would allow you to have more choice and therefore you have the opportunity to opt for a more suitable job. The status of the people within your network predicts the status of the job offers that they are likely to lead you to. So the message for our clients is that to find a suitable, high-level job, they should fill their network with high-status people who don't know each other very well.

The research on networks and networking seems to be giving us conflicting messages. Van Hoye suggests that it leads to jobs with a poor person–organization fit, while Griffeth's findings suggest the opposite. Van Hoye's study suggests that a high level of networking is actually less likely to find you a job, but Wanberg's meta-analysis suggests that networking does lead to more job offers and a greater chance of being employed. So how do we as practitioners make sense of these apparent contradictions and how can we use the research to support our clients? Van Hoye's work on the nature of networks holds a possible key. There is no single concept of 'networking'. A network can be a very few close family and friends, or it can be the 500+ LinkedIn group, populated by everyone you've ever encountered in a personal and professional context, plus specially targeted potentially useful contacts you've never met before. And the process of 'networking' can range from letting a few people who ask know that you are looking for a new job to proactively targeting everyone you know, encouraging them to ask their contacts, and asking them to keep an eye out for opportunities for you. This diverse range of concepts perhaps means that research looking at 'networking' as a single entity only gives us limited understanding of the process and how it actually works. Van Hoye's study looking at the relative effectiveness of different types of networks is interesting, and the academic community should be encouraged to do more along these lines.

In order to maximize their chances of getting a job, clients should:
- Develop networks full of people they don't know very well.
- Adopt a 'focused' or an 'exploratory' job hunt.
- Surround themselves with supportive people.
- Develop their job search self-efficacy.
- Have high scores on extraversion and conscientiousness.
- Put in more effort to their job hunt.

To maximize their chances of getting a 'good' job, clients should:
- Use networks to find out about job leads.
- Develop networks full of high status people.
- Put extra effort in at the career planning phase.
- Make links with organizations before applying.
- Adopt a 'focused' job hunt.
- Combine logical decision making with intuition.
- Make fewer applications but put more effort into each one.

The academics have not made it easy for us. The research around job search strategies is complex and sometimes contradictory. Terms that sound the same actually mean something different and although there are many different theories, they are not always backed up by evidence, nor are they consistently helpful in our practice. But by unpicking it carefully, there are some messages that you can take to your clients. First and foremost is that time put into goal setting and planning a strategy will not be wasted, although you shouldn't always ignore the advice from your inner voice. People can make a great difference to the process. Widen your networks: don't feel that you should limit your networks to people that you know well, but rather make an active effort to get to know people on the periphery of your acquaintance. In addition, make contacts at organizations you are considering applying to and surround yourself with supportive friends while you are going through the process. Finally, work smarter, not just harder, tailoring each application to the particular opportunity and again devoting some energy to making contact with the organization before you apply.

While we wait for a clearer picture to emerge from the academic world, these are useful, practical and tangible messages to be passed on to clients.

REFERENCES

Blau, G. (1993) Further exploring the relationship between job search and voluntary individual turnover. *Personnel Psychology*, 46: 313–330.

Blau, G. (1994) Testing a two-dimensional measure of job search behavior. *Organizational Behavior and Human Decision Processes*, 59: 288–312.

Brown, D. J., Cober, R. T., Kane, K., Levy, P. E. and Shalhoop, J. (2006) Proactive personality and the successful job search: A field investigation with college graduates. *Journal of Applied Psychology*, 91(3): 717–726.

Crossley, C. D. and Highhouse, S. (2005) Relation of job search and choice process with subsequent satisfaction. *Journal of Economic Psychology*, 26: 255–268.

Griffeth, R. W., Hom, P. W., Fink, L. S. and Cohen, D. J. (1997) Comparative tests of multivariate models of recruiting sources effects. *Journal of Management*, 23: 19–36.

Kanfer, R., Wanberg, C. R. and Kantrowitz, T. M. (2001) Job search and employment: A personality–motivational analysis and meta-analytic review. *Journal of Applied Psychology*, 86(5): 837–855.

Kirkman, B. L. and Rosen, B. (1999) Beyond self-management: Antecedents and consequences of team empowerment. *Academy of Management Journal*, 42: 58–74.

Knouse, S. B. (2009) Targeted recruiting for diversity: Strategy, impression management, realistic expectations, and diversity climate. *International Journal of Management*, 26(3): 347–353.

Koen, J., Klehe, U., Van Vianen, A. E. M., Zikic, J. and Nauta, A. (2010) Job-search strategies and reemployment quality. *Journal of Vocational Behavior*, 77(1): 126–139.

Nelson Bolles, R. (2012) *What Color Is Your Parachute?* New York: Ten Speed Press.

Rynes, S. L. (1991) Recruitment, job choice, and post-hire consequences: A call for new research directions. In M. D. Dunnette (ed.), *Handbook of Industrial and Organizational Psychology*, 2nd ed. Palo Alto, CA: Consulting Psychologists Press, pp. 399–444.

Saks, A. M. and Ashforth, B. E. (2002) Is job search related to employment quality? It all depends on the fit. *Journal of Applied Psychology*, 87: 646–654.

Saks, A. M. and Ashforth, B. E. (2000) Change in job search behaviors and employment outcomes. *Journal of Vocational Behavior*, 56: 277–328.

Saks, A. M. (2006) Multiple predictors and criteria of job search success. *Journal of Vocational Behavior*, 68: 400–415.

Song, Z., Wanberg, C., Niu, X. and Yizhong, X. (2006) Action-state orientation and the theory of planned behavior: A study of job search in China. *Journal of Vocational Behavior*, 68: 490–495.

Stevens, C. K. and Turban, D. B. (2001) Impact of job seekers' search strategies and tactics on search success. Paper presented at the annual conference of the Society for Industrial and Organizational Psychology.

Šverko, B., Galić, Z., Seršić, D. M. and Galešić, M. (2008) Unemployed people in search of a job: Reconsidering the role of search behavior http://www.sciencedirect.com/science/article/pii/S0001879107001212 - item1. *Journal of Vocational Behavior*, 72(3): 415–428.

Van Hoye, G., van Hooft, E. J. and Lievens, F. (2009) Networking as a job search behaviour: A social network perspective. *Journal of Occupational and Organizational Psychology*, 82(3): 661–682.

Van Hoye, G. and Lievens, F. (2009) Tapping the grapevine: A closer look at word-of-mouth as a recruitment source. *Journal of Applied Psychology*, 94(2): 341–352.

Wanberg, C. R., Kanfer, R. and Banas, J. T. (2000) Predictors and outcomes of networking behavior among unemployed job-seekers. *Journal of Applied Psychology*, 85: 491–503.

Zottoli, M. A. and Wanous, J. P. (2000) Recruitment source research: Current status and future direction. *Human Resource Management Review*, 10(4): 353.

Chapter 17

CV coaching

One of the most sought-after services that a career coach can offer is help with constructing a winning CV. There are several reasons for the popularity of this kind of service. First of all, everyone needs one. Even those whose career paths are clearly mapped out will usually need to draw one up at some point, and most of us will need a suitable CV at each job or career change throughout our working lives, so there is a lot of demand. Second, seeking professional help for a CV can constitute an unthreatening first step towards getting assistance with a bigger issue. Making a career choice can be a daunting prospect and the idea of going to see a career coach to get some support with this major change can be intimidating enough to put people off altogether. Booking an appointment to have your CV looked at, in contrast, can feel much less personal and much less overwhelming, so is often used as a safe starting point.

And the CV is still important. Although many industries and organizations are now using application forms instead of them, they are still very widely used at the first stage of selection, and there is some evidence that the impression the recruiter gets of the applicant at the CV stage has an impact on their perceptions of that candidate at interview. Dougherty *et al.* (1994) showed that interviewers actually change their interviewing behaviour to allow them to confirm the impressions they have gleaned from the CV. So a good CV can do more than just get you an interview, it can support you right through to a job offer.

Sadly, despite their popularity, they are not particularly reliable as selection tools. Employers tend to infer certain personality characteristics from reading a CV, but these inferences have been shown to be neither terribly reliable, nor valid. Cole *et al.* (2009) conducted a large-scale study looking at employers' inferences of candidates' personality traits and found that there was poor inter-rater reliability (i.e. two recruiters reading the same CV would interpret their personalities quite differently) and that the employers' ratings did not correlate well with candidates' actual personality scores. Nevertheless, employers' ratings of candidates' personalities on paper had quite an impact on the employers' ratings of the candidates' personalities at and after interview.

The first part of the chapter will be devoted to what makes a good CV, focusing on the empirical evidence for what makes a successful one. We'll then move on to discuss the practicalities of non-directive CV coaching, introducing the EPIC model as a framework.

WHAT MAKES A GOOD CV?

The evidence

There is extraordinarily little empirical evidence about what makes a winning CV. Over a decade ago, Thomas *et al.* (1999) commented that 'unfortunately, there is little empirical evidence that provides clear résumé guidance' (1999: 339–40) and the research conducted in the last ten years has only gone so far in redressing this. They point out that 'although much advice has been given about how to write and structure a résumé, conflicting opinions regarding résumé characteristics are commonplace', highlighting the gulf between what we think we know and what we actually know. But not only is there a limited supply of good quality empirical evidence available, we also need to be cautious in generalizing the findings from the studies that have been produced. Much of the research done in this field has focused on asking recruiters what they like in a CV rather than conducting research projects that measure what kinds of CVs actually lead to interviews. Although this is interesting and we could easily imagine a link between what employers say and what they do, we can't be sure. Then there is an issue of the geographical provenance of the research. Nearly all the research published has come from the United States, with just a smattering of papers from Europe and Australia, and what is desirable in a CV seems to be so varied between these regions that we should be very cautious about generalizing from other cultures. Finally, most of the research has been conducted on groups of college graduates as they find their first substantive jobs. This tends to be a very over-studied group, as they are so readily available to the university academics who conduct most of the published research. While they are useful group to research – they are relatively homogenous and are looking for work at the same time – it is hard to know to what extent any findings are generalizable to other groups.

With those caveats in place, let's move on to a summary of the key findings.

What to include

The three key areas which are shown consistently to have an impact on employers' ratings of candidates are their academic qualifications, work experience and extracurricular activities. The relative importance of these three areas, however, is still the subject of some debate. A few studies suggest that employers may place more weight on work experience than on educational achievements (e.g. McNeilly and Barr 1997; Cole *et al.* 2004) although Kinicki and Lockwood (1985) argue that academic and extracurricular activities are given greater weight for entry-level jobs as the work experience that most candidates have at this stage tends not to be very relevant to the job.

There seems to be some evidence that employers are impressed with information that is specifically relevant to the position for which the candidate is applying. Knouse (1994) showed that it is the relevance of the experience in the CV that is key to impressing employers, and Thomas *et al.* (1999) found some evidence that employers are interested in a description of academic course work if it can be directly related to the job.

When it comes to academic achievements, it seems that it is advisable to specify grades or marks if they are impressive, but better to leave them out altogether otherwise. Thomas *et al.* (1999) found that employers responded most positively to the inclusion of high secondary school grades (US Grade Point Average of 3 and above); the second highest scores went to CVs which didn't specify grades, and least positively to the inclusion of low grades.

Employers also use biodata such as information about interests and work experience to allow them to assess candidates' personalities, even though the reliability of this kind of measure is questionable. The research has reported mixed findings, and there is even some evidence that the specific qualities that employers infer from the biodata depend on the kinds of role they are recruiting for. Brown and Campion (1994), for example, found that employers felt that experience in sales implied good interpersonal skills when they were recruiting for a job that involved significant work with people, but did not think it implied interpersonal skills when recruiting for a job in accounts. Nemanick and Clark (2002) showed that employers are influenced by the number of activities and the number of leadership positions held by an applicant, finding candidates who have taken positions of responsibility in a significant number of activities impressive. It is thought that

Brown and Campion (1994) conducted a study into what attributes are inferred from which different kinds of biodata in US college students and found some interesting results.

If you want to convince an employer that you have drive and energy, pretty much anything will do – good grades, work experience, elected offices, specific achievements in a job. If you want to show your interpersonal skills, then elected offices, college clubs and athletics captains have the strongest links in employers' minds. To demonstrate leadership skills, you need to include experience of supervising others in a work context – this carries more weight than leadership within extracurricular activities. If you're running short of time at college and don't have time to do everything, then the single most useful activity would be to make it as a sports captain, which ticks the most boxes, demonstrating interpersonal skills, physical skills, and drive and motivation. One perhaps surprising finding was that playing sports in itself (i.e. without leading a team) does not seem to be impressive to employers, with no links emerging between sports and employer perceptions of interpersonal skills, drive or motivation.

this effect is a result of an association in employers' minds between leadership, motivation and interpersonal skills, and people who seek out responsibility in their leisure time. This effect holds regardless of the nature of the interests involved (Rubin *et al.* 2002).

How to express experience and skills

Although the evidence for how best to express experience and skills on a CV is thin on the ground, the research consistently points to a need for specific examples that are tailored to the particular vacancy or organization.

There is some evidence that when screening applicants' CVs, employers place a high value on specific examples and concrete statements; unsubstantiated, self-flattering adjectives and generalities fail to impress. Knouse *et al.* (1988) found that tangible examples of a desirable skill or trait created a favourable impression with employers, but a list of positive words such as 'highly motivated, excellent communication skills, energetic' were seen negatively by employers.

Thomas *et al.* (1999) conducted a large-scale study into which specific factors in a CV were more likely to lead to an invitation to an interview. They found that having a career objective in a CV worked well if it was specific and targeted (for example 'now seeking an entry-level management position in a major fashion retail chain'), but that a general objective (such as 'seeking a stimulating job in a growing company') resulted in a lower rating than a CV that included no objective (Thomas *et al.* 1999: 346). This is a useful piece of information to be able to share with clients, who often find the opening section of a CV challenging to compose.

The study also found that including what they call an 'accomplishment statement' or specific examples of achievement after each role held, such as (1999: 347) 'not one customer complaint in two years', contributed to a call to interview.

How to send the CV

Traditionally, CVs were printed out by the candidate, preferably on good-quality white paper, and sent along with a covering letter by post to the employer. In the modern age of e-communication, it's much more common to email a CV or email a link to a website, but this leaves us with questions about whether to email the document as an attachment, or in the body of the email, and what to do about a cover letter. Schullery *et al.* (2009) conducted a survey of major graduate recruiters in the US to find out how they preferred their CVs to be presented. Their respondents by far preferred CVs to be emailed as attachments, with five per cent wanting the CV to be copied and pasted in to the body of the email, and seven per cent preferring a hard copy. None of their respondents was keen on having to click onto a candidate's own website. Just over half of their respondents (56 per cent) wanted a cover letter, although the study did not explore whether this cover letter should be attached, or if the email itself should constitute the cover letter.

The way your CV is submitted appears to have an impact on the way that a reader rates you. Elgin and Clapham (2004) showed that their participants were more likely to rate a candidate who had submitted a CV online as intelligent, technologically advanced and with high qualifications. The same CV submitted in hard copy led to readers rating the candidate as more friendly, although less intelligent.

If we thought there was little empirical evidence underpinning our understanding of CVs, there really are slim pickings when it comes to cover letters. In one of the few published studies, DeKay (2006) compared the results from different types of cover letter, all submitted electronically together with a CV. The study found that a brief one line 'please find attached my CV for your consideration' type cover letter resulted in no interviews, but longer cover letters that clearly demonstrated some emotional engagement with the job itself resulted in invitations to interview.

How the CV should look

Layout is one area that is often covered in books offering CV advice. Arnulf *et al.* (2010) conducted a piece of research that compared CVs laid out in a traditional format to those more creatively designed and found that the more traditional design printed on white paper was the most attractive to employers. A formal layout on coloured paper was the next most popular option, but the creative design the least likely to lead to an interview. This study did not include employers specifically from the creative industries, who might view an imaginatively designed CV in a different light, although it did include employers who requested 'creativity' as a desirable quality.

In Thomas *et al.*'s study (1999), the success rates of two-page and one-page CVs were compared and one-page CVs were found to be more likely to result in an invitation to interview than their longer counterparts.

What recruiters say and what they do

As noted above, the most common way to establish what works in a CV has traditionally been to ask recruiters what they look for and what they value. It is well known that people don't always do what they say they do, but nevertheless this approach to identifying what is going to work best in a CV has some obvious credibility and face validity. But as studies are emerging that compare employers' stated views with their behaviour, we are realizing that the picture is more complex. Cole *et al.* (2004) conducted an extensive study into what makes an employer rate a candidate as highly employable. Their most intriguing finding indicated that what employers say they value isn't always what they actually base their decisions on. In this study, employers said that they placed most value on work experience and academic qualifications. In practice, however, their decisions were based almost exclusively on extracurricular activities, and employer perceptions of how employable a candidate was were negatively correlated to high academic qualifications. So although they stated that they were looking for highly qualified candidates, in fact, candidates whose qualifications were run of the mill were more likely to get an interview. This seems completely counter-intuitive, but the finding was replicated in another study (Rynes *et al.* 2003) which showed that while recruiters said that they were looking for people skills and specific skills-based coursework, the evidence of these skills in the CV actually had little impact on their perceptions of candidates' employability.

Although employers primarily look for factual evidence of candidates' experiences, skills and qualifications, they also make inferences about candidates' personalities as we have seen. Kirkwood and Ralston (1999) demonstrated that employers make judgements about candidates' personalities based on their paper applications, and Cole *et al.* (2004) demonstrate that employers base their ratings of candidates' employability on the suitability of the personality traits that they have inferred, judging, for example, candidates they perceive as extravert to be more suitable for enterprising jobs.

Bricoult and Bentley (2000) have provided some evidence that employers discriminate against candidates who disclose a disability on their CV. They found that employers rated candidates whose CVs did not mention a disability as the most employable, with those disclosing a physical disability as the next most employable group and those disclosing a mental health disability (such as schizophrenia) as the least employable. There has been some evidence of sex discrimination from CVs, with most of the evidence (e.g. Riach and Rich 2006) suggesting that men are discriminated against when applying to female-dominated professions, such as secretarial roles, and that women are subject to discrimination when applying to traditionally male spheres, such as engineering. The numbers in these studies are relatively small but as the authors comment, this is disturbing because it is:

> discrimination of a particularly decisive form; the denial to the individual of the opportunity even to present herself/himself in a competitive fashion before an interview panel; the screening out of applicants at the very outset of the hiring process.
>
> (Riach and Rich 2006: 9)

A few studies have explored whether candidates are discriminated against on racial grounds, but no conclusive evidence has been published.

CV COACHING – HOW TO DO IT

Career practitioners tend to be committed to non-directive practice in nearly every kind of professional interaction but I am always surprised by the strong desire in clients, policy makers and practitioners to be directive when it comes to CV checks. Perhaps this is an arena where people imagine that there are hard and fast rules, and where the careers professional is seen as the holder of the knowledge. Or perhaps it's a more practical issue, in that there tends to be quite a demand for this service and stakeholders are keen to capitalize on this popularity by treating it as an 'easy win'. Even practitioners who would generally shy away from giving advice or information feel that with a CV, a more directive approach is appropriate.

There is no more reason to be prescriptive about a CV than any other part of the career process, and here I want to provide you with a framework that you can use to provide non-directive CV coaching.

Your aim when CV coaching is to get your clients to see their CV the way that an employer might. You are not there to tell them what *you* think of it, whether you would select them for interview or whether you'd have laid your own CV out in that way, but to ask them the questions that allow them to critically reflect on and analyse the impression given by their document.

You can certainly do an excellent CV coaching session without looking at the CV at all, but my usual approach is to spend the first part of the session talking and the second part looking together at the document. I find that reading the CV allows me to ask the right questions and focus the session on the most apposite issues.

We will look now at the EPIC (Employer, Perspectives, Impact, Changes) model, a four-stage framework to help to structure CV coaching.

1. Employer

My first questions are usually about who the CV is aimed at. Which employer, or which kind of employer, is their target audience? And what kind of job is my client hoping to get with this CV? The clarity with which people answer these questions varies widely, from those who are quite specific through to those who haven't yet considered who might read the document. It is helpful to establish at this stage where your client is in their job search. The desire to sort out your CV can grab you at any stage in the process, from way before you're ready to think about making a career choice, through to after the decision has been made. CV coaching tends to be most helpful when the choice has already been made, and when there is a specific role in mind. If clients are not targeting a specific vacancy, I would usually ask them to suggest a particular employer to use for the purposes of the session, stressing that we are working on the underlying principles that they can then apply in any situation. If individuals are at the early stages of thinking about a career choice, I might offer them the option to change the nature of our session, and re-focus it on helping to make a career choice.

Typical questions you could use in this phase might include 'What sort of job are you applying for?', 'Who will you be sending this CV to?', 'Who are you hoping will read this CV?'

2. Perspectives

Employer perspective: The next stage is to get your clients to put themselves in the shoes of the employer and think about what an employer might be looking for in a candidate. You could use the person specification and job description to help the discussion here. Perceptual positions (described in more detail in Chapter 13 within the context of transactional analysis) can be a helpful tool.

Typical questions might include: 'What do you think the employer would be hoping to see on this CV?'; 'What kinds of qualifications would most impress?'; 'Imagine that you've got a huge pile of CVs. You're half-way through. What is going to make the next CV stand out?'

Client perspective: Then ask your clients to think about their own history, and highlight the elements that are going to be most relevant to this particular role. Here I might ask: 'Of all the things that you have done in your life, what do you think are the most relevant to this job?'; 'What do you think you have to offer that might make you stand out from the other candidates?'; 'What skills have you got that would make you particularly suitable for this role?'

For some clients, making these links can be quite straightforward. Other clients can find it more difficult to articulate their own skills, or might have career histories that mean that the answers are not quite as obvious. It can be worth devoting some considerable time to this section, as the thinking will also help your clients with their interview performance and could enhance their confidence and self-efficacy in their ability to get the job they are applying for.

3. Impact

Next ask your clients to look at their own CV from the employer's perspective and see what message they get. Following the answers that they provided in the previous section, ask them whether the skills, experience and qualifications that they themselves highlighted as the most important, are the ones that stand out when they look at the page.

You might ask: 'You said earlier that your most relevant experience was your time at the Post Office. How clearly does that come across here?'; 'When you look at your CV, what do you first notice?'; 'You said that organization skills would be important in this role. Have a look at your CV and tell me how organized you think it looks.'

The way you choose to handle this section can vary, depending on your style and your perception of the needs of your client. You could choose not to look at the CV yourself, and encourage your client to take full responsibility for the process and the decisions. Alternatively, you could choose to run this part of the session more collaboratively, looking at the document together and each of you suggesting thoughts and reactions based on the information the client has provided.

4. Changes

In the final phase of the session, you encourage your client to specify what they need to do improve the CV. As with any action-planning stage, the more specific the changes are, the easier it will be for the client to implement them, so do encourage them to come up with specific words or phrases that they could use. It may feel appropriate at this stage to use some of your own knowledge and experience of CVs to broaden your client's thinking – for example, showing them some examples of different layouts, fonts, styles or language that other people have used. In my experience, we can feel somewhat rule-bound when it comes to CV writing, as though there are some definitive directives about what is allowed and what isn't, and clients can sometimes need some encouragement to think a little more creatively about what they could or should do. Showing other clients' examples of styles and layouts can often encourage them to inject more of their personality into these otherwise dry documents.

There is a lot that we have yet to learn about what kind of CV is most likely to lead to an invitation to interview. Given the amount of contradictory advice about CVs that our clients will be exposed to, it's useful for us to have some idea of the evidence that exists. But do remember that the evidence is limited; a CV is a very personal document. You make a hundred choices when you compile it, about what to include and what to leave out; what to highlight and what to play down; how to express it and how to lay it out. Each one of these decisions is a personal one, and it says something about you and your response to a particular role. There are very few absolute rights and wrongs in a CV and what 'works' is down to an almost chemical click between applicants (as they appear on paper) and the recruiter, who will inevitably have their own views on what they are looking for, and how they want to see it expressed. There are myriad books, websites and CV-writing services that people can access if they are looking for someone to tell them what to write on their CV, but as career coaches, we should be confident that our non-directive approach is the best way to help our clients to make their own thoughtful and considered choices.

REFERENCES

Arnulf, J., Tegner, L. and Larssen, Ø. (2010) Impression making by résumé layout: Its impact on the probability of being shortlisted. *European Journal of Work & Organizational Psychology*, 19(2): 221–230.

Bricout, J. C. and Bentley, K. J. (2000) Disability status and perceptions of employability by employers. *Social Work Research*, 24(2): 87.

Brown, B. K. and Campion, M. A. (1994) Biodata phenomenology: Recruiters' perceptions and use of biographical information in résumé screening. *Journal of Applied Psychology*, 79(6): 897–908.

Cole, M. S., Feild, H. S., Giles, W. F. and Harris, S. G. (2004) Job type and recruiters' inferences of applicant personality drawn from résumé biodata: Their relationships with hiring recommendations. *International Journal of Selection & Assessment*, 12(4): 363–367.

Cole, M. S., Feild, H. S., Giles, W. F. and Harris, S. G. (2009) Recruiters' inferences of applicant personality based on résumé screening: Do paper people have a personality? *Journal of Business & Psychology*, 24(1): 5–18.

DeKay, S. H. (2006) Expressing emotion in electronic job cover letters. *Business Communication Quarterly*, 69(4): 435–439.

Dougherty, T. W., Turban, B. B. and Callender, J. C. (1994) Confirming first impressions in the employment interview: A field study of interviewer behavior, *Journal of Applied Psychology* 79: 659–665.

Elgin, P. D. and Clapham, M. M. (2004) Attributes associated with the submission of electronic versus paper résumés. *Computers in Human Behavior*, 20(4): 535–549.

Feild, H. S. and Holley, W. H. (1976) Résumé preparation: an empirical study of personnel managers' perceptions. *Vocational Guidance Quarterly*, 24: 229–237.

Johnson, E. and Lahey, J. (2011) The résumé characteristics determining job interviews for middle-aged women seeking entry-level employment. *Journal of Career Development*, 38(4): 310–330.

Kinicki, A. J. and Lockwood, C. A. (1985) The interview process: An examination of factors recruiters use in evaluating job applicants. *Journal of Vocational Behavior*, 26: 117–125.

Kirkwood, W. and Ralston, S. (1999) Inviting meaningful applicant performances in employment interviews. *Journal of Business Communication*, 36(1): 55–76.

Knouse, S. B. (1994) Impressions of the résumé: the effects of applicant education, experience and impression management. *Journal of Business and Psychology*, 9: 33–45.

Knouse, S. B., Giacalone, R. A. and Pollard, H. (1988) Impression management in the résumé and its cover letter. *Journal of Business and Psychology*, 3: 242–249.

McNeilly, K. M. and Barr, T. (1997) Convincing the recruiter: A comparison of résumé formats. *Journal of Education for Business*, 72(6): 359.

Nemanick, R. C. and Clark, E. M. (2002) The differential effects of extracurricular activities on attributions in résumé evaluation. *International Journal of Selection and Assessment*, 10: 206–217.

Oliphant, V. N. and Alexander III, E. R. (1982) Reaction to résumés as a function of applicant determinateness, applicant characteristics and sex of raters. *Personnel Psychology* 35: 829–842.

Riach, P. A. and Rich, J. (2006) An experimental investigation of sexual discrimination in hiring in the English labor market. *B.E. Journal of Economic Analysis & Policy: Advances In Economic Analysis and Policy*, 6(2): 1–20.

Rubin, R. S., Bommer, W. H. and Baldwin, T. T. (2002) Using extracurricular activity as an indicator of interpersonal skill: Prudent evaluation or recruiting malpractice? *Human Resource Management*, 41: 441–454.

Rynes, S. L., Trank, C. Q., Lawson, A. M. and Ilies, R. (2003) Behavioral coursework in business education: Growing evidence of a legitimacy crisis. *Academy of Management Learning and Education*, 2: 269–283.

Schullery, N. M., Ickes, L. and Schullery, S. E. (2009) Employer preferences for résumés and cover letters. *Business Communication Quarterly*, 72(2): 163–176.

Singer, M. S. and Bruhns, C. (1991) Relative effect of applicant work experience and academic qualification on selection interview decisions: A study of between-sample generalizability. *Journal of Applied Psychology*, 76: 550–559.

Thomas, P., McMasters, R., Roberts, M. R. and Dombowski, D. A. (1999) Résumé characteristics as predictors of an invitation to interview. *Journal of Business and Psychology* 13(3): 339–356.

Chapter 18

Interview coaching

Most of us dread interviews. We fear going blank at the crucial moment or spouting gibberish to the very people we're trying to impress. We also fear rejection, which, however many times we are advised not to 'take it personally', always takes its toll on our self-esteem. Interviews are by far the most common method of selection and are used by more than 99 per cent of organizations to recruit staff. It's clearly important to an organization to make sure that it selects the right people for the job, as mistakes can be costly and hard to rectify, and it is partly for this reason that a considerable amount of research has gone into finding out how to make interviews more effective.

The traditional 'unstructured' interview, during which the candidate and employer just sit and have a chat, is still very widespread but has been shown to have really quite low validity; in other words, you have quite a low chance of selecting the right person to do the job if you choose your employees in this way. In contrast, structured, competency-based interviews that are based on the criteria needed to do the job well, that ask the candidate for evidence and that use the same set of questions for each competing candidate, have been shown to be more or less the most effective selection method there is. That said, at a validity of just over 0.5 (i.e. you have a 50 per cent better than random chance of picking the right person), there is still plenty of room for improvement!

Clients often come to career coaches looking for tips on how to succeed at interviews, or for some practice and feedback on their interview technique. A clear understanding of the interview process can give us some great insights to what is actually going to work in an interview context, and can allow us to increase our clients' chances of success.

This chapter provides an overview of what we know about the interview process. In the first part, we will look at the qualities that are actually measured by a job interview and whether these assessments are accurate, and then go on to examine what kinds of qualities and behaviours are most likely to lead to a job offer. The chapter ends with some suggestions for using this wealth of research to improve our clients' chances of getting the position they want.

WHAT EXACTLY DO INTERVIEWS MEASURE?

Ostensibly, there are hundreds of different qualities that job interviews could measure. After all, there is no limit to the vast range of questions that a candidate could be asked, and job descriptions and person specifications differ widely. In practice, though, it seems that job interviews for the most part tend to assess the same handful of qualities. Huffcutt *et al.* (2001) identified seven types of constructs that interviews commonly gauge and found that basic personality and applied social skills were by far the most evaluated qualities. Within these categories, the most frequently judged single trait is conscientiousness, followed by interpersonal skills. Between them, these two account for nearly 30 per cent of everything anyone assesses in any interview.

The next most frequently assessed category of characteristics is mental capability, followed by job knowledge and specific job-related skills. Further down the scale come interests and preferences, organizational fit and finally physical attributes.

The categories come in more or less the same order for both structured and unstructured interviews, but this broad similarity masks some interesting differences in the detail. It is well documented that structured interviews are more likely to select applicants who are going to perform well in the job than unstructured ones, and Huffcutt *et al.*'s (2001) meta-analysis gives us a clue as to why. The two types of interviews tend to evaluate slightly different facets of personality and experiences, and the characteristics assessed in structured interviews tend to be more job-related than those assessed in unstructured interviews. For example, while unstructured interviews will look at both candidates' occupational interests and their hobbies outside work, structured interviews are interested only in occupational interests. Unstructured interviews assess candidates' levels of general intelligence, whereas structured interviews are more interested in their applied mental skills – so how their general intelligence translates into a work context. Finally, physical appearance, which is given significant weight in unstructured interviews, is practically negligible in structured interviews.

Traditional careers interview support has held that interviewers are trying to find the answers to just three questions:

1. Can you do the job?
2. Will you do the job?
3. Will you fit in?

Research (Huffcutt *et al.* 2001) provides some evidence to back this up. 'Can you do the job?' is answered by finding out about candidates' mental capacity and their job skills. 'Will you do the job?' is covered by job knowledge and conscientiousness, and 'Will you fit in?' is answered by exploring candidates' applied social skills, personality traits such as extraversion, agreeableness and organizational fit. This is a useful framework to share with clients as a structure for helping them to prepare interview answers.

These, broadly, are the qualities interviewers are looking for. But how good do interviewers tend to be at rating these qualities accurately?

Even though we don't quite understand the cognitive processes that underpin selection interviews, we do know that interviewers, particularly in structured interviews, are relatively accurate at judging candidates.

Specifically, interviewers in general do a reasonably good job at assessing candidates' personalities (Barrick *et al.* 2000), generating ratings that correlate moderately with candidate's self-ratings on all of the 'Big Five' personality traits. Initial impressions are quite powerful within the interview process, with candidates who make good first impressions being more likely to get job offers and be recommended for higher starting salaries (Barrick *et al.* 2010). Reassuringly, there is considerable evidence that interviewers are skilled at making quick judgements about people, making fairly accurate assessments of candidates' competence in as little as one hundred milliseconds (Willis and Todorov 2006). Interviewers also tend to provide reasonably accurate assessments of applicants' levels of person–organization fit, identifying with considerable validity whether a candidate's values will chime with those of the organization.

Much research has been conducted into how to make selection interviews fairer and more valid, and as noted above, employers can make relatively valid assessments within a structured interview. Despite this, employers in general prefer to base their decisions on subjective, personal evaluations, rather than the tests that have been shown to increase validity (Lievens *et al.* 2005). Employers often prefer unstructured interviews, have their own favourite interview questions and prefer to rely on their instincts rather than the evidence that they have gathered. Even those who embrace the more valid structured interview like to start the interview with some rapport-building (Chapman and Zweig 2005), which instantly reduces the validity of the process.

DISCRIMINATION DURING INTERVIEWS

The issue of unfair discrimination during interviews has received a significant amount of attention both within the academic literature and within the HR departments in organizations who have been campaigning with some success to decrease inequitable practices within recruitment. The literature gives us an interesting perspective.

Discrimination against people with disabilities seems still to be present in employment selection. The nature of disabilities varies widely and not all are perceived in the same way by employers (Premeaux 2001). When compared to all candidates with disabilities, candidates with physical disabilities tend to be rated most favourably in job interviews, and receive the highest employability ratings and the highest number of job offers. The next most highly rated group are candidates with sensory impairments, while the least likely to be given a job offer are those with psychological disorders. This reflects the stigma that is still very much associated with mental ill health and the corresponding widespread lack of understanding and awareness in society.

Knowing whether to (or when to) disclose a disability can be a tricky decision. Although there is now considerable legislation to help protect the employment rights of those with disabilities, some people with a 'hidden' impairment (such as dyslexia or depression) prefer not to mention it at all in order to prevent the negative attitudes and discrimination that they may feel they are bound to encounter. Others prefer to disclose upfront, not wanting to drag themselves through a stressful process only to be rejected when their disability finally emerges. You might feel that you stand more of a chance of getting the job if you don't disclose until after the job offer is in the bag, but you then risk starting your working relationships with your new employers on the wrong foot, as they may feel resentment at being misled.

We can look to the research for some advice on how best to handle the issue. Candidates with visible disabilities (most studies have been conducted with wheelchair users) tend to do better in interviews if they make some verbal reference to the disability during the meeting (Macan and Hayes 1995), but interviewers are more comfortable if this reference is made towards the end of the interview. Candidates with a non-visible disability, based on Roberts and Macan's 2006 study, are rated more highly in terms of how qualified they are and how likable they are if they disclose their disability at the start of the interview rather than at the end. The difference is that employers may feel that they have been deceived in some way if they feel that this piece of information has been withheld from them throughout the interview.

Evidence on whether there are gender biases for candidates at the interview stage is mixed, with some studies finding that men and women have equal chances at interview, some finding a bias against women and some a bias against men. Hardin et al.'s (2002) meta-analysis concluded that although there are no sex differences in interview ratings, men tend to be given higher salary recommendations.

The sex of the interviewer does seem to make a difference, however. Graves and Powell (1995) found that the underlying gender issue in interviews is down to a sense of perceived similarity. It is well documented throughout psychology that people are drawn to people who are similar to themselves. The similarity makes us feel more comfortable with who we are, and it tends to lead to more predictable social interactions. It should come as no great shock, then, to hear that male interviewers tend to favour male candidates. More surprising is that this study found that female interviewers too gave more positive ratings to the male characteristics for exactly the same reasons – that they found greater perceived similarities between themselves and the male candidates than they did between themselves and female candidates. The researchers offer no explanation for this intriguing finding, but Schein's (1973) work on the perceived links between managers (and most women on interview panels will be managers) and male characteristics may be relevant.

Encouragingly, there is some evidence that positive action and equal opportunity policies in the workplace do make a difference in attitudes towards recruitment of underrepresented groups (Ng and Wiesner 2007).

As with gender, empirical evidence about the impact of race on hiring decisions has been mixed and even where effects have been found, they are not significant. Lin *et al.* (1992) did find some evidence about the impact of the race of the interviewers, based again on the attraction of perceived similarity, in that interviewers showed strong preferences for candidates of the same race as themselves in conventional structured interviews. This effect was considerably reduced in situational interviews and with interview panels featuring a range of ethnicities.

Despite social stereotypes of older people being of less value in the workplace due to reduced motivation, creativity and productivity (Dedrick and Dobbins 1991), these negative associations translate only marginally into fewer job offers (Gordon *et al.* 1988).

The chapter so far has looked at the interview process more from the perspective of the employer, looking at what interviews do and whether they do it well. We will now move on to looking at the topic from the candidates' perspective, looking at what kind of person and what kind of behaviour lead to job offers.

WHO DOES WELL IN INTERVIEWS?

Successful candidates can be characterized in terms of their personalities and the specific behaviour they demonstrate within the interview.

Personality

Two of the biggest predictors of job interview success are the personality traits of extraversion and conscientiousness. The explanation here is that as job interviews are basically social interactions, people who feel more comfortable interacting socially (extraverts) are likely to excel. Those with a preference for conscientiousness tend to put more effort into preparing for the interview, and thus are more likely to perform well and feel more confident about the interview process. This sense of confidence is important; a high degree of interview self-efficacy leads to higher chances of success at interviews. A further advantage that those scoring high on extraversion have is that they are more likely to engage with tactics to impress at interview (Kyl-Heku and Buss 1996). Extravert candidates are more likely to smile and come across as relaxed and enthusiastic. They tend to have better short-term memories, lower social anxiety, lower language anxiety and better resistance to stress in high-information flow environments. They tend to talk more, so provide more information.

Specific interview behaviour

Organizational citizenship

Interviewers are currently very keen to select good organizational citizens. The term was coined by Organ (1997: 95) who describes organizational citizens as those demonstrating behaviour which 'supports the social and psychological environment in which task performance takes place'. Evidence has emerged about links with a range of positive outcomes in the workplace, including high productivity, low turnover and efficiency, so no wonder it is becoming something that employers are looking out for in selection interviews. Three of the key elements of organizational citizenship behaviour are helping, voice and loyalty, and candidates who demonstrate these kinds of behaviour in their interviews are more likely to get job offers, and are also more likely to secure higher starting salaries (Podsakoff *et al.* 2011).

Table 18.1

Organizational citizenship behaviour	What it means	What you might say
Helping	Going out of your way to support colleagues with work or solving problems	'My colleague was struggling to meet her deadline, so I offered to stand in on the helpdesk for her to give her some more time to finish.'
Voice	Giving your opinion or suggestions for positive changes that could benefit the organization even when everyone else disagrees	'Everyone I spoke to seemed really happy with the status quo but I was convinced that there was a more efficient way to run the service, so I asked for some time in a team meeting and presented a few of my ideas.'
Loyalty	Putting the needs and reputation of the organization above the individual	'My team seemed to really distrust the senior managers, so I spent a lot of time in my first year trying to build bridges, and to get them to understand how the directors worked and why they worked like that.'

This concept is a useful one to share with clients, so that they have an opportunity to prepare examples of their own organizational citizenship behaviour before the interviews.

Self-presentation

We all know that success at interview is based not just on what we have to say, but on how we present ourselves. A clear understanding of the self-presentation factors that influence the interviewers can be particularly helpful to career coaches; some of them are within the clients' control, so sharing this information can have a significant impact on their interview success.

Self-presentation covers all aspects of how you come across in an interview, and with such a broad definition, it's no wonder that the literature ends up looking somewhat complicated. Barrick *et al.* (2008) have helped us to make sense of it by conducting a meta-analysis that provides us with a neat framework within which to understand the different elements, as well as some evidence of how influential each of the different behaviours are in the selection process. The most influential of the self-presentation tactics were found to be physical attractiveness (how good-looking you are) and professional appearance (how well groomed and appropriately turned out you are). The next most influential group were impression management tactics, followed by verbal and non-verbal cues.

We'll look at each of these groups in more detail below, but it's worth mentioning briefly the validity of these judgements. Although some of them sound superficial, discriminatory and irrelevant, there are in fact some links between the qualities underlying the elements of self-presentation and the qualities needed in the workplace. We spend much of our working lives trying to influence people – colleagues, managers, clients and customers. It follows that those who can manage to influence their interviewers may also perform well when faced with managing others. More specifically, there are some links between particular elements of self-presentation and job performance. Conscientiousness, for example, is a personality trait that is strongly correlated with positive job performance, and this quality might also lead a candidate to turn up to an interview polished and well groomed.

The links between these kinds of self-presentation tactics and job performance are relatively weak, but it may give us some comfort to learn that they are there at all.

Let's look in more detail at the three groups of self-presentation tactics that Barrick *et al.* (2009) identified: appearance, impression management and verbal and non-verbal skills.

Appearance

Attractive people do better than unattractive people in job selection interviews in a variety of ways. They score more highly in terms of initial impressions (Jackson *et al.* 1995), hiring recommendations (Gilmore *et al.* 1986), predicted job success

(Morrow 1990) and pay (Frieze *et al.* 1991). Hosoda *et al.* (2003: 451) sum up the unpalatable truth, that 'physical attractiveness is always an asset for individuals'. The empirical evidence suggests that as a society we're still firmly wedded to the 'if it's beautiful it must be good' paradigm, as we imbue attractive candidates with all sorts of positive job-related personal qualities. Recruiters rate attractive candidates as having significantly higher social skills, greater cognitive abilities (especially male candidates) and more integrity and concern for others than their less attractive rivals.

One factor that is even more influential than how you look is how you *think* you look. Feingold (1992) showed that self-ratings of attractiveness have more of an impact than actual physical attractiveness, suggesting that part of what we are judged on in interviews is how being attractive (or thinking you are attractive) makes you behave.

On top of your basic good looks, employers are also swayed by the image that you choose to portray at interview. Appropriate attire and a well-groomed appearance will increase your chances of a job offer, and for women, there is some evidence that a more masculine choice of clothing has traditionally been more likely to get you a senior level job offer (Forsythe *et al.* 1985).

One glimmer of hope that the literature will concede is that the attractiveness effect does seem to be diminishing over the years.

Impression management

Impression management has received a lot of attention in the literature over the last decade or so. The phrase describes a range of tactics that we deliberately produce in an attempt to make ourselves more desirable as candidates in a job interview. The use of these tactics is extremely widespread and researchers have shown (e.g. Levashina and Campion 2007) that nearly all of us employ some impression management technique or other at almost every interview.

The broad concept of impression management has been framed in various different ways. The table overleaf illustrates one framework (Jones and Pittmen 1982). Swider *et al.* (2011) provide an alternative conceptualization, separating impression management tactics into 'self-promotion' and 'image creation'. Self-promotion is used by candidates to illustrate skills, qualities and attributes that they already possess. It is about making the most of what you've got and these tactics are 'generally seen as honest attempts to manage positive information' (Swider *et al.* 2011: 1277). They might include taking credit for one's achievements and highlighting experiences that demonstrate relevant skills and attributes. In contrast, image creation is less authentic. Tactics here might include intentionally exaggerating experiences, taking credit for others' successes and entirely making up events. It is about creating an image of oneself that is more attractive to the interviewer than the reality and is intentionally misleading.

It is a victory for the interview process and for integrity itself that while a moderate amount of self-promotion increases your chances of a job offer, outright

Table 18.2

Impression management tactic	What it means	What you might say
Self-promotion	Exaggerating or highlighting experiences to make yourself seem more competent or more suitable	'I used my determination and business acumen to turn the company's fortunes round and I increased profits by 25 per cent.'
Ingratiation	Flattering the interviewer to make them like you more	'I've had a look at your profile and you've had an amazing career.'
Intimidation	Acting in an intimidating way to impress	'I used to just turn up at client offices and ask them why they hadn't paid, and I would just stay there until they did.'
Supplication	Making yourself look vulnerable or needy to get the interviewer on your side	'I had to make the whole team redundant, and I found it really hard.'
Exemplification	Making your behaviour seem exemplary in order to present yourself as a role model	'My success led to being awarded the company's sales manager of the month, and I was asked to mentor a new member of the team.'

Adapted from Jones and Pittmen (1982).

image creation lowers your chances. Employers expect candidates to talk positively about their experiences and want them to highlight their most relevant skills, and this kind of impression management really makes a difference to employers' views. Image creation, however, is negatively correlated to interviewers' ratings of candidates; the more image creation a candidate engages in, the less likely they are to get a job. The reason for this is not that candidates give themselves away or that interviewers pick up on the lie, but rather that it is much harder work for our brains to make something up than it is to tell a real story. As a consequence, our brains are so busy devising the narrative, making up the detail and controlling our emotions, that we have no cognitive space left over to give a full and interesting answer. Fictitious interview answers tend to be shorter and less detailed than honest answers, and it is this that leads to lower interview scores.

Verbal and non-verbal skills

Verbal skills cover everything about how you talk other than what you're saying. They include voice intensity, pauses, use of fillers such as 'um' or 'er' and fluency. Non-verbal skills cover body language of all sorts, including eye contact, smiling, hand gestures and posture. Both are significantly linked to interview ratings and job offers, with non-verbal behaviours marginally more influential than verbal ones.

Various verbal styles are perceived as being indicators of specific qualities (DeGroot and Gooty 2009). A low-pitched voice signals dominance, and use of a wide range of pitch is thought to signify charisma. Fluency is thought to be (and there is some evidence that it actually is) linked to IQ, and fast speech is seen as a sign of competence and extraversion. Pauses are good to stress a point, but need to be combined with moderately fluent speech for maximum effect. There is a curvilinear relationship between speech rate and perception of sociability, meaning that up to a point, the faster you talk, the more sociable you are thought to be; after that point, the direction of the correlation reverses and the faster you talk, the less sociable you are thought to be. There is a similar relationship between volume and perceptions of sociability, extraversion and dominance, which to a certain level increase as the volume goes up, but then decrease as confident voice projection turns into shouting.

One non-verbal cue that has been given some attention recently is the handshake. A good handshake conveys sociability, friendliness and dominance. A poor one is thought to indicate introversion, shyness and neuroticism. There is some empirical evidence to back this up: in particular, the links between a good handshake and both extraversion and emotional stability are fairly robust (Chaplin *et al.* 2000). A 'good' handshake, according to the research conducted by Stewart *et al.* (2008) is firm, has a good grip and is accompanied by eye contact. Women in particular are given high ratings in interviews for a good handshake.

Non-verbal cues tend to produce more accurate assessments than verbal cues, because they are more likely to be processed automatically. As verbal cues tend to be processed cognitively, they can be subject to cognitive overload (Ambady and Gray 2002) and this makes judgements less accurate.

Interview practice

The traditional career-support process for clients going to interviews has been the mock interview. This tends to involve the coach role playing the interviewer and asking a series of appropriate questions that the clients answer. The coach then feeds back on the clients' performance and makes recommendations.

There is a lot of common sense to this approach, but the research provides no evidence that these run-throughs help interview success. It seems that experience of real interviews makes a significant difference to interview success, but mock interviews have no such impact. The experience of going through lots of real interviews has been shown to improve your chances of landing the job: experienced interviewees make fewer mistakes and tend to have smoother performances. Going for interviews where you are successful is the best preparation of all, as not only does this give you some practice, but it also feeds into the interview self-efficacy loop and enhances your chances of doing well next time round.

Mock interviews haven't been shown to have much of an impact on future chances of success, so more specific skills training on how to convey enthusiasm, perfecting your handshake and making sure you look the part might have more of an impact.

INTERVIEW COACHING

The client-centred principles that underpin our one-to-one work should be as core to an interview coaching session as to any other kind of coaching intervention. Time and access to resources are often cited as reasons for making interview sessions more directive than other coaching sessions, but if you really believe that a client-centred approach is the most effective way to a behaviour change, you will be letting your clients down if you start telling them what they should be doing, rather than encouraging and enabling them to find the answers themselves.

The very best way to get clients to become aware of their own behaviour within an interview session is to record a mock interview (preferably conducted by someone other than you), and then watch the recording together. Your role, as is traditional within client-centred coaching, is to ask questions and provide reflections that will allow clients to explore their own thoughts and opinions. In this context, you might want to be in charge of the 'pause' button, and stop the recording every so often to ask the clients how they felt about an answer, or perhaps to get them to think about the conclusions that the interviewer might draw from a particular response and explore whether there could have been a different example that they might have used.

Sharing some of your expertise on the interview process can be productive. You could talk to your clients about the value that interviewers tend to place on organizational citizenship behaviour and see if they could think of some instances of this from their work lives that they could use. You could share some information about the impact of non-verbal behaviour with your clients and suggest that you could watch parts of the interview with the sound down to see what sort of impact their body language makes. Your understanding of the crucial role that the first few minutes play within the interview context could lead you to watch the opening of the interview in order to analyse what kind of initial impression your clients make.

As usual, within a coaching intervention, your clients might find it useful to make some notes about their thoughts throughout the session, and it might be appropriate to identify some action points that they could work on either before or during their next interview to help them come across as well as they can next time round.

Despite decades of research, our collective understanding of the interview process is still pretty patchy. Given the complex nature of how we present ourselves and the complex systems that we employ to interpret other people's behaviour, perhaps it shouldn't surprise us. What we have learned, though, are some insights that we can pass on to clients to help them improve their chances. Good preparation, relevant experience, appropriate skills and articulate fluency will always be the keystones for a successful interview, and as a career coach, it's useful to have a clear understanding of the other factors more readily within clients' control that have a significant impact on their chances of success. A few examples of organizational citizenship, a carefully honed handshake and well-polished shoes are straightforward for clients to engineer and may make a significant difference to their interview score.

REFERENCES

Ambady, N. and Gray, H. (2002) On being sad and mistaken: Mood effects on the accuracy of thin slice judgements. *Journal of Personality and Social Psychology*, 83(4): 947–961.

Barrick, M. R., Shaffer, J. A. and DeGrassi, S. W. (2009) What you see may not be what you get: Relationships among self-presentation tactics and ratings of interview and job performance. *Journal of Applied Psychology*, 94(6): 1394–1411.

Barrick, M. R., Swider, B. W. and Stewart, G. L. (2010) Initial evaluations in the interview: Relationships with subsequent interviewer evaluations and employment offers. *Journal of Applied Psychology*, 95(6): 1163–1172.

Barrick, M. R., Patton, G. K. and Haugland, S. N. (2000) Accuracy of interview judgements of job applicant personality traits. *Personnel Psychology*, 53(4): 925–951.

Campion, M. A., Palmer, D. K. and Campion, J. E. (1997) A review of structure in the selection interview. *Personnel Psychology*, 50: 673–702.

Chaplin, W. F., Phillips, J. B., Brown, J. D., Clanton, N. R. and Stein, J. L. (2000) Handshaking, gender, personality, and first impressions. *Journal of Personality and Social Psychology*, 79: 110–117.

Chapman, D. S. and Zweig, D. I. (2005) Developing a nomological network for interview structure: Antecedents and consequences of the structured selection interview. *Personnel Psychology*, 58: 673–702.

Dedrick, E. and Dobbins, G. H. (1991) The influence on subordinate age on managerial actions: An attributional analysis. *Journal of Organizational Behavior*, 12: 367–377.

DeGroot, T. and Gooty, J. (2009) Can nonverbal cues be used to make meaningful personality attributions in employment interviews? *Journal of Business & Psychology*, 24(2): 179–192.

Feingold, A. (1992) Good-looking people are not what we think. *Psychological Bulletin*, 111: 304–341.

Forsythe, S., Drake, M. F. and Cox, C. E. (1985) Influence of applicant's dress on interviewer's selection decisions. *Journal of Applied Psychology*, 70(2): 374–378.

Frieze, I. H., Olson, J. E. and Russell, J. (1991) Attractiveness and income for men and women in management. *Journal of Applied Social Psychology*, 21(13): 1039–1057.

Gilmore, D. C., Beehr, T. A. and Love, K. G. (1986) Effects of applicant sex, applicant physical attractiveness, type of rater and type of job on interview decisions. *Journal of Occupational Psychology*, 59(2): 103–109.

Gordon, R. A., Rozelle, R. M. and Baxter, J. C. (1988) The effect of applicant age, job level and accountability on the evaluation of job applicants. *Organizational Behavior and Human Decision Processes*, 33: 174–186.

Graves, L. M. and Powell, G. N. (1995) The effect of sex similarity on recruiters' evaluations of actual applicants: A test of the similarity attraction paradigm. *Personnel Psychology*, 48 (Spring): 85–98.

Hardin, R. J., Reding, K. F. and Stocks, M. H. (2002) The effect of gender on the recruitment of entry-level accountants. *Journal of Managerial Issues*, XIV(2): Summer.

Harris, K. J., Kacmar, K. M., Zivnuska, S. and Shaw, J. D. (2007) The impact of political skills on impression management effectiveness. *Journal of Applied Psychology*, 92(1): 278–285.

Higgins, C. A., Judge, T. A. and Ferris, G. R. (2003) Influence tactics and work outcomes: A meta-analysis. *Journal of Organizational Behavior*, 24: 89–106.

Hosoda, M., Stone-Romero, E. F. and Coats, G. (2003) The effects of physical attractiveness on job-related outcomes: A meta-analysis of experimental studies. *Personnel Psychology*, 56(2): 431–462.

Howard, J. L. and Ferris, G. R. (1996) The employment interview context: social and situational influences on interview decisions. *Journal of Applied Social Psychology*, 26: 112–136.

Huffcutt, A. I., Conway, J. M., Roth, P. L. and Stone, N. J. (2001). Identification and meta-analytic assessment of psychological constructs measured in employment interviews. *Journal of Applied Psychology*, 86(5): 897–913. doi:10.1037/0021-9010.86.5.897

Jackson, L., Hunter, J. and Hodge, C. (1995) Physical attractiveness and intellectual competence: A meta-analytic review. *Social Psychology Quarterly*, 58(2): 108–122.

Jones, E. E. and Pittmen, T. S. (1982) Toward a general theory of strategic self-presentation. In J. Suls (ed.), *Psychological Perspective on the Self.* Hillsdale, NJ: Erlbaum, pp. 231–261.

Kraiger, K. and Ford, J. K. (1985) A meta-analysis of rate race effects in performance ratings. *Journal of Applied Psychology*, 70: 56–65.

Kyl-Heku, L. M. and Buss, D. M. (1996) Tactics as units of analysis in personality psychology: An illustration using tactics of hierarchy negotiation. *Personality & Individual Differences*, 21: 497–517.

Levashina, J. and Campion, M. A. (2007) Measuring faking in the employment interview: Development and validation of an interview faking behaviour scale. *Journal of Applied Psychology*, 92: 1638–1656.

Lievens, F., Highhouse, S. and De Corte, W. (2005). The importance of traits and abilities in supervisors' hirability decisions as a function of method of assessment. *Journal of Occupational and Organizational Psychology*, 78: 453–470.

Lievens, F. and Sackett, P. R. (2012). The validity of interpersonal skills assessment via situational judgement tests for predicting academic success and job performance. *Journal of Applied Psychology*, 97(2): 460–468.

Lin, T., Dobbins, G. H. and Farh, J. (1992) A field study of race and age similarity effects on interview ratings in conventional and situational interviews. *Journal of Applied Psychology*, 77(3): 363–371.

Macan, T. H. and Hayes, T. L. (1995) Both sides of the employment interview interaction: Perceptions of interviewers and applicants with disabilities. *Rehabilitation Psychology*, 40: 261–278.

Morrow, P. C. (1990) Physical attractiveness and selection decision making. *Journal of Management*, 16(1): 45–60.

Ng, E. and Wiesner, W. (2007) Are men always picked over women? The effects of employment equity directives on selection decisions. *Journal of Business Ethics*, 76(2): 177–187.

Organ, D. W. (1997) Organizational citizenship behaviour: It's construct clean-up time. *Human Performance*, 10: 85–97.

Perry, E. (1994). A prototype matching approach to understanding the role of applicant gender and age in the evaluation of job applicants. *Journal of Applied Social Psychology*, 24(16): 1433–1473.

Pinar, M. and Hardin, J. (2005) The effect of gender on recruiting for sales positions. *Services Marketing Quarterly*, 27(2): 15–32.

Podsakoff, N. P., Whiting, S. W., Podsakoff, P. M. and Mishra, P. (2011) Effects of organizational citizenship behaviors on selection decisions in employment interviews. *Journal of Applied Psychology*, 96(2): 310–326.

Premeaux, F. (2001) Impact of applicant disability on selection. The role of disability type, physical attractiveness and proximity. *Journal of Business Psychology*, 16: 291–298.

Roberts, L. L. and Macan, T. (2006) Disability disclosure effects on employment interview ratings of applicants with nonvisible disabilities. *Rehabilitation Psychology*, 51(3): 239–246. doi:10.1037/0090-5550.51.3.239

Schein, V. E. (1973) The relationship between sex role stereotypes and requisite management characteristics. *Journal of Applied Psychology*, 57: 95–100.

Stewart, G. L., Dustin, S. L., Barrick, M. R. and Darnold, T. C. (2008) Exploring the handshake in employment interviews. *Journal of Applied Psychology*, 93(5): 1139–1146.

Swider, B. W., Barrick, M. R., Harris, T. B. and Stoverink, A. C. (2011) Managing and creating an image in the interview: The role of interviewee initial impressions. *Journal of Applied Psychology*, 96: 1275–1288.

Roth, P. L., Van Iddekinge, C. H., Huffcutt, A. I., Eidson, C. R. and Bobko, P. (2002) Corrections for range restriction in structured interview ethnic group differences: The values may be larger than researchers thought. *Journal of Applied Psychology*, 87(2): 369–376.

Tay, C., Ang, S. and Van Dyne, L. (2006) Personality, biographical characteristics, and job interview success: A longitudinal study of the mediating effects of interviewing self-efficacy and the moderating effects of internal locus of causality. *Journal of Applied Psychology*, 91(2): 446–454.

Willis, J. and Todorov, A. (2006) First impressions: Making up your mind after a 100-ms exposure to a face. *Psychological Science*, 17: 592–598.

Final thoughts

Positive psychology tells us that happiness is finding a balance of meaning, engagement and pleasure. I'm not sure that I can think of many professions that are likely to meet all three in the way that career coaching can. Delving into people's minds and enabling them towards career fulfilment is interesting, intriguing and it matters. It's a very exciting time for our profession. The need for good quality career support has never been higher, and with the changes in both government policy and the demands of the workplace, the onus is on us to recreate a profession that is fit for purpose. Research needs to be at the very heart of this reconfigured landscape and will ensure that we maintain credibility and provide first-class service to our clients. Research into career and coaching theory is growing and shifting almost daily. We need to keep learning, keep trying things out and reflecting on what is working and what isn't. I hope that the ideas you have encountered in this book will help. I hope they have given you food for thought and inspired you to try something new in your practice. New ideas will keep us fresh and will enhance our chances of giving our clients the best support possible.

Index

Page references in *italic* indicate Tables and Figures.

Taylor & Francis

eBooks
FOR LIBRARIES

ORDER YOUR FREE 30 DAY INSTITUTIONAL TRIAL TODAY!

Over 23,000 eBook titles in the Humanities, Social Sciences, STM and Law from some of the world's leading imprints.

Choose from a range of subject packages or create your own!

Benefits for you

▶ Free MARC records
▶ COUNTER-compliant usage statistics
▶ Flexible purchase and pricing options

Benefits for your user

▶ Off-site, anytime access via Athens or referring URL
▶ Print or copy pages or chapters
▶ Full content search
▶ Bookmark, highlight and annotate text
▶ Access to thousands of pages of quality research at the click of a button

For more information, pricing enquiries or to order a free trial, contact your local online sales team.

UK and Rest of World: **online.sales@tandf.co.uk**

US, Canada and Latin America:
e-reference@taylorandfrancis.com

www.ebooksubscriptions.com

ALPSP Award for BEST eBOOK PUBLISHER 2009 Finalist

Taylor & Francis eBooks
Taylor & Francis Group

A flexible and dynamic resource for teaching, learning and research.